June Sprigg

UNIVERSITY PRESS OF NEW ENGLAND
HANOVER AND LONDON

BY SHAKER HANDS

The art and the world of the Shakers—
the furniture and artifacts,
and the spirit and precepts
embodied in their simplicity,
beauty, and functional practicality

*The University Press of New England
is a consortium of universities in New England dedicated to
publishing scholarly and trade works by authors from
member campuses and elsewhere. The New England imprint
signifies uniform standards for publication excellence
maintained without exception by the consortium members.
A joint imprint of University Press of New England
and a sponsoring member acknowledges the publishing
mission of that university and its support for the
dissemination of scholarship throughout the world.
Cited by the American Council of Learned Societies
as a model to be followed, University Press of New England
publishes books under its own imprint and the imprints of
Brandeis University, Brown University, Clark University,
University of Connecticut, Dartmouth College,
Middlebury College, University of New Hampshire,
University of Rhode Island,
Tufts University, University of Vermont,
Wesleyan University.*

Printed in the United States of America

∞

*Library of Congress Cataloging-in-Publication Data
Sprigg, June.
By Shaker Hands : the art and world of the Shakers . . . / June Sprigg.
p. cm.
Subtitle: The furniture and artifacts, and the spirit and precepts
embodied in their simplicity, beauty, and functional practicality.
Reprint. Originally published: New York : Knopf, 1975.
Includes bibliographical references and index.
ISBN 0-87451-542-4 (alk. paper)
1. Shakers. I. Title.
[BX9771.S67 1990]
289'.8—dc20   90-50316
CIP*

5   4   3   2   1

*This book
is respectfully
and lovingly
dedicated
to the memory of
Sister Lillian Phelps
(1876–1973),
of Canterbury,
New Hampshire,
who made all aware
that above all else
the Shaker way
meant love,
on earth
as it is in heaven.*

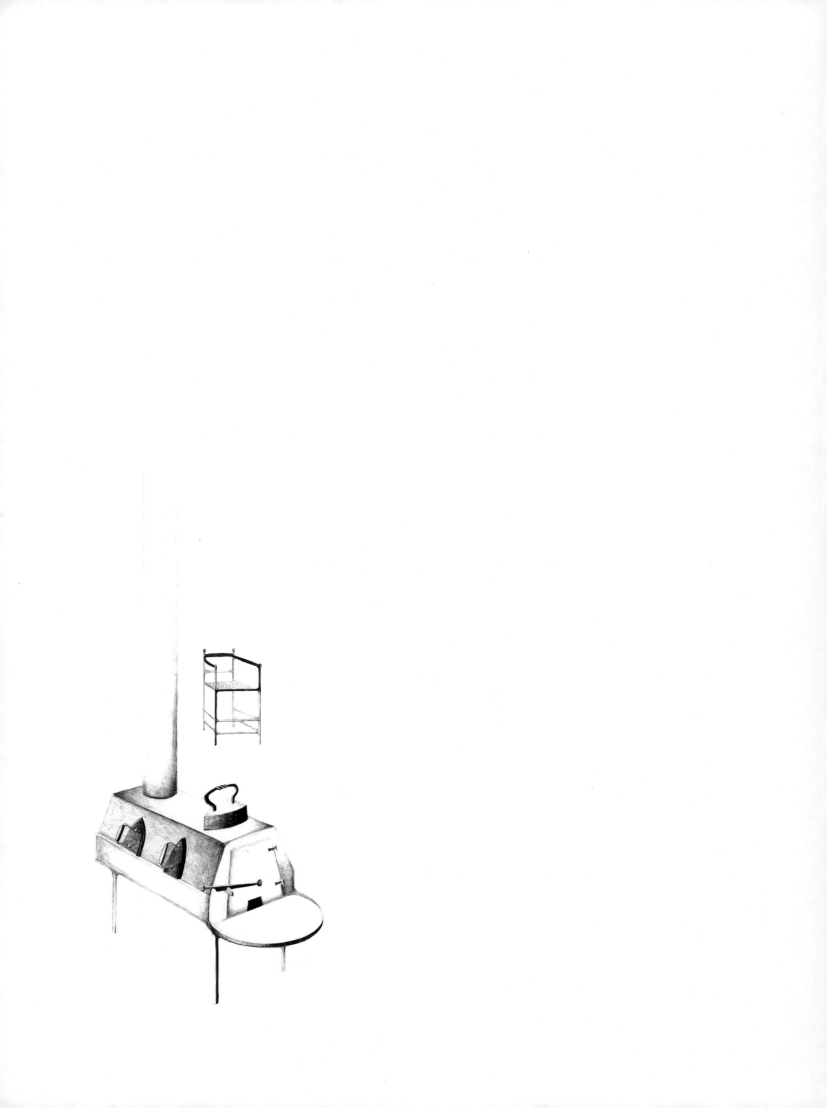

Contents

Motifs from Shaker spirit drawings are used for chapter headings.

pages 3, 77, and 159
Probably the best-known Shaker spirit drawing is Sister Hannah Cohoon's *Tree of Life, received as a vision and recorded in 1854.*

pages 33 and 87
It is easy to imagine the watch-toting angel singing,

> There is no time to sleep I say,
> Now in this great and glorious day
> Don't be sleeping there so sound,
> Get up yourselves and stir around
> For if you want to keep awake
> Arise and give a mighty shake.
> —Shaker hymn, 1850

The watch was a reminder that man's days on earth are numbered.

pages 49, 107, and 137
The spiritual purity symbolized by a rose emblem was matched by the Shakers' spotless cleanliness.

pages 63, 115, and 153
*The lamp design—*The Heavenly Father's Lamp of Eternal Brightness—*signified truth.*

pages 99 and 171
The "spiritual machine" is symbolic of progress to modern eyes. Among birds, trees, and other natural symbols, mechanical contraptions like this show how easily Shakers accepted progress in the material world as a true reflection of progress in the spiritual world.

The heading for the Notes is a detail of a Shaker-printed horseradish label. Heading the Selected References is the Mount Lebanon chair stamp, also shown on page 89. The Index heading is a detail of Elder Henry Blinn's map of Canterbury, shown on pages 20–21.

Many thanks to the many who helped me . . . John Ott, Director-Curator of Shaker Community, Inc., Hancock, Massachusetts; Robert Meader, Director of The Shaker Museum, Old Chatham, New York; Theodore Johnson, Director of The Shaker Museum, Sabbathday Lake, Maine; Suzanne Toomey, Curator of the Shaker Historical Society, Shaker Heights, Ohio; Mrs. K. E. Thomas, Trustee, Shaker Historical Society, Shaker Heights, Ohio; Kermit Pike, Chief Librarian of the Western Reserve Historical Society, Cleveland, Ohio; Frank Sommer, Head of Libraries of The Henry Francis du Pont Winterthur Museum, Winterthur, Delaware; David Proper, Librarian of the Memorial Libraries, Deerfield, Massachusetts; and Daniel Evans, Assistant Reference Librarian of Lafayette College, Easton, Pennsylvania, who did more digging than a clammer at low tide to unearth the works I needed.

Special thanks to the special . . . Gus and Alice Schwerdtfeger, makers of miniature Shaker furniture and beloved friends, who interested me in Shakers in the first place, introduced me to the Canterbury Shakers—and got as fine thanks five years of putting up (with) the kid from Pennsylvania; Peter Parnall, my art teacher and friend, who time and again pointed me in the right direction, usually back to the drawing board! To my mother and sister, who cheerfully endured eraser crumbs in the soup and artist's moods, and even more cheerfully waved me goodbye on research trips. I love them for their interest and encouragement. And to Angus Cameron, my editor, who rewarded my visit with his faith, a contract, writer's cramp, and the deep satisfaction of creating this book.

But it is the people of Shaker Village in Canterbury, New Hampshire, that I thank with all my heart . . . Bud Thompson, Director, who has shared willingly all that he has—knowledge, ideas, unique insight, even his best punch lines . . . without him, this book would never have been. Eldress Bertha Lindsay, who has generously shared her home, her experience, and herself with love and good will. I can thank, but never repay, the Shakers themselves, who have taught me more about the Shaker way by just being themselves than any book I've ever read.

By Shaker Hands

Introduction

My heavenly home is here,
No longer need I wait
To cross the foaming river,
Or pass the pearly gate;
I've angels all around me,
With kindness they surround me,
To a glorious cause they've bound me,
And my heavenly home is here.

—*Hymn from Mount Lebanon, N.Y., 1884*

In 1828, a visitor knocked at the door of a plain but neat building. He'd heard about the Shakers, those strange folk who lived off in their own communities—how they didn't marry, but lived together in purity and celibacy; how they danced and sang in worship of the Lord; and how they were convinced that a woman who'd come to America more than fifty years earlier had taught them to live as God's people. And, too, they were remarkable farmers and builders—he could see that already for himself. Still lost in thought, he watched as the door opened and a Brother smiled a greeting and welcomed him inside.

What he found were not religious fanatics or strange somber creatures—he was welcomed by simple, good, hard-working *people* who loved God and life so much that they wanted to make their own lives reflect the beauty and perfection of God's heaven. The day the visitor spent in the Shaker village showed him a hum of industry, from farming to baking to carpentry, in some of the neatest and cleanest workshops he'd ever seen. But what struck him most was a sense of harmony and joyousness in the way these people lived. Neat Sisters in their bonnets and Brothers in their straw hats spun or hoed busily, but not once did he hear a complaint or a cross word. The faces that he saw were content, with a serenity he'd rarely seen elsewhere. Off in the kitchen he heard a Sister sing,

I love my faithful brethren more
Than any souls I've seen before;
Their spirits are so clean and pure,
They are so kind and clever.

They were simple people, to be sure, working hard at ordinary jobs; but there was something special about the way they worked together. When he left at the day's end, he turned to the Brother who'd greeted him and impulsively commented on what he'd sensed. The Brother nodded and replied, "We think that man cannot hope to attain a spiritual heaven, until he first creates a heaven here on earth." Suddenly, the spirit of the Shaker way of life clicked inside him. When he went home that night, he wrote, "Although everything is plain, there is about the whole village an air of plenty, neatness and comfort which gives it the appearance of a little paradise as it were." He couldn't forget that "little paradise" and its faithful inhabitants, and when he came the next time, it was to stay.

There were once nineteen Shaker villages flourishing in America, in eight of the states from Maine to Kentucky. Visitors to any one of them one hundred twenty-five years ago would have seen an average of three hundred members busy in mills, shops, and gardens, putting their hands to work at everything from sawing to smithing to cooking to weaving.

The village at Canterbury, New Hampshire, was a typical one. Remote from what the Shakers called "the great and wicked cities," the Canterbury Shakers relied on themselves and their lands as much as they could for everything that they needed. Visitors might have seen Brothers busily scooping clay from the pond banks to make the bricks that they used and sold. Other members like Brother Micajah Tucker might have been hard at work prying granite from the land to cut into foundations, steps, fence posts, and sidewalks. Businessmen from the cities bustled into the Office to place orders for Shaker dried apples, patent medicines, even a water-powered mechanical washing machine.

Across the street in the Infirmary, Brother Thomas Corbett bandaged a toe and went back into the Medicine Room to put up more bottles of Shakers' Sarsaparilla Syrup. The lowing of a hundred thoroughbred cattle accompanied the bleating of fine Merino sheep at evening time, while in the day the village rang with the blows of the blacksmith and the whine of the sawmill. Sisters in the Bake Room hummed as they finished dozens of apple pies, using the fruits of the harvest from the orchards near the Schoolhouse; children rustled to attention as their school bell clanged. It was home for nearly four hundred men, women, and children who shared their work, love, and worship. They considered themselves part of one family under Christ, so they called each other Brother and Sister.

Shakers had a dream of independence from the outside world, and the down-to-earth common sense to achieve it. They were so practical, hard-working, efficient, and inventive that they produced for themselves almost everything that they used, in the early days. Only a few things—glass for windows, chinaware, sheets of tin, for example—were bought from the World, as the Shakers called the outside towns. Through hard work and thrift, Shaker villages grew large, prosperous, and orderly; Canterbury, for example, once had 4,000 acres of fertile fields and forest, and over a hundred neat buildings. From an economic standpoint, the Shakers were a remarkable success.

But self-sufficiency and financial success were only means to an end for the Shakers. More than anything else, they sought freedom to work and worship in a world of harmony and brotherly love that most people thought could exist only in heaven. Their motto was "Put your hands to work, and your hearts to God."

Since they felt that the homes they created were a true reflection of the inner spirit, they practiced the ideals that they preached. Whatever they held most important for the good of their souls—honesty, utility, simplicity, purity, progress, order, precision, economy—they felt should be a part of the things that they made and the way that they lived every day. One Shaker said it for all when he said, "Heaven and Earth are threads of one loom."

The Shaker way of life was not always so ordered, prosperous, and peaceful, however. There was a time when being a Shaker meant persecution, poverty, even imprisonment. When young Ann Lee, in the 1750s, joined a group of former Quakers to worship in Manchester, England, she began a lifetime of hardship and scorn as the founder of a new faith called Shakerism. They were seeking, as a member later said, "to know by daily experience . . . the peaceable nature of Christ's Kingdom." Born in 1736 in the run-down section of Manchester called Toad Lane, Ann Lee became convinced through visions that she and others could serve God and each other best if they led celibate lives devoted to virtue and work. Soon the others recognized her as the spiritual leader of the group, and she became known as Mother Ann. Although they felt that she had brought the spirit of Christian love to earth once again, they didn't worship her as a second Messiah.

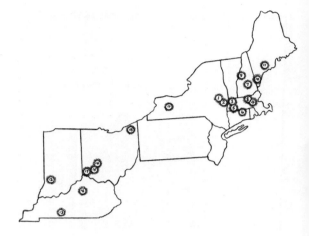

1 Watervliet, N.Y.	1787–1938
2 New Lebanon, N.Y	1787–1947
(in 1861 became Mount Lebanon)	
3 Hancock, Mass.	1790–1960
4 Harvard, Mass.	1791–1919
5 Tyringham, Mass.	1792–1875
6 Enfield, Conn.	1792–1917
7 Canterbury, N.H.	1792–
8 Shirley, Mass.	1793–1909
9 Enfield, N.H.	1793–1918
10 Alfred, Maine	1793–1931
11 Sabbathday Lake, Maine	1794–
12 West Union, Ind. (Busro)	1810–1827
13 South Union, Ky.	1811–1922
14 Union Village, Ohio	1812–1910
15 Watervliet, Ohio	1813–1900
16 Pleasant Hill, Ky.	1814–1910
17 Whitewater, Ohio	1824–1907
18 North Union, Ohio	1826–1889
19 Groveland, N.Y.	1836–1892

Glass was one of a few things the self-sufficient Shakers didn't make. A view from the Dwellinghouse (1793) at Canterbury, New Hampshire, shows the slate roof of the North Shop (1841) through the old wavy panes. Slate was something else the "Granite State" Shakers had to buy, so they purchased fine Welsh slate to make roofs as durable as their buildings.

She herself said humbly, "Do not kneel to me; kneel to God. I am but your fellow-servant."

In these earliest days of the faith, members moved by the spirit were often seized with shaking and whirling in their religious fervor—a form of worship that gave them their name (originally "Shaking Quakers") and that conservative members of the English Church found hard to understand or accept. In spite of beatings and imprisonment for their unusual beliefs and worship, Ann and her followers persisted in their faith. Finally it became clear to her through visions that the American colonies could offer the Shakers the freedom and members they needed to pursue their godly lives in peace.

When Mother Ann and her group of only eight followers left England in 1774, Shakerism became a religion and a way of life in its own right. No members continued on to form Shaker communities in England or Europe; and although the Quakers and the Shakers continued to share beliefs in pacifism, equality of people, brotherly love, and sharing in worship, once the Shakers settled in America they became a uniquely American communal system.

In May 1774, Mother Ann and her small group set sail on the *Mariah* for a voyage of three difficult months. Even on board they couldn't escape persecution, this time from superstitious sailors who blamed all hardships on the Shakers and their strange manners and worship. When a storm broke and the ship sprang a leak in mid-Atlantic, the frightened sailors were ready to toss Mother Ann overboard to rid the ship of what they felt was the cause of God's wrath. Mother Ann, however, never gave up hope. Receiving strength from a vision of angels at the helm calming the waters, she convinced the sailors that the ship would safely reach its destination. As the story goes, the plank that waves had torn loose washed miraculously back into place with the next blow of the water; and when the storm calmed, the sailors treated the Shakers with new respect.

When Ann and her eight faithful landed in New York on August 6, 1774, they must have felt as if they had reached the Promised Land. But the way was still not easy. They had no homes, no money, knew no one, and had nothing to give them hope of success. For the first years, they didn't even have a single convert to their faith. Since they neither married nor had children, they needed converts to fill their ranks with members. It must have been discouraging, but they worked hard: Mother Ann as a washerwoman, her brother William as a blacksmith, and her devoted follower and eventual successor, James Whittaker, as a weaver. By 1776 they had earned enough for a home of their own, at Niskeyuna, New York (later called Watervliet), in the wilderness near Albany.

Unhappily, Mother Ann and her followers could not escape persecution in America, either. They came from England just before the Revolution, and people accused them of being British spies. As always, the superstitious felt that it was unnatural for anyone willingly to give up marriage or his Worldly possessions to share in common with others, and Mother Ann was accused of being a witch.

But persecution and poverty to the point of near starvation could not defeat the Shakers' faith in Mother Ann or in God during those difficult years. With the only powers they had—the faith in their hearts and the work of their hands—they managed to accomplish a success that seemed miraculous enough to them to give them renewed faith in their chosen way. By the mid-1780s, converts were "flocking in like doves," as Mother Ann had predicted. Within less than thirty years after their arrival in America, more than half of the eventual nineteen villages stood solidly across the New England States, with over a thousand members. By the Civil War, all nineteen were firmly established, with over six thousand members from Kentucky to Maine.

Sadly, Mother Ann died in 1784, only ten years after her arrival; she was just forty-eight years old. She never lived to see the flourishing of the Shaker way of life. After her death, one of her faithful followers from England became the leading spirit. As he had once saved Ann from starving in an English prison, James Whittaker again saved Ann's faith from passing with her. For three years "Father James" helped the faith grow; when he died in 1787, Joseph Meacham—a Yankee convert from Enfield, Connecticut—became one of the early leaders responsible for the order and practicality of the Shaker way. He chose Lucy Wright, another devoted convert from Pittsfield, Massachusetts, as the Sisters' leader. Under "Father Joseph" and "Mother Lucy," the order of the Shaker community became a working way of life.

What were the beliefs of the men and women who made these villages successful? Most importantly, they believed in sharing, especially in worship. They didn't believe in sitting dumbly in church while one man did all the preaching; the "tithingman's stick" that knocked the noggins of nodding parishioners in colonial churches was unnecessary in a Shaker Meetinghouse. They expressed their love of God by rising together and joining in singing and dancing. A visitor to the Meetinghouse one hundred fifty years ago would have seen rows of singers and lines of Brothers and Sisters dancing in neat ranks or circles, usually the men on the left and the women on the right. From some of the shaking motions that accompanied their early dances when they would "shake out sin" or "shake out the Devil," they had been called Shakers. In spite of the scorn that originally accompanied the name, they accepted it, feeling that their faith was indeed mighty enough to shake the heavens and the earth. The name they chose to give themselves later was the United Society of Believers in the First and Second Appearing of Christ; they called themselves the Society or Believers, but most often just plain Shakers.

In the earliest years of the faith, the visitor would not have witnessed such orderly participation in worship. He would have seen every member moved to feel the presence of God in his own spontaneous way, whether whirling like a dervish or shaking mightily. One of the earliest commentators on the Shakers wrote in 1781 (just seven years after their arrival in America) that during "the best part of their worship" the spirit moved each member to almost any form of worship. He watched in dismay and later wrote that

> one will stand with his arms extended, acting over odd postures, which they call signs; another will be dancing, and sometimes hopping on one leg about the floor; another will fall to turning round, to twist if it be a woman, her cloaths will be so filled with the wind, as though they were kept out by a hoop; another will be prostrate on the floor; another will be talking with somebody; and some sitting by, smoaking their pipe; groaning most dismally; some trembling extremely; others acting as though all their nerves were convulsed; others swinging their arms, with all vigor, as though they were turning a wheel, &c.

No wonder he was convinced that this was the work of the Devil. What he didn't understand was that these people had enough love and trust for each other to share their deepest religious emotions freely.

Spiritual fervor intensified during the early years of settlement until its climax from about 1840 to 1850. At this time, Shaker worship was characterized by what members felt was direct communication with God; the emotional impact was so powerful that for a time visitors were not permitted to observe. Outdoor services became a regular part of the Shakers' spiritual celebration. Members marched reverently to a select spot or "feast ground" several miles from the village and there sang, shouted, and clapped in joyous submission to God. A "holy stone" or "fountain stone" inscribed with words of the Lord marked the spiritual "fountain" where Believers received spiritual "gifts" of inspired dancing, heavenly visions, or speaking in tongues.

By the late Victorian years and throughout the twentieth century, the visitor wouldn't have seen dancing at all, but he would have heard all the Shakers singing together and individual members freely speaking out prayers or messages as the spirit moved them.

So although the exact form of worship changed over the Shakers' two hundred years here, the same spirit of sharing in worship moved

Variations on a theme are Shaker hand-turned wall pegs. The mushroom cap is the most characteristic shape; screw pegs were easily replaceable. The unusually graceful long peg with the rounded end is from the Canterbury Trustees' Office (1831). (Canterbury, N.H.)

them all. As one Shaker Sister wrote in 1880, "We aim to cultivate simplicity and freedom in our meetings, and all, both brethren and sisters, are expected to take an active part; to sing, speak and give utterance to their best thoughts and devotional feelings."

Another belief of the Shakers was in sharing their property. People who joined brought whatever they had; no matter what it was, the convert was welcome because of his willingness to share.

The story of the settling of the village at Canterbury gives a good idea of how most of the villages came into existence. Families listened to Shakers passing through the neighborhood on their preaching missions in the earliest years in America, and those who were moved by the Shaker spirit began to practice Shaker beliefs like celibacy and charity in their own homes. Soon converts in the area would begin to share worship in each other's homes. At Canterbury, the Whitcher family—Benjamin, his wife, Mary, and their three sons and a daughter—began to hold worship meetings at their small farm home in the 1780s. For ten years, they "most generously and conscientiously opened their doors and spread their tables in welcome to every one who came to seek for the truth"—sometimes over forty Believers would stay on Saturday night and worship together on Sunday, the women sleeping in the small house and the men in the Whitcher barn.

In 1792, these faithful worshippers decided to share their lives as one Shaker Family. They chose Benjamin Whitcher's farm as their home since it had the best land and water. He gave his entire farm of 100 acres to share with others; others sold their lands and gave the money to buy surrounding acres. The point was that whatever the convert brought was welcome because it was given with love for all to share. The 127 pounds of cheese that Solomon Frizzle brought to the Harvard Shakers in Massachusetts and the single pound of chocolate that Mehitable Grace could afford meant as much as Whitcher's whole farm.

Sharing work was another important part of the Shakers' worship and way of life. As they worked together to build their barns and homes, they built a spirit of communal love and brotherhood at the same time. The Shaker knew that he was working for the good of all his

The Shaker motto was "Hands to work, hearts to God." Sisters shared stints in the kitchen on an alternate basis; pie-baking for a Family of several hundred was typically efficient, progressive, and ingenious. Opposite, the Sister on the right prepares dough on a handy work surface–storage area kitchen table, while another carries a pie from the famous iron and brick revolving oven at Canterbury, New Hampshire. On the left, a pie safe from South Union, Kentucky. Tin panels in the doors were pierced from the inside to let air in but help keep insects out.

Brothers and Sisters, not just to put a shirt on his back or money in the bank. So, for the Shaker, work was not a necessary evil. He went to work willingly, glad to devote his time and effort to making a better way. One member wrote:

> *I'll work 13 hours, in each 24*
> *Or more if necessity call;*
> *In point of distinction, I want nothing more*
> *Than just to be servant of all;*
> *I peaceably work at whatever I'm set,*
> *From no other motive but love,*
> *To honor the gospel and keep out of debt,*
> *And lay up a treasure above.*

Elder Frederick Evans spoke for all Shakers when he put it this way: "While my work has ever been before me, my reward has always been with me."

Work was one joyful and satisfying form of worship because it gave the Shaker a chance to put his beloved ideals into practice. People today admire Shaker furniture and architecture because of its simplicity, honesty, grace, utility, and sturdiness. These are the qualities that characterize the things they made, because these were the ideals

Probably the most famous Shaker invention was the flat broom, shared freely with the World because the Shakers thought patenting was selfish. Brother Theodore Bates of Watervliet, New York, watched the Sisters sweeping in 1798 with their common round brooms and realized that they were wasting time and effort. He didn't offer to help sweep, but he did flatten the brooms to make them more efficient.

that the Shaker felt were a part of God's heaven and his home. As one member said, "What are goods worth unless they are full of genuine religion?"

Work was just as much a part of the Shaker's worship as worship was a part of his work. No one ever told him that living as God wanted was going to be anything but hard work. The Shaker knew that his spiritual work was even more demanding than the work of his hands. One member observed, "A good many Christians pray that the world may be converted and then sit down and wait for God to answer their prayers. But if they are farmers, they never pray that God will plough their corn fields, and then get up on the fence and wait to see the dirt fly."

"Labor" was the word they used to describe the way they worshipped in their Meetinghouse—they "labored" at their dancing to come closer to God. Mother Ann said, "Labor to make the ways of God your own." The Shaker felt simply that work and worship were inseparable, and put his hands to work and his heart to God where he worked *and* where he worshipped. How significant that the Shaker Meetinghouse looked like a simple workshop with its plain wooden floors and white walls, and that the huge Shaker barns looked as majestic as cathedrals with their lovingly polished beams and great wooden vaults.

The sharing of ideas was just as important to the Shaker way of life. It seems incredible that a small group of people who never numbered more than six thousand at a time could have produced so many inventions and so much plain and simple ingenuity. The flat broom, the circular saw, metal pens, the everyday clothespin, the notion of selling seeds in paper packages, the swivel foot on chairs . . . so many of the good ideas we take for granted today are attributed to the ingenuity of Shaker men and women. Walk into a Shaker room and you see convenient drawers built into the walls; the handy row of pegs on the wall; a clever pulley door to save steps outside; even a window in the side of a cupboard just where it's needed for light inside. It seems that the Shakers always figured out exactly the best way to do anything; and so most people think that Shakers must have been smarter than ordinary people.

Well, the Shakers *weren't* any smarter than most of us. What they were was more loving and more willing to share. They were simple farmers, tradesmen, craftsmen, and housewives who had just a few advantages over everybody else. For one thing, they shared their ideas freely, through visits or letters. If a Brother in Maine thought up a better way to do something, it was soon bound to spread from his village to them all, as far as Kentucky. Shaker leaders traveled to each other's villages and kept detailed journals of all the good ideas they saw; when they came home, they brought home a record of ideas that worked.

For another thing, the celibate Shakers had certain advantages in relying entirely upon converts for members. People of all trades joined together in one Family and shared all the skills they had, from medicine-making to bricklaying to dyeing and beekeeping. This is one explanation for the Shakers' celebrated self-sufficiency. Another reason was that members shared turns at many different jobs through job rotation every few weeks. All the men shared turns at farming, tailoring, woodworking, and the like, while Sisters spent alternate stints in the kitchens, laundry, gardens, sewing shop, and so on.

Sharing through communication was so important that the Shakers even published their own newspaper (printed at Canterbury) during the end of the nineteenth century. From 1871 to 1873 it was called *The Shaker;* in 1873, women's liberation hit and it became *Shaker and Shakeress.* Four years later the name changed again to *The Shaker Manifesto;* in 1888 it became *The Manifesto* and stayed that way until its last issue in 1900. Shakers wrote and read inspirational articles, home notes from all the villages, an obituary column, letters to the editor, book reviews, and good hints on better ideas in farming, working, and housekeeping.

The Shakers believed just as strongly in sharing their good ideas with others; Shaker inventions like the flat broom, the clothespin, and the circular saw were given freely to the World because Shakers did not believe in patenting, feeling that it was selfish and un-Christian. They were honest but shrewd tradesmen and refused to cheat or be cheated; later in the nineteenth century, certain Shaker inventors did patent some of their major contributions like the water-powered washing machine and the revolving oven, but only with great reluctance. No more than a half-dozen Shaker ideas were patented during two centuries of free sharing.

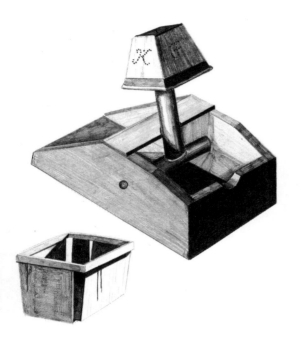

Shakers believed in making the right tool for every job to save time, like this berry box form. Thin wood sheets folded across each other over the box-shaped wooden form; then the whole form swung down on its arm to turn in the groove while a Brother nailed on the wooden rim. Iron plates crimped the nails underneath as he turned the box. The simple initial "K" marked the maker; Shakers rarely signed their work, believing in personal anonymity for the sake of the community. (Canterbury, N.H.)

❋

One of the steadfast beliefs of the Shakers was in celibacy; they neither married nor had children. Outsiders often wondered if this weren't an unnatural and loveless way of life, but they couldn't have been more wrong according to the Shakers. Members felt that celibacy freed them from limits on their ability to love—rather than devoting all his love to a personal family of four or five, the Shaker was free to love all the members of his large Shaker Family equally. Since Shaker Families numbered several hundred, he felt that he was giving and receiving infinitely more love: he called it "universal love." To the Shakers, celibate love meant a more perfect kind of love, without covetousness, envy, or lust.

Although Shaker Brothers and Sisters didn't have their own children, they were never deprived of the love—or spared the trouble—of raising youngsters. One of the most important functions of the Shaker village was to provide good loving homes for any homeless or unwanted child who would otherwise have been at the mercy of the World. Sometimes, too, a man and wife would join the Shakers and bring their children with them. Then the man would live with the Brothers, the woman with the Sisters, and the children would find a good home in the Children's Order. In any case, during the nineteenth century there were always plenty of children to liven the village. When they grew up, they were just as free to choose the Shaker life or not as any other convert; at twenty-one they could make their decision.

Since the Shakers didn't rely on children for their members, they had to attract converts to their faith. Once they had settled into their villages, they gave up preaching in the outside "great and wicked cities" and felt that the best way to gather in new members was to share their worship services and their hospitality with visitors. On a typical Sunday morning, carriages and wagons lined the way to the Meetinghouse, with often over a hundred visitors inside, sitting on benches and watching the Shakers dance. On June 14, 1874, the Sabbathday Lake Shakers in Maine had what must have been a record crowd of "five hundred spectators or more." Wrote the recorder, "The House could not hold them all and it was surrounded on three sides by a gaping crowd at all the windows."

Many visitors, moved by the spirit they felt, stayed on and became

Shakers themselves; others seem to have been moved by curiosity, sympathy—or hunger! At one time it seems that certain visitors enjoyed Sunday dinner with the Canterbury Shakers so much that the Shakers circulated a notice welcoming visitors to their services but requesting them please not to expect to stay to dinner every week.

Sharing together and living together as a community meant that members had to treat each other as equals. No one was slighted and none was given special treatment: leader, "hand-minded" member, man, woman, black, white, old person, or child—all were treated with the same dignity, and all were expected to give their hands to work and their hearts to God.

No one thought he was better than anyone else, and the sense of union and brotherhood that resulted meant that individual pride was a sin which could not be tolerated. Open a Shaker hymnal and you won't find the name of the individual composer; you'll read simply the name of the community where he lived. Examine Shaker tools and it's seldom that you will see more than initials to identify the maker. According to the religious rules of the Shakers,

> No one should write or print his name on any article of manufacture, that others may hereafter know the work of his hand.
>
> The names of individuals may not be put upon the outside of the covers of books, of any kind.

Little did it bother a Shaker carpenter that his name would someday be forgotten; he wanted it to be that way. Anonymity and obscurity were not the curse for Shakers that they are for most creators. They were deliberate, and to the Shaker they meant a blessing because he had succeeded in putting his ego second to the good of his community. The Shaker cemeteries in most of the communities today don't even have individual tombstones—one monument to the "Shakers" reminds all who pass that the Shakers chose to live and work as a community.

The leaders in a Shaker village were not privileged characters; they shared work and rules along with everyone else, besides having the added responsibilities of leadership. Each Shaker Family had three sets of leaders, for spiritual, business, and domestic concerns. The spiritual

Brothers made nested oval wooden boxes, perhaps most symbolic of the Shaker way in their perfection, beauty, and practicality. Light and delicate as they are, they were designed to last forever, with "finger" joinery. Shakers knew that wood swells across the grain when damp, so they cut wooden fingers—the joint "breathes" without warping or buckling, and the lids slide on as perfectly today as they did when new. Copper nails wouldn't rust and ruin the wood.

leaders (and the leaders of the village in general) were the Elders and Eldresses—two Brothers and two Sisters chosen to lead the village in matters of worship and conduct. They also heard confession of sins regularly from other members.

For business matters, the Shakers entrusted two men and two women to act as Trustees to manage buying and selling. They worked in the business Office of the village and were during the early years the only Shakers allowed to go into the World on business errands. Two Deacons and two Deaconesses were in charge of all the practical matters of village life, from overseeing in industry, to organizing the schedules of cleaning and farming, to seeing that everyone was properly fed and clothed.

Although Shakers believed in treating all people as equals, they never pretended that all people *were* equal. Shakers from the beginning chose to have the wisest and best among them guide them along the path of God's way. Shaker Elders and Eldresses were often outstanding men and women of their time. There were men like Elder Henry Blinn of Canterbury (1824–1905), who was master of over a dozen skills from printing to beekeeping; he corresponded with the Oneida community about communal living. His fitting counterpart at Canterbury was Eldress Dorothy Durgin (1825–98), a dynamic and progressive educator and close friend of Mary Baker Eddy, the founder of the Church of Christ, Scientist; she brought the first musical instrument into the Shaker world when she persuaded a music store proprietor to share a little pump organ with the Shakers in 1871.

The leaders of the village at Mount Lebanon, New York, were the "Parent Ministry" over all the Shaker villages. Some of these men and women were the most remarkable of all. Elder Frederick Evans (1808–93) went to England to lecture on vegetarianism and ventilation; he also persuaded Abraham Lincoln to free the Shakers from the military draft, and shared ideas with Tolstoy through correspondence.

Another strong tenet of the Shakers was a belief in the importance of order. The village itself was arranged into several "Orders" or "Families." Each Family had its own Dwellinghouse, workshops, and set of leaders, but the main or Church Family was the location of the one Meetinghouse that served them all; the Church Family leaders were the ones responsible for the village as a whole.

One of the Families was called the "Gathering Order," where a person interested in joining the Shakers was encouraged to try the life and see if it were best for him. After all, becoming a Shaker was no light matter; it meant giving up marriage, personal gain, and the natural tendency to put oneself first. Instead of letting people join quickly only to decide later that they had made a mistake, Shakers chose to have converts make up their minds at a pace that was fair both to themselves and to the village.

Everything and everyone had a proper place in the village, and all parts worked together for the good of the whole. One of the ways that Shakers maintained order was by living according to certain set standards. In the early years, the *Millennial Laws* played an important part in keeping order. These rules, received as divine revelation from heaven by a member in 1821 and slightly revised in 1845, told the Shaker the right way to do most things. Both practical and spiritual, they advised on everything from the color he painted on the trim of his different buildings, to the way he should pray, to the way he made his furniture.

Many of the minor rules in these *Millennial Laws* applied only to the early years of the faith—for example, the very minor ones which

Shaker beliefs in simplicity, celibacy, and equality of the sexes were reflected in their simple double-doored Dwellinghouses, like this one built in 1817 at the East Family of Pleasant Hill, Kentucky. Brothers used the left side, Sisters the right.

specified that members should fold their right thumbs over their left for the sake of uniformity when clasping hands; or the very stringent ones which forbade musical instruments, flowers, literature, or communication between the Brothers and Sisters. Today, you won't find Shakers eating in monastic silence or refusing to offer their hands to people from the World; these rules have long since been found unnecessary. On the whole, though, most of the laws had a basis in common sense or spiritual sense that held good throughout two centuries of Shakerism, and they give a fascinating glimpse into the way the Shakers put their ideals into daily practice. Other inspired works that guided Shakers were *The Gospel Monitor*, written in 1841 and printed two years later, a guide for raising children; and *The Youth's Guide in Zion*, received and printed in 1842.

The appearance of the Shaker village was also the result of a belief in proper order. A typical Shaker village had various buildings that were considered essential for the Shaker way of life. First and most important was the Meetinghouse, the place of worship. The largest building in the Family was the Dwellinghouse, where members ate and slept. The Meetinghouse and Dwellinghouse nearly always had double doors; the Dwellinghouse, which often had as many as five storeys, usually had double hallways and staircases inside to boot. The two doors reminded Shakers and visitors alike that Brothers and Sisters were equal but decidedly separate: the left side of the buildings was occupied by Brothers, and the right side by Sisters.

Inside the Dwellinghouse, members slept dormitory-style with two or three occupants in a room. There were usually huge storage attics and plenty of closets, and always a worship hall, meeting rooms, a common dining hall, and large kitchens and bakeries—normally in the lowest floor near the cool food cellars.

The only people who didn't live in the Dwellinghouse were the Elders and Eldresses and the children. The Elders and Eldresses originally lived in the two upper floors of the Meetinghouse, but by the later nineteenth century there was usually a separate house for them called the Ministry's Shop. Elders lived downstairs, Eldresses upstairs. If you had walked into Canterbury's Ministry's Shop a hundred years ago, you might have seen Elder Henry Blinn pulling teeth in his Dentist's Shop in the back room, or playing marble games with the children who were so fond of him.

Girls lived in a separate Girls' House until age fourteen with several Sisters chosen as Caretakers; boys had their own Boys' House with Brothers to care for them. At fourteen, young people moved into the Dwellinghouse. Both boys and girls received excellent education in the Shaker Schoolhouse for nine years, or until they were about fifteen. Although you may read in old stories how the little girls' long pigtails usually wound up in the inkwells of the boys behind them, that probably would never have happened in a Shaker school—because until the turn of the twentieth century boys and girls went to school at different times of the year. Boys went for the three winter months, and girls during the three months in the summer. As a rule, Brothers taught the boys, and Sisters the girls; but they were taught the same things.

Most of the Shakers' day was not spent in the Dwellinghouse, but in workshops. Their motto was "Hands to work and hearts to God," and they practiced what they preached. The Canterbury Shakers, for example, built their Meetinghouse in 1792 as the first community building, where they could put their hearts to God as a Family. The next building they raised was a tannery, where together they could put their hands to work. Only in 1793, the following year, did they consider themselves ready to build the Dwellinghouse where they ate and slept.

Every Shaker village had certain standard workbuildings. There were always a cow barn, a horse barn, and the assorted outbuildings that go with them; a blacksmith shop; a laundry; a business office; sawmill and gristmill; a spinning and weaving shop; a carpenter shop; and a schoolhouse. Most villages had a separate infirmary building. Shakers everywhere worked in orchards and large vegetable gardens.

The one other standard feature of a Shaker village was the cemetery. Shakers understood and accepted death as naturally as they did life—as one Shaker put it, "Death is but taking off the coat"—so the graveyard was not marked with solemn monuments. Simple stone or metal markers stood together in some villages; in others, only a single marker inscribed "Shakers" indicates where several hundred members lie at rest. From the time of Elder Frederick Evans (in the late nineteenth century), Shakers saw no point in wasting time and effort carving and maintaining stones for each member. Elder Frederick

A Shaker rocker was typically light, simple in line, easy to clean, and sturdy. (Old Chatham, N.Y.)

The Church or Center Family at Canterbury, New Hampshire, begun in 1792, was mapped by Elder Henry Blinn in 1848, when Canterbury and Shakerism in general flourished at their peak. Shaker villages were as straight and foursquare in layout as the Shakers themselves. (Buildings marked ★ still stand.)

1	Meetinghouse★	1792
2	Ministry Shop★	1848
3	Carriage House	
4	Girls' House★	
5	Spin Shop★	⎫
6	Elder Sisters' Shop★	⎬ 1816
7	Dwellinghouse★	⎫
8	Elder Brothers' Room★	⎬ 1793
9	Meeting Room★	⎭
10	Overseers' Rooms★	
11	Kitchen★	
12	Ministry's Kitchen★	
13	Bake Room★	
14	Sick House	⎫
15	Dairy	⎬
16	Brethren's Shop	⎫
17	Elder Brothers' Shop	⎬
18	Lower House★	1811
19	Yellow Building★	⎫
20	Garden Seed Room★	
21	Granary★	⎬ 1825
22	Carriage House★	
23	Wood House★	⎭
24	Brethren's Shop★	⎫
25	Doctor's Shop★	
26	Shoemaker's Shop★	⎬ 1824
27	Joiner's Shop★	
28	Farmer's Shop★	⎭

29	Boys' House and Wood House (note wind sock weathervane)	
30	Wood House★	⎫
31	Weave Room★	⎬ 1841
32	Store Room★	⎭
33	Wash House★	⎫
34	Steam Engine★	⎬ 1816
35	Distillery★	1795
36	House for the Fire Engine	
37	Best of Red-cheeks	
38	Shop for Pressing Herbs★	1806
39	Home Orchard	
40	Cart House★	
41	Ox Barn	
42	Cow Barn	
43	Cow Watering Trough	
44	Ox Watering Trough	
45	Engine, Wood Shed	
46	Hen House	
47	Hen Yard	
48	Peter Ayre's House	
49	Sheep Barn	1814
50	Sheep Yard	
51	Bird House	
52	Plum Orchard	
53	Dry House for Lumber	

54	Cider Mill	
55	Botanical Garden (to the east)	
56	Garden Barn	1828
57	Wood House	
58	Printing Shop (where Elder Henry printed the first Shaker books and the Shaker newspaper)	
59	Schoolhouse★	1823
60	Horse Barn★	1819
61	Horse Stand	
62	Red Building or Office Store and Carriage House	
63	Office★	1831
64	Wood House	
65	Wood and Coal House	
66	Blacksmith's Shop	1811
67	Tinker's Shop	
68	Office Garden (to the south)	
69	Hog Pen	
70	Hog Pen	
71	Old Horse Mill	

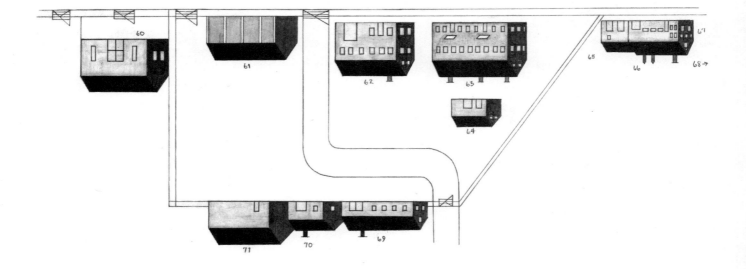

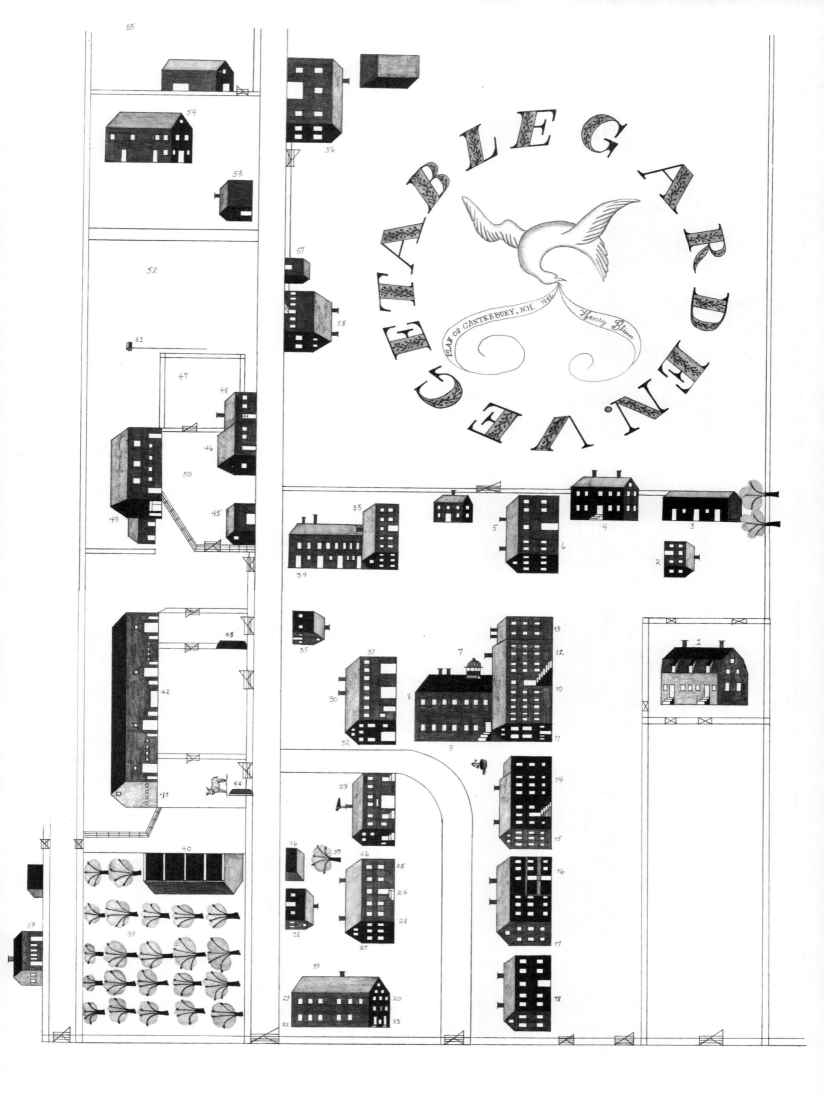

VEGETABLE GARDEN

PLAN OF CANTERBURY, N.H. 1848   Henry Blinn

Sharing in work was as important as sharing in worship. Two Sisters shared one sewing desk with drawers on the front and side. Typically simple and beautifully made, the desk has a space-saving slide-out cutting board and narrow drawer below for patterns. (Canterbury, N.H.)

said, "Let our lives be our memorials." Today these Shakers share one stone in death as they shared one home in life.

The Shakers believed strongly in pacifism. They were proud of America and happy to be citizens, since America had been their chosen land of freedom. But in spite of their patriotism, they refused to bear arms for their country because they firmly believed that all men were brothers. Their devotion to nonviolence caused them much suffering during wartime, especially in the Civil War. Shakers hated slavery, but they loved peace even more; so they chose to fight slavery with words and prayers, not guns.

Americans tended to forget all the good that Shakers had freely shared, however, and sometimes thought that the Shakers were ungratefully neglecting their duties as good citizens. The Shakers in Kentucky suffered particularly, since their devotion to helping their fellow men meant that they fed and sheltered the men in blue or gray alternately, whoever occupied their territory at the time. The hearts and consciences of many hardened soldiers must have been touched during those war years in the simple Shaker homes. In 1862, one officer leaving the dinner table thanked a Sister named Hannah for the meal, adding in jest, "I fear you will kill us with good victuals. She replied, better that, than with a bullet. This seemed to take him by the heart, She passed on."

The military draft was even more of a problem for Shaker Brothers. Elder Henry Blinn of Canterbury was one of the Brothers called in for his examination in 1863. The good Elder suffered patiently, standing during the long delay in the waiting room, and kept quiet in spite of the rough behavior of the crowd. The only time he opened his mouth at all, in fact, was when the doctor inspected his teeth, and then he had to hold it open so wide that he said later he felt like "the man who attempted to swallow an island," while the doctor peeked and poked.

But finally even Elder Henry's patience came to an end. When the doctor asked him to strip for his physical, Elder Henry felt "this was a little too sweeping to correspond to the rules of propriety"—and the modest Elder firmly "threw in a Christian remonstrance" which caused the doctor to relent and settle for a partial disrobing.

The healthy condition of Shaker Brothers like Elder Henry might have proved disastrous, since he was found more than acceptable physically for the army, had not Shakers been granted "indefinite furloughs" during the war. Thanks to the appeal in person of Elder Frederick Evans of Mount Lebanon to President Lincoln, Brothers were classified as the equivalent of conscientious objectors. Besides pleading reasons of conscience, Elder Frederick pointed out that many earlier Shakers who had fought in the Revolution had done the government a favor already by refusing to collect the pensions for which they were legally eligible. Honest Abe was sympathetic with their belief in peace and pacifism and granted them exemption, but added with regret that what the country needed was "whole regiments of just such men as these."

Another belief of the Shakers was abstinence from Worldly politics. They did not participate by running or campaigning and didn't vote in any elections. Since they wanted to be independent, they always felt that they had no right to tell the country how to pick its leaders or run its affairs unless they were willing to have the World do the same to them.

And besides, Shakers felt that God was their leader above all Worldly politicians, and that they were better off living in peace in His kingdom than disrupting their harmony by arguing politics among themselves every time the nation went to the polls. During the campaign between Clay and Jackson, one Brother commented wryly how glad he was the Shakers had more sense than to fool with politics. Going into town, he said, "There is a great many people gathered here as it is election day; and they seem to be very talkative and sometimes seem to entertain a slight variation of opinion so much that I fear they will get to deciding it by hard knocks before they get through!"

More than anything else, perhaps, the Shakers believed in freedom—from sin, from sickness, from passion, jealousy, bad habit, hatred, filth, and chaos. Despite the strict discipline of work, celibacy, and humility, the Shakers always considered themselves the freest people in the world because the Shakers' way of life was always a *chosen* way, never an imposed one.

Since they were celibate, no one was ever born automatically into

For the pacifist Shakers, a "revolver" was a revolving or swivel chair, said to have been the innovation of Shakers in Enfield, New Hampshire. The back spindles are made of wood or metal.

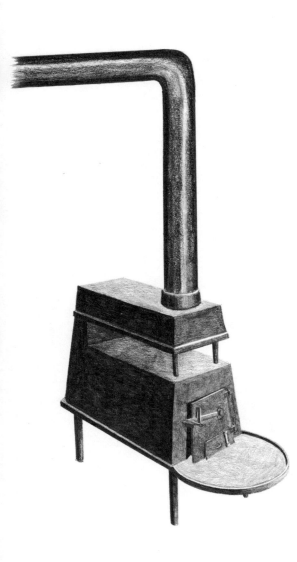

The distinctive Shaker wood-burning stove was typically simple, efficient, and progressive. The stoves were so efficient as heaters that one was found in nearly every Shaker room instead of a fireplace. Some villages had their own foundries. This double model from New Lebanon, New York, was especially efficient, since the upper chamber radiated heat too. (Old Chatham, N.Y.)

the faith. Anyone—at any time—could leave freely if he felt that the Shaker way was no longer best for him. No one ever had to stay in discontent because he couldn't afford to go; the Shakers provided him with the wherewithal to get him started on his new life. The Shakers had no walls around the village cloistering them in; the converts who came were held only by bonds of love. The result was an enthusiasm and devotion to their disciplined way of life that made two centuries of successful work and worship possible such as no other American utopian community has equaled.

One reason for leaving was the desire to get married. If a young Brother and Sister fell in love, they were given a period of some months to decide if they really wanted to give up their Shaker home for marriage. They were free to marry if they chose, but necessarily had to find a new home as non-Shakers. Shakers didn't look down on marriage, or expect the World to convert to celibacy; they just felt that it was their particular calling. Nathaniel Hawthorne wrote a short story, "The Canterbury Pilgrim," about two young people from Canterbury who decided to marry. They sat on the great granite water trough which still stands at the foot of the hill and wondered what their future as man and wife instead of Brother and Sister would bring.

Shakers were as free to come as they were to go—members who left were always accepted back if they chose to return. If they had truly undergone a revelation they were welcomed as lost sheep back to the fold. But even if they were what the Shakers called "bread-and-butter" or "winter Shakers" (who came when work was light and then left in the spring), there was always a possible chance for redemption that the Shakers couldn't throw away. Brother Thomas Damon of Enfield, Connecticut, may have sniffed to himself when he wrote in his diary in 1845: "William Shaw left the community of Shakers to shirk for himself." But if erstwhile Brother William had come back, no doubt Brother Thomas would have done what he could to help him along the way. There was always an open door, and it swung both ways.

Discipline in a Shaker village was not a matter of spying, and members were not threatened with punishment—discipline came from within. Shakers had no courts or jail systems; no judge, no jury, and no stocks like the Puritans. If a member were not successfully living up to Shaker ideals, it was the duty of the Elder or Eldress to speak to him and help him change his ways. Shakers were quicker to criticize their own faults than others'; one member at Hancock, Massachusetts, wrote in the Family Record: "When a man does all he can do not blame him Tho he succeeds not well." Anyone who simply couldn't mend his ways was asked to leave for the good of all and himself, too.

Even in Shaker schools, discipline was a matter of love and not punishment. Shaker teachers used wooden rulers for measuring only—they were not allowed to hit the children. They thought that an ounce of prevention was worth a pound of cure and tried to avoid problems before they started. On rainy days, recess time was not the zoo it could have been with first to ninth graders in one room; children brought their handwork to keep them quietly busy. The original Schoolhouse at Canterbury, for example, was designed with an eye to discipline. The teacher could observe even the last row: the desks were raised in tiers toward the back. At one time the Canterbury Schoolhouse had a small bed in the back of the room where a tired, cranky child could rest and not disturb the rest of the class (teachers didn't share the privilege).

If you look at a record of Shaker workers, you won't find a single painter or sculptor listed as such; but nothing could be further from the truth than to say that there were no Shaker artists. The satisfaction that Shakers felt in creating a better way of life is evident in the beauty of form of the furniture and the superb woods and quiet but rich color and texture that mark a Shaker room. Who can look at the massive steps of elegant proportions that Brother Micajah Tucker of Canterbury hewed from single huge granite blocks and call him just a stonecutter? Were the Sisters who stitched fine broadcloth into cloaks that draped perfectly merely seamstresses? And how about any of the nameless Brothers who shaped the curving banisters and graceful chair finials, or Brother Micajah Burnett who swirled two magnificently simple staircases from cellar to attic at Pleasant Hill in Kentucky? Although they didn't make paintings for their walls or statues for their churches, no one can say that Shakers didn't have artists or didn't believe in beauty in their lives. Beauty was just one more heavenly ideal that Shakers saw fit to practice in their villages.

Even the lands where they chose to settle were magnificently

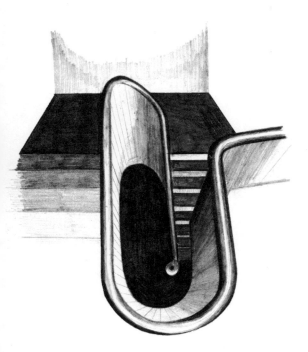

The Schoolhouse stairs at Canterbury, New Hampshire, are typically graceful and utilitarian: the banister is the right size and height to be really functional. Shakers didn't waste any space; the narrow niche below was just big enough for two coat hooks.

beautiful, often hills commanding glorious views. A hill location is good for drainage? Yes—but if you think that's the only reason the practical Shakers settled there, you're missing an important point about their ways. Hills are good for drainage, but they're even better for the soul; and the Shakers knew that as well as they knew that they loved the God who made hills and valleys.

In the early years of Shakerism, you could have walked into a Shaker home anywhere and not seen one picture on the wall. For the early Shakers, paintings were "superfluous"—just another useless thing to catch dust. The only form of drawing or painting that was part of the Shaker world was a "spirit drawing," and even these were not hung but kept privately as sacred images.

These spirit drawings were recordings of heavenly visions that some of the members received as "gifts" from heaven; most of them date from 1840–60, when Shakerism peaked in numbers as well as accomplishment. Often they included emblems of trees, birds, trumpets, or harps, and flowers; inspirational messages from biblical figures made up part of the designs. Most of them were very detailed and gaily colored.

From the time of Mother Ann, direct heavenly revelation was an important part of the Shaker way. Such revelation was something that could and did happen anywhere, at any time, not just in the Meetinghouse. In the early years, members recorded visits from heavenly spirits in their diaries as matter-of-factly as they recorded the daily weather.

Shaker music was also the result of direct divine inspiration. Members like Eldress Dorothy Durgin of Canterbury who had the "gift" of music kept slates by their beds to record the music or verses that would come to them at night; she alone wrote over five hundred inspired hymns. Shakers wrote all their own music and printed their own hymnals; probably the best-loved Shaker song is "Simple Gifts." Aaron Copland liked it so much that he made it a theme in his *Appalachian Spring*.

Shakers received many other gifts during their years of worship. Some members, such as Philemon Stewart, wrote inspirational books while under the gift; others had gifts of leaping or whirling. One young Brother at South Union, Kentucky, simply had a "wonderful gift of laughing." Whatever the gift, Shakers rejoiced in the closeness they felt with heaven. Their feet were planted firmly on the ground, but their souls soared infinitely upward in search of oneness with God.

The Shakers built so permanently and accomplished so much during their two centuries here that it seems a surprise to find that today most of the Shaker villages which once flourished on American land are almost entirely gone. Where one of them once stood is now an airport—the fate of Watervliet, New York. The village at Enfield, Connecticut, is now a prison. Sometimes only the name remains to tell where Shakers once lived and worked. Shaker Heights, Ohio, was once the home of the North Union Shakers; today not a single Shaker building remains.

The village of Mount Lebanon, New York, once the home of six hundred Shakers and the chief community in America, is now a private school. Alfred, Maine, and Enfield, New Hampshire, have become the homes of Catholic orders. Several others, notably Hancock, Massachusetts, and Pleasant Hill and South Union, Kentucky, have become museums where rooms filled with Shaker things seem to await the return of Shaker people.

Only two of the original nineteen villages—Canterbury, New Hampshire, and Sabbathday Lake, Maine—remain as Shaker homes today for the Shakers left in America. As this book goes to press, twelve Shakers still exist, all Sisters who are, for the most part, in their sixties and seventies; not even a single Brother remains since Brother Delmer Wilson died at Sabbathday Lake in 1961. The mills are gone, the carpenter shops are closed, and the bells no longer ring to call in workers at mealtime. The holy stones that marked the worship grounds were long ago removed or destroyed.

What happened from 1774 to 1974 that made the Shakers rise against all odds, and then come full circle to the point where there are scarcely more Shakers in America today than there were when Mother Ann landed in 1774?

The answer that seems most obvious at first glance is their celibacy. "Of course," people say, "how did they expect to continue if they didn't marry and reproduce?" The same way that all celibate religious orders have maintained their ranks for hundreds of years, one could reply. Nuns and priests don't marry, either, but there have

The best-known Shaker song is "The Gift to Be Simple," written in Alfred, Maine.

Shaker tinsmiths made dustpans for use and for sale; this one hung in plain sight from a handy peg near a stove or woodbox. Shakers never swept across a threshold, but swept each room at a time. No wonder a visitor to New Lebanon in 1857 wrote, "The floor, made of white pine, was as clean as a dining table." (Canterbury, N.H.)

been nuns and priests since the days after Christ because some people have always felt called to devote their lives to God in celibacy. The difference was that everybody in the Shaker way lived according to standards that other religions reserve for their leaders alone.

For nearly a century, celibacy did not mean the end of Shakerism; from 1774 until the Civil War, the number of Shakers increased steadily in the country. Celibacy was not really the cause of their decline; rather, it was one of the main reasons for their success. The people who became Shakers *wanted* to be Shakers; the result was a tremendous spirit of enthusiasm.

The causes for their decline came not so much from within as from outside. One of the most likely reasons for the Shakers' gradual decline—from six thousand members before the Civil War to only one thousand at the turn of the century—was the change in America from a nation of farmers and craftsmen to a nation of factory workers and businessmen. During the first half of the nineteenth century, the Shakers could afford to make their cloth, furniture, and everything by hand because the rest of America was doing things with the same slow-paced methods. Even so, the Shakers at that time were not producing for the outside market as much as they were for themselves and their newly settled homes; and they were living at a time when self-sufficiency was still possible and practical in America for most of the population.

But when factories began to make everything faster and cheaper—and shoddier—the Shakers continued to make things with the same standards of perfection. They were working not for the market, but for God and themselves. Shakers did mechanize some of their hand-work if the machines proved more efficient, but on the whole they realized that no machine could put as much care or perfection into any article as an individual could.

The things they did produce for the market were so well made that the continuing demand guaranteed by planned obsolescence was no part of the Shaker world. The washing machine made at Canterbury and sold to hotels in the 1850s and later, for example, was so durable that hotels simply didn't replace them.

Gradually it became harder for Shaker goods to succeed competitively in a market flooded with cheaper machine-made goods. By the 1870s, it was evident that Shakers just couldn't afford to compete, and the eventual fate of Shaker industries began to become clear. Rather than sacrifice the handmade perfection of their boxes, chairs, or anything else, the Shakers began to drop industries one by one as they became unprofitable. In 1875 Elder Frederick Evans said with sadness,

> We used to have more looms than now, but cloth is sold so cheaply that we gradually began to buy. It is a mistake, we buy more cheaply than we can make, but our home-made cloth is much better than that we can buy; and we have now to make three pairs of trousers, for instance, where before we made one. Thus our little looms would even now be more profitable—to say nothing of the independence we secure in working them.

As they dropped industries, naturally the Shakers began relying more and more on the World for things. Shaker rooms dating from the Victorian era and later often have metal latches and hooks instead of handmade wooden pulls and pegs; iron stoves made in outside foundries; even commercially purchased chairs and carpets.

There were fewer jobs for Shaker hands as the industries dropped off, and less to attract young members; as the older members passed

The innovative Shakers believed in progress, feeling that greater efficiency meant more accomplished and more time for good works. They were among the first to experiment with static electricity machines, like this one, early in the nineteenth century.

away, numbers declined steadily. By the twentieth century, it became necessary to hire outside help for heavy work on the farms.

During the nineteenth century, Shaker villages changed as surely as the World did. In the first half of the century, to be sure, Shakers lived in utter simplicity in the type of room we see now in restored villages and museums, filled with simple straight chairs and wood-burning stoves.

But the next half century witnessed a broadening of that simple life. For the first time, Shakers began to feel that they could enjoy art and hang pictures on their walls, as well as express their talents in painting and appreciate the music of organs and other instruments which had once been forbidden as "superfluous." The Canterbury Shakers even had a fine collection of early recordings of classical music.

They began to appreciate flowers for the sake of their beauty alone, not just for utilitarian purposes as medicines or dyes; they collected fine libraries when once all books except the Bible and Shaker works had been forbidden. Instead of forbidding all members except the business leaders to visit outside, Shakers were encouraged to travel and learn about the World, besides cultivating friendships with people outside the community. Elder Henry Blinn summed up the new spirit when he visited Kentucky Shakers in 1873:

> Really it seems that they work harder than the Brethren & Sisters do at the north, and have less time for mental, moral or spiritual cultivation. This being the case where is the advantage of a residence in a southern clime? If to obtain a milder winter, that indeed, is but poor compensation.

And instead of discouraging communication between Brothers and Sisters by forbidding them to talk or work together, by this time Shakers had such confidence in the faith of members to their chosen celibacy that the strict rules separating men and women in the earliest days could be left behind. Also for the first time, some Shakers began to use ornament in their handwork. A few Victorian Shaker rockers have rope-twisting on the posts; here and there a desk has carving on the drawer pulls.

Some choose to explain this broadening of the Shaker way as a corruption of the original simplicity of their spirit. But the Shakers

Shaker chairs progressed, too—from the classic ladderback (c. 1840) to the Canterbury Windsor to the Victorian chair by Brother Thomas Fisher of Enfield, Connecticut (late nineteenth century)—but these three, opposite, all have the Shaker "tilting button" on the hind legs. The half-round wooden swivel foot, another Shaker invention, was pegged in with a piece of leather thong and made tilting back easier on both sitter and floor.
(Canterbury, N.H.)

themselves saw it in a different light. The simple life, they felt, did not have to mean a narrow life; and they never changed the spirit of their devotion to God and mankind. A Brother from Enfield, New Hampshire, concluded that by clinging to past custom for its own sake, Shakers ran "the danger of becoming fixed and fossilized"—and a "fossil Shaker," he added, was "not a very attractive character."

The Shakers never gave up their standards of honesty, celibacy, thrift, or dedication to the spirit of Christian love; they never gave up their ideals. They continued to provide loving homes for children during the twentieth century, even when it became apparent that most of the youngsters were almost certain to leave the Shaker villages when they became of age.

So although some of the earliest Shakers would undoubtedly have been puzzled to see paintings on Shaker walls or televisions in Shaker rooms, they would have felt that the true spirit of Shakerism had not been laid aside. Above all else, the Shaker way of life has always represented a challenge. In the days of Mother Ann, the challenge was

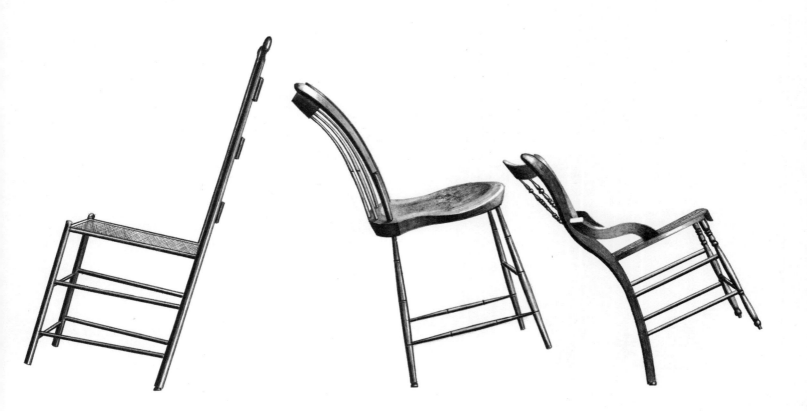

to establish a unique way of life in the face of poverty and persecution by the World. In the nineteenth century, it was to maintain the simplicity and perfection of that way in the face of prosperity and the threat of Worldliness.

For the twentieth-century Shakers, the challenge has been maintaining faith in a way of life that seems to be coming to an end. Perhaps there will never be any twenty-first-century Shakers. Mother Ann herself predicted more than two hundred years ago that there would come a time when the Shakers would not have enough members left to bury their own dead, as she put it. For the most part, the Shakers accept the fact that their ranks will someday close. They don't feel that just because the Shaker way of life will come to an end means that it has failed. Far from it. Like any living thing, Shakerism was born, it flourished, and someday it will pass from the earth. Even God's Son passed from earth.

But like the spirit of Christ or the spirits of the faithful, they feel that the spirit of Shakerism will live on. As they say, "The hands drop off, but the work goes on."

Mother Ann made another prediction: that when there were as many members left as a child could count on his fingers of one hand, there would again be a revival and new members would flock like doves. Interest and respect for the Shaker way of life are growing every year. If Mother Ann's vision is fulfilled, perhaps new members won't return to the established Shaker villages and the old ways—but, like Mother Ann and her original eight, will have the courage and the faith to set out for new homes and new challenges. A Shaker proverb says: "New bees don't return to the old hive."

And though there are only a handful of Shakers left, the spirit of those who remain is just as strong as that of Elder Giles Avery of Mount Lebanon, who wrote in his journal in 1837:

> *Those who're faithful just & true*
> *Firmly speak it—I'll go thro'*
> *And in answer not a few*
> *Firmly say I'll go with you*
> *Tho' the number in the hive*
> *Should be lessened down to five*
> *I shall of this number be*
> *Then we'll say so let it be.*

The beehive emblem from a spirit drawing sums up the Shaker spirit best: the communal life, the hum of busy hands, and the efforts of each member to do his best for the good of everyone.

When Mother Ann and the eight original Shakers landed in New York some two hundred years ago with hardly anything but the clothes on their backs, it must have seemed impossible to anyone that the little group would ever amount to anything. Yet within twenty-five years after their arrival without friends or fanfare, nearly half of the nineteen communities had been firmly established. Within the next fifty years the Shakers had proved themselves the successful creators of growing homes and busy workshops and were soon to number about six thousand members as willing workers for their faith.

The original Shakers had nothing to give but their faith and their time—yet what could have been more important?

From the days of Mother Ann, the Shaker's willingness to devote his time—all the days of his life—made the difference for the Shaker way of life. Mother Ann said, "Do all your work as though you had a thousand years to live on earth, and as you would if you knew you must die tomorrow." The Shaker kept busy every minute; yet he took the time necessary to build his faith, his home, and the things that he used in such a way that they could be done as perfectly as possible.

Open a Shaker chest today, and all of a sudden the simple act of pulling out a drawer becomes a pleasure. It doesn't stick, but slips in and out smoothly and quietly; it works as well today as it did when it was made one hundred twenty-five years ago. Look closely at anything the Shakers made—a cloak, a basket, a box, a tool—and the same perfection is there. The beauty of these simple things is not in fine materials or in detailed ornament; it has nothing to do with paint and it can't be pasted on.

What renders these things beautiful and rare to us today is the *time* that has obviously been spent in making them perfect. The Shaker didn't work to punch a time clock, he worked with patience to do something right. We shake our heads and say, "People don't have time to make things that way any more"—but who has ever had more free time than we do? Only in the twentieth century has it become possible for the average man to afford a work week of 40 hours out of a 168-hour week and still have food for his table, clothes for his back, and a car and two TV's besides. We have more time than any other culture has ever had; what's missing is the patient pace and the willingness to spend time on our work the way the Shakers did. We save time with mechanical wonders and keep the time we save for

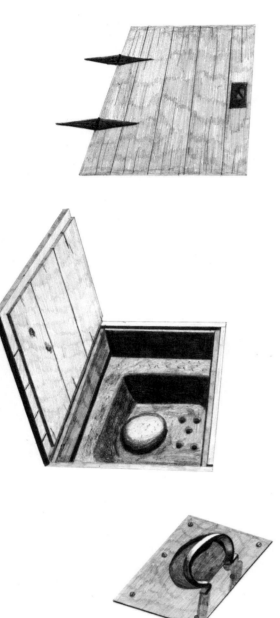

The time saved by this solid granite drain for floor-scrubbing Sisters in the South Kitchen (added in 1867) of the Canterbury Trustees' Office is almost as impressive as the time it took a Brother to carve it. The iron handle on the trap-door cover folds flush with the floor for safety; the round stone, when set atop, kept the holes from clogging.

our own; the Shaker saved time with his efficient ways, and then gave the time he saved away to his Brothers and Sisters in good works.

Even though the Shakers were working on earth for salvation and eternity they never forgot that time on earth is reckoned in days, hours, and minutes. They valued the minutes as much as they did eternity and felt that God gave eternal life as a reward only to those who had made the most of the little time He'd given them here. This general attitude was summed up—fittingly enough—by Brother Isaac Youngs (1793–1865) of Mount Lebanon, a noted clockmaker, who wrote on one of his clocks,

> *O let each one his moments well improve*
> *To gain abiding bliss in realms above.*

The Shaker attitude toward time was summed up in four simple rules: they never procrastinated; they used every minute; they never rushed; and they always provided time to unwind. The result for the "timely wise" Shakers was a time for everything.

From the beginning, Mother Ann urged her followers to avoid idleness. She told her listeners, "You must not allow the children to be idle; if you bring up your children in idleness, the devil will set them to work." Mother Ann's ability to make her faithful followers get things done promptly was one of the things most remembered about her by those who had known her. Dana Goodrich, who later became an Eldress at the Hancock village, remembered how "in mending our clothes, she was very particular. She taught us to mend them in season, and not let them go till it would take double the time, cloth and thread to repair them." A stitch in time, for sure.

The Shakers not only felt it their duty to get things done promptly, they were actually eager to get at the job. An inspirational work called the *Holy Laws of Zion* recorded in 1840: "When there was a building to repair or be built, when the signal was given, all would lend a liberal hand, and feel an interested desire to see how quick it would be accomplished." The real success was not just the barn or shop getting built—it was the proof that they could *want* to do what they knew they should do, when it should be done. As the Shaker hymn went,

> *Now's the time to travel on*
> *Now's the time to labor*

> *Now's the time for everyone*
> *To be a good Believer.*

What the Shakers sang about on Sunday, they put into practice on Monday and the rest of the week. Another hymn from Watervliet, Ohio, circa 1833, gives a good idea of the Shaker's work-day schedule:

> *I sleep seven hours, with little recess,*
> *And O how refreshing they seem:*
> *At four in the morning I get up and dress,*
> *Regardless of vision or dream.*
>
> *When meeting is over I chuse to give way,*
> *And be at my work very soon,*
> *And more than one half that's laid out for the day,*
> *Must always be done before noon.*

"Now" was also the time to put every minute to good use. Any "pestiferous scoundrel" who wasted the time God gave him was called an "Old Slug." Mother Ann had told her followers, "You must not lose one moment of time, for you have none to spare," and her advice continued to influence the way the Shakers thought when the villages stood solidly on American land. Isaac Youngs had something to say about this, too, as usual inscribed on the back of one of his clocks:

> *O swiftly see! each moment flies!*
> *See and learn, be timely wise*
> *Seize the moments as they fly,*
> *Learn to live and know to die.*

Spare minutes were always put to good use, for example, in some light industry like making wool carders. According to the Shakers' newspaper, *The Shaker Manifesto,* in a typical village: "Even the farmers and teamsters would eagerly catch every spare opportunity to assist in the setting of card teeth. All the family were very much interested in the work, and their mornings and evenings and even the few minutes while waiting for their meals were utilized in this employment." Even mealtime was put to good use at Canterbury. In the earliest years the Canterbury Shakers ate in silence, like other Shakers, but later during the nineteenth century they realized how much time they could save if one person read the newspaper aloud to everyone

Two members at a time used the curved footscraper on the Canterbury Dwellinghouse (1793). Leaving dirt outside meant less work cleaning inside.

during the meal. Long before the days of radio, Shakers had their own efficient, time-saving "broadcast" system.

One of the Shakers most remarkable for using every minute was Brother Calvin Goodell of Canterbury, who "had no moments to waste in idleness. He would make calculations to have something to do on his way to and from the mill, or while he was waiting at the house for his meals." For Brother Calvin, no time was too short to use, and no job too trivial for his spare minutes: "A few crooked, headless pins were made serviceable in putting up sheets of wool, and by this means save buying new ones." Brother Calvin, typically, couldn't abide waste of time or material.

"Haste makes waste" was another simple rule taken to heart by most members, who steadfastly refused to rush. Brother James Johnson of Canterbury was one Shaker who learned the hard way that short-cuts don't always pay. One winter, Brother James

attempted to cross the Bark Mill pond on the ice, as the shortest way to the Turning mill where he worked.

He had not walked far from the edge before the ice broke and let him into the water. From this cold bath and the fright he screamed for help, but no one was near to hear him. He now began in earnest to break the ice, and luckily made his escape from what seemed so sure to become his grave.

Brother James in later years (he lived to be eighty-four) remembered the incident with a chuckle. He would always say, "I guess the bath did me good"—but he learned a valuable lesson about hurrying, and "did not venture again upon the pond that season."

Brother James and his fellow Shakers found that haste was a mistake in crossing ponds, cutting cloaks, or turning chair legs. A few extra minutes made more sense when the result was something done right, and so they took the time necessary. Shakers simply did not hurry. A sense of control is evident even when a member like Issachar Bates wrote, "My whole stay at Lebanon was not much over an hour, for we did business quick. I ate quick and talked quick, heard quick and started home quick, for I was quickened." He moved right along, but significantly *he* was setting the pace and not frantically scrambling to catch up.

Since Shakers put their ideals—like eternity—into practice in their daily lives, it was only natural for them to seek and achieve a kind of "timelessness" in their villages. The village atmosphere was so calm and unrushed that one could at least in imagination have "a thousand years" of tomorrows for work and worship. Even Shaker furniture at one time was allowed only "two figures for a date," according to the *Millennial Laws* (for example, 47 or 82). The century was not even indicated—that's how little a hundred years mattered, with the Shakers' belief in eternity.

A visitor to Canterbury in 1877 sensed this quality of timelessness. He wrote:

> Whether you pass along the streets, or enter the houses, or wherever you go, you feel that you are beyond the realm of hurry; there is no restlessness, or fret of business, or anxiety about anything; it is as if the work was done, and it was one eternal afternoon.

That was not to say that the Shakers weren't busy at their work; but, as the visitor continued, "even when you are in the midst of their industries, and the making of cheese, the milking of cows, the washing and ironing, and baking, and harvesting," there was a sense of otherworldly peace.

Another visitor expressed it simply: "Even in what is seen of the eye and heard of the ear, Mt. Lebanon strikes you as a place where it is always Sunday."

One good way of economizing on time yet keeping from rushing was to set up a definite daily schedule. The daily schedule was the same every day except Sunday. Generally, it meant being up at dawn to work for about an hour and a half before breakfast—the Sisters at housecleaning and stripping the beds, the Brothers in the barn, and the kitchen Sisters at making breakfast and baking the daily bread. After breakfast, members went to workshops until dinnertime; after dinner, work until suppertime; then perhaps some more work, a meeting or worship service (in latter days, a night for games like checkers or dominoes); and to bed about 9 P.M.

On Sunday, there was no work, a later rising, and worship in the Meetinghouse; in the evening, private time for prayer or writing.

There were several advantages to this ordered system. For the Shakers, following a definite daily schedule eliminated aimless mo-

Above: Kitchen Sisters saved time with the double rolling pin—and rolled crust with half the effort. (Old Chatham, N.Y.)
Opposite page: To save time planting corn, a Brother filled the tin can on the side of the planter, at top, with kernels, then walked down the rows pulling the handles open and shut. The curved iron arm turned a disk inside the can, letting one kernel out the chute with every push. Metal disks of different gauges suited different kinds of seeds. The sower pushed dirt over the seed with one foot and pressed it down with the other. Fast work and easy on the back—no stooping meant no stopping. Iron corn shellers, at bottom, featured curved blades of various shapes and sizes. Shelling the cob was a quick matter of pulling it over the blades.

Shakers quickly peeled apples for drying with a screw-base apple peeler, above. An apple stuck onto the prongs and turned with the handle was shaved in seconds by the razor-type blade on the flexible jointed arm.

ments of wondering what to do next: it organized them. A journal from Sabbathday Lake recorded the following daily schedule for 1881:

> Elder William Dumont announced the summer arrangement of ringing the bell. For rising in the morning at one-half past four o'clock. Quarter before six for breakfast. Dinner, quarter before twelve o'clock. Supper, quarter before six o'clock and half past seven o'clock for gathering into the house.

"Old Slugs" who found it hard to rise with a glad heart at half-past four in the morning had their consciences poked with verses like these:

> Slug:
> *A lazy fellow it implies,*
> *Who in the morning hates to rise;*
> *When all the rest are up at four,*
> *He wants to sleep a little more.*
> *When others into meeting swarm,*
> *He keeps his nest so good and warm,*
> *That sometimes when the sisters come*
> *To make the beds and sweep the room,*
> *Who do they find wrap'd up so snug?*
> *Ah! Who is it but Mr. Slug.*

Anyone with habits like this was sure to receive a lesson in punctuality, another Shaker ideal that members like Daniel Goodrich put seriously into practice. No matter what business he was up to, even if it were dealings with Worldly businessmen, "he would never allow any thing to prevent him from attending to his own order." When that dinner bell rang, "Daniel would never wait to close a bargain by stopping from his meal, but would leave all, and afterwards attend to his dealing concerns." Did Worldly business suffer as a result? No, according to the account; on the contrary, "The world all knew his punctuality in these matters, and respected him for it." (Whether it was entirely his own sense of proper order and punctuality or partly an understandable wish to get to the good Shaker cooking, Daniel had the right idea.)

Visitors themselves, while hospitably received, were politely but firmly requested to follow the schedule to prevent unnecessary breakup of daily order. A list of *Rules for Visitors* included:

THIRD. Those who live near and can call at their own convenience are not expected to stay more than a few hours; but such as live at a great distance, or cannot come often, and have near relatives here, can stay from one to four days, according to circumstances. This we consider sufficient time, as a general rule.

FOURTH. All visitors are requested to rise to take Breakfast at half past Six in the Summer, and half past seven in the Winter.

With hours like those, most visitors were probably not too unhappy about staying only one to four days.

The Shakers' weekly schedule was just as orderly in plan. Weeknights in the nineteenth century probably ran something like this: on Monday, an information meeting, when letters between the villages were read; on Tuesday, perhaps a singing and dancing worship meeting. Wednesdays were likely to be for conversation meetings to exchange ideas; while on Thursday, a "Laboring" worship meeting might have been in order. Friday was another night for singing and dancing meeting; Saturday, a worship meeting; and Sunday, "union meetings" between small groups of Brothers and Sisters for socializing.

If it seems impossible for the Shakers to have had time for all their work *and* time for all those meetings, too, it's because we don't realize just how much time the Shakers' "timely wise" habits saved them. One important way in which they saved time (fascinating to Americans smitten with labor-saving gadgets) was to design their tools, buildings, and furnishings to avoid unnecessary steps or wasted motion. A classic example is the famous round barn at Hancock, Massachusetts, built in 1829 and rebuilt in 1865. The farmer could walk around the center of the barn and feed the whole herd in a few short steps. Most of the illustrations in this chapter are examples of Shaker-made things designed to save time—and good examples of the way a Shaker ideal, like economy of time, was also a part of their daily life and work.

Another way of improving the use of time was to keep careful records of how each day had been spent: the Shakers encouraged journals, diaries, and account books. According to their *Millennial Laws,* "A JOURNAL of all the work done and proceedings of a temporal nature in the family, may be kept by order of the Deacons and

Peeled apples were mounted on the spike of the corer-and-quarterer, below. (Brother Sanford Russell of South Union, Kentucky, invented one such model.) When the long handle was pulled down, spring action drew the apple to be cored and quartered by the blade on the handle. This apple design is from the labels Canterbury Shakers printed for their applesauce tubs. (Canterbury, N.H.)

Deaconesses, or Caretakers—Those appointed to transact business of a temporal nature, should keep all their accounts booked down, regular and exact." This system made it easy to figure out which days had been better spent, and why. Members like Sister Elizabeth Lovegrove of New Lebanon felt there was always room for improvement. On the last day of 1838, she wrote in her journal, "I must . . . consider how well I have spent it, and if I have spent it well, begin the next month with an increase."

Shaker daybooks like Sister Elizabeth's often prove to be more than just accounts of hours spent. Recording each day was a good way of keeping the Shakers aware of the significance of each moment. Brother Henry Hewitt wrote in his journal,

August 1836   I began to make myself a new desk for writing on:

> *And so it is while time does last,*
> *I find enough to do,*
> *With busy hands can't work so fast,*
> *But what there's more to do.*

Brother Isaac Youngs, the clockmaker, was even more acutely aware of the hours that he put to use:

October 1816. 19. Finished a cheap kind of timepiece, having made it in about 22 hours.

July 1820. 4th Finished a striking clock. No. 8. I began it in May 1819 & worked at it by little at a time & I reckoned it took me about 40 days to make the clock & case.

I meant to have written some useful remarks in this book from experiments. But alass time flies & I am no more in time!

Notice how Brother Isaac counted the timepiece "cheap" not because of cheap woods or because not much money was spent—he was talking about time spent.

Shakers like Brother Isaac never found themselves wondering what to do next for lack of pressing chores to begin; it was more of a question of deciding which job to do next. Sometimes, according to Isaac, it seemed that there was too much to do:

> *I'm overrun with work and chores*
> *Upon the farm or within doors*
> *Which ever way I turn my eyes;*

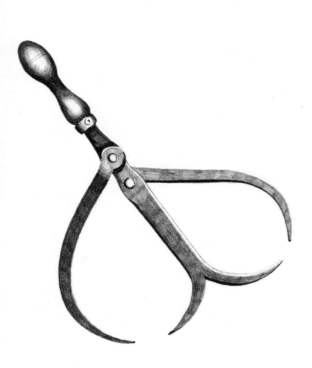

Double calipers saved time for the carpenter because he could record two different measurements at once.

Enough to fill me with surprise.
How can I bear with such a plan?
No time to be a gentleman!
All work-work-work, still rushing on,
And conscience too still pushing on.
When will the working all be done?
When will this lengthy thread be spun?
As long as working *is the cry*
How can I e'er find time to die?

Complaints like Brother Isaac's would have disrupted the peace of Shaker villages if the Shakers hadn't provided themselves time to unwind. After all, the Shakers lived in the same world that we do, where if something can go wrong it usually will. As calm as they kept while working at a fast efficient pace, frustration and tension must have been an occasional problem in Shaker workshops, too. Blades can and will snap; dye bottles can and will upset; and sometimes it's easier to love one's Brother—no matter how blackened with sin—than it is to have patience with a wayward mechanical contraption.

The Shaker believed that a few minutes spent each day putting his heart to God while resting his hands from work made very good sense. The prosperity of Shaker villages was remarkable because industry did not mean sacrificing peace of mind. Every Shaker felt with St. Mark that gaining the world only to lose his soul was no profit at all.

To help Brothers and Sisters restore serenity and successfully put aside their tensions with their tools at the close of the work day, the Shakers from the earliest years had what they called "retiring time." For one half-hour, after the day's work and before worship, all the members would sit in silent meditation "to banish from the mind all thoughts of a secular nature, as well as all vain imaginations or worldly temptations."

Not surprisingly, clocks and watches seem to have had a certain fascination for the Shakers, especially in many of their spirit drawings where they probably represented mortality or the responsibility to prepare for the Lord's coming. The harmonious operation of the community was seen sometimes as regular clockwork order. According to an 1887 issue of *The Shaker Manifesto*, "The clock is an emblem of a Shaker community because everything goes on time. . . .

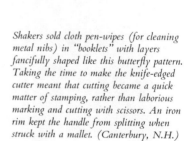

Shakers sold cloth pen-wipes (for cleaning metal nibs) in "booklets" with layers fancifully shaped like this butterfly pattern. Taking the time to make the knife-edged cutter meant that cutting became a quick matter of stamping, rather than laborious marking and cutting with scissors. An iron rim kept the handle from splitting when struck with a mallet. (Canterbury, N.H.)

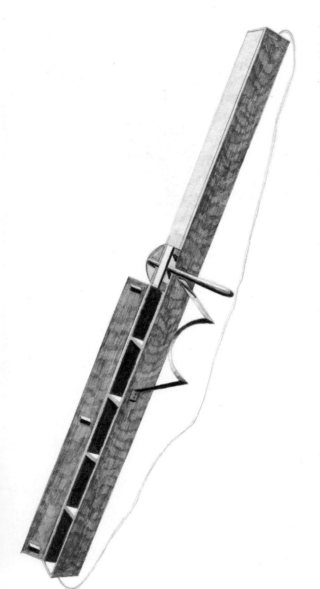

Shakers saved time and seed with a 10-foot wooden seeder. Filled with small seeds, it hung from the sower's neck by the cord and was balanced in front with the curved iron waist band. As he walked, the sower moved the lever, connected to a long-toothed wooden strip inside, forcing the seeds through holes in the tin strip on the bottom. The seeds sprinkled out so evenly that none was wasted, and the field was seeded in a faction of the usual time. (Canterbury, N.H.)

Promptness, absolute punctility, is a *sine qua non* of a successful community." For the Shakers, a perfectly regulated schedule reflected the perfection of heavenly order, and a timepiece represented both. A hymn called "Heavenly Display" went, "The wheels of a time-piece imitate the flows of the heavenly love that flows in heaven."

But all the "promptness" and "absolute punctility" in heaven and earth couldn't make clockwork order unless everyone knew what time it was. As early as 1790, the Mount Lebanon Shakers had a clockmaker Brother. The earliest record of clocks indicates that they were in use around 1830, although they may have been clocks that converts brought with them. Clockmakers and repairers from Isaac Youngs to Brother Ricardo Beldon (1870–1958)—one of the last members of the Hancock community—supplied the villages.

The most significant thing about clocks and watches in a Shaker village, however, was their virtual absence in the earlier days. There were several reasons why this was thought best. For one thing, they weren't really needed, since bells called workers in to meals or to meetings together. It was only when members such as the Trustees ventured into the outside World that watches became necessary. Bells also furthered a sense of brotherhood in the village—everyone depended together on the bell, since in the earliest years no one had his own watch except the Elders.

According to the *Millennial Laws,* there weren't even to be any clocks in the dwelling rooms or workshops. Shakers couldn't be time-wasting clock-watchers; they were free instead to consider their days in terms of the work they accomplished instead of the hours they spent. Without clocks, no one rushed to finish a job hoping to get it done before the end of the work day. Some perceptive soul has commented that work expands to fill the time in which it has to be completed. For the Shakers, work lived a natural life, not squashed or stretched into arbitrary time units . . . and how much more satisfying to think of a day's work in terms of fulfillment and creativity, rather than filling a time slot.

Watches as well as clocks were "contrary to order" until the late 1830s, for several reasons. Often they were simply too fancy. According to the *Millennial Laws,* "Superfluities not owned" on account of their decoration included "Silver pencils, silver toothpicks, gold pencils, or pens, silver spoons, silver thimbles (but thimbles may be lined with silver,) *gold or silver watches,* brass knobs or handles of any size or kind," and *"Superfluously finished, or flowery painted clocks."* The line from Brother Isaac's verse—"No time to be a gentleman!"—sums up pretty well the feeling that these things weren't worth the time to make or buy them.

Besides, without watches, the members could develop a healthy self-reliance on their own senses. Elder Henry Blinn of Canterbury was always impressed when he was a boy by Brother Moses Johnson—the Shaker architect who framed the gambrel-roofed Meetinghouses in seven of the villages—who could tell time perfectly without a watch. Elder Henry remembered, "When at work some two miles from home, it was nice to know the time of day, and Moses would pace on his shadow, and tell us within a very few minutes when the Village bell would ring for noon." Elder Henry added that "to young minds it was a mystery," and that Brother Moses used it as a good chance to tell the young boys to study latitude and longitude—which Elder Henry said made it more of a mystery!

Some fine bells were purchased by the villages for telling time, including a Revere bell still hanging in the tower of the Canterbury Dwellinghouse. When the Sabbathday Lake Shakers hung their bell in 1872, they put it up so promptly that it seemed to serve as an example for others to act as promptly whenever they heard the bell. In 1872, the Shakers' journal read, "Elder Otis Sawyer and Brother Hewitt Chandler went to Portland and returned same day. Brought with them a fine bell weighing 108 pounds, costing 45 cents per pound." The journey by wagon must have taken them several hours, since Portland, Maine, is a good 25 miles from Sabbathday Lake. The bell was "for Brother Granville Merrill to attach to a clock which he has put up in the south attic of the Brethren's shop." By seven o'clock that same evening, they heard the bell's "clear, shrill, melodious tone through the whole village.... So much for promptness. Much praise for Brother Granville," concluded the account. The clock he made was for community use—it struck the hours, but had no face. Odd? Not really; the idea was not to show the minutes ticking away, but to signal the progress of daily events.

When the villages didn't have bells, large conch shells brought from the ports did the trick nicely. Someone with a healthy set of lungs would blow through the shell to call in workers off in the fields

Brother Benjamin Youngs (d. 1818) of Watervliet, New York (uncle of the poet-clockmaker Isaac Youngs), made this wall clock, called an "alarum" clock. (Western Reserve Historical Society, Cleveland)

at mealtimes. In order to avoid confusion, sometimes the different Families in a village would use different signals. The Church Family at Canterbury had a "large frog shell" for its members, but the Second Family had none. Good old Yankee ingenuity saved the day, however, when "an impromptu thought brought out a cruet, and this served for a whistle to call the family, and it worked admirably."

As usual, the "Old Slug" of the group managed to make himself a bother, even without clocks to watch:

> *When he conceits meal-time is near,*
> *He listens oft the trump to hear;*
> *And when it sounds, it is his rule*
> *The first of all to drop his tool;*
> *And if he's brisk in any case,*
> *It will be in his homeward pace.*

Like any other happy family, a Shaker Family had to share and share alike. A member's time was literally not his own. As the *Millennial Laws* put it, no Shakers could "work as hirelings, gaining time, and counting it their own, to spend and use as they please ... but every one should work diligently with their hands, according to their strength, for the public good of the Society." Even the Trustees who went into the cities on business trips were discouraged from spending too much time away from home, even though their business was for the good of the community: "Neither Trustees, nor any one in their employ should be gone from home among the world, on trading business, more than four weeks, at one and the same time." Of course, it kept them safer from the influence of the "great and wicked cities." But it also helped limit the time that the Shaker would have to spend in a world where everyone was convinced that his time was his own to use or fritter as he pleased.

Any thinking in terms of personal possessions was dangerous to the communal spirit. An inspirational message from 1841 warned of just this danger:

YOUNG brethren and sisters scarce ever consider, that they are not their own, that their *time* is not their own.... Some are always

Who ever thought taffy-pulling was worth simplifying to save time? The Shakers did, and pulled over large iron hooks like this. It took fewer Sisters to pull the taffy, leaving others free to stir up another batch. (Canterbury, N.H.)

ready to take advantage of a thing like this, and spend days and days, to provide themselves with a piece of furniture. . . . Then they are ready to say, "the time was their own, that they took to make the article. I gained it, and I had a right to it." Then the word is, *"My writing desk! my chest, my tools! my Book! my bench!"* etc.

The Shakers gave all their time to make their way of life a success. They thought a lot about time—how to spend it, how to save it, how to make the most of God's gift. But more than anything else, the Shakers thought about the time ahead. One Shaker said that man's eyes pointed forward and so did his feet . . . and there was a good lesson in that.

Their name, especially, indicates something about their forward-looking attitude toward time. They were the United Society of Believers in the First and Second Appearing of Christ and felt that under the guidance of Mother Ann the Christian spirit had come again to stay. The Shakers weren't waiting for anything to happen, or for Resurrection Day to come—they were convinced that the time was *here.* It was this spirit that made them acutely aware of the millennium to come.

The time given to any individual member was short; in this sense, a Shaker did his work as if he "must die tomorrow." But as a growing and continuing community, Shakers felt they could expect to be a part of the next millennium, and so they also had "a thousand years to live." In this sense the seeming paradox of Mother Ann's words was resolved. The words of the Shakers' *Youth's Guide* heralded to all the promise of the new day:

Brother Isaac Youngs of New Lebanon, New York, the Shaker clockmaker, designed a five-pointed pen to save time writing music—one pull across the page and the whole staff was completed. The pen case is made of cherry.

> The morning of righteousness has but just begun to dawn; and ye, O little ones of your Mother, have been called at an early hour of the day. Look a thousand years forward, and consider the souls who will be called to the gospel. They will look back to your days on earth, and by them ye will be considered even of the first founders of the work of God in time.

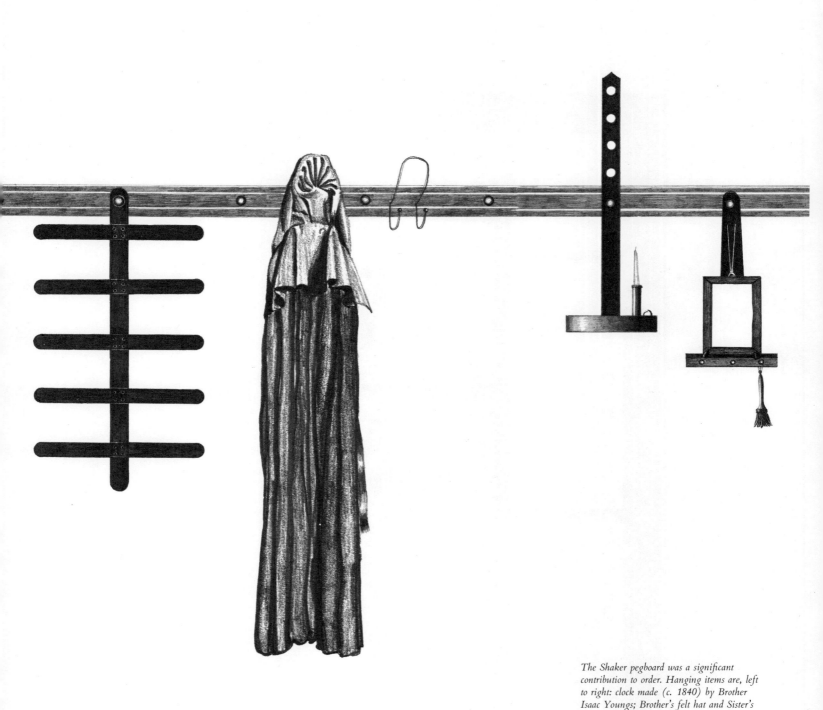

The Shaker pegboard was a significant
contribution to order. Hanging items are, left
to right: clock made (c. 1840) by Brother
Isaac Youngs; Brother's felt hat and Sister's
bonnet above a graceful coathanger;
five-armed coathanger (note the four wooden
pegs, not nails, in each joint); famous
broadcloth "Dorothy cloak," designed by
Eldress Dorothy Durgin of Canterbury, and
made both for Sisters and for sale; special
wire hanger on which the hooded cloaks were
hung to keep their shape; height-adjustable
candleholder made by Western Shakers with
a rim on its round base to keep the candle
from falling off; wall mirror whose tilt always
suited the individual because an adjustable
cord altered the viewing angle (note the small
pegs on the mirror itself).

One of the first things that people (especially mothers) notice when they walk into a Shaker room are the built-in cupboards and drawers, the wall pegboards, and the neatness and order of the room itself—every tool in place and every chair in order. "How did the Shakers manage to keep it so neat?" is a common cry. Mother Ann had told her followers to keep all their things in such order that they could find anything day or night, but unlike the mothers of *this* world, she didn't have to nag. The Shakers thought up efficient and simple ways of keeping their homes in perfect order.

At Canterbury, for example, every building was given a letter and every room inside a number. Look on the back of Canterbury tools and you will usually find a letter and a number—a fork marked L17, a yardstick marked G7—according to where the thing was used. There was no excuse for not putting it back in the right place. Drawers were numbered, and so were tools, according to size; Shaker chairs made at Mount Lebanon for sale had sizes ranging in order from 0 to 7. Visitors to Shaker villages were often invited to look into the drawers in the children's houses to see how neatly the children kept their things. No wonder when Elder Henry Blinn praised Sister Sarah Ward for her orderliness, he said she was "so neat that she looked as though she had been taken from the bureau drawer."

Shaker worship during most of the nineteenth century consisted of orderly rows of people dancing and singing. The Shaker love of order even affected the names their members used. If a new Sister was named Molly and there was already a Sister Molly in the village, very often the new member would take her middle name or another name she liked, to avoid confusion.

Order in Shaker homes and workshops was practical, of course, since several hundred people living together as one Family had to be organized if they were to get anything done right. But most of all, the Shakers chose order as an ideal because they wanted to imitate the perfect order that they felt was a part of God's kingdom. They said, "A place for everything and everything in its place"—then made this ideal a part of their everyday life in every way, from numbering drawers to selecting leaders to making the right tool for each job. Brother Alonzo Hollister of Mount Lebanon spoke for all Shakers when he wrote in his journal, "Every great man, every genuine man, is by the nature of him, a son of order, not of dis-

order.... He is here to make what was disorderly in a thing, ruled, regular."

From the beginning, Mother Ann was very mindful that order was a must in the Shaker way of life. Even more important to Mother Ann and her early followers than order in their homes, however, was the challenge of convincing people that she was indeed fitting as the leader of a new faith. Think for a minute how remarkable it was that a woman was acknowledged at all as the leader of a faith. Even now, two centuries later, the notion of God is as masculine as it was two thousand years ago, and the idea of a female minister still seems strange.

It was the notion of proper order—"a place for everything and everything in its place"—that helped Mother Ann convince new converts. She pointed out how natural and fitting it was, instead of how remarkable, for a woman to follow a man—in everyday life as they knew it, and also according to the Book of Genesis. She told her listeners,

> Where they both stand in their proper order, the man is the first, and the woman the second in the government of the family. He is the father and she the mother; and all the children, both male and female, must be subject to their parents; and the woman, being second, must be subject to her husband, who is the first; but when the man is gone, the right of government belongs to the woman: So is the family of Christ.

The man that she herself followed was, of course, Christ.

In another way, too, the Shakers felt that a woman was fitting as a new Christian leader. She could redeem womankind for the first time since Eve had caused all the trouble:

> *To accomplish this purpose on* Order's *great plan,*
> *As woman at first had been taken from man,*
> *And done all the mischief, it seemed to be fair,*
> *That she should be called on the loss to repair.*

Moral or spiritual order was even more important to the Shakers than domestic order. They believed in a universe of divine order, ruled by a God who saw to it that all things were in their proper order so that everything worked best for the whole. Since the Shakers wanted to follow God's perfect example in whatever they did, naturally the same kind of order was a part of the Shaker way. Eldress Aurelia Mace of Sabbathday Lake, Maine, wrote in 1899 that the Shakers were assured through heavenly visions that the angels in heaven themselves were as ordered as a Shaker drawer, adding, "How could these be held together unless there was perfect order, and each had his place assigned to him and kept himself in it?"

In this sense, moral order meant to the Shakers that in their villages, just as in God's heaven, there was a proper place for everyone, high or low. Elder Richard Pelham of Union Village, Ohio, explained this in terms of building a home—or a faith. "The great Architect," he said, "has various grades of workmen, all necessary in their places, in order to carry on the work and complete the building." Humility was an important part of this kind of order, Elder Richard continued.

> Let not those whose business it is to work in the mud, and make brick, imagine that theirs is the all-important business, and strive to pull down the bricklayer, the plasterer, the painter, and those qualified to give the finishing touches of taste and ornament, into the mud and drudgery of brick-making. Nor let these brick-makers imagine that they can do the work of all the other classes of workmen, and make bricks too. Let every one, of each class, work on in his own calling till the Master shall call him to another grade of duty....

Shakers—Elders and "hand-minded" members alike—took this advice. For example, Elder Giles Avery of Mount Lebanon was a mason—and a cooper, joiner, carpenter, plumber, and wagonmaker—both before and during his call to leadership as an Elder.

The notion of "a place for everyone and everyone in his place" meant that there was a remarkable sense of contentment in the village, with everyone satisfied to serve where he was most fit. In particular, the Shakers' sense of order meant that Elders and other leaders were not privileged unduly over the "hand-minded" members. Father Joseph Meacham, who as one of the earliest Shaker leaders helped establish the orderly structure of the Shaker village and government, explained,

> All the members of the Church have a just and equal right to the use of things, according to their order and needs; no other dif-

Special forms were in order for Shaker oval boxes, opposite. Brothers steamed fine hardwoods like maple and cherry (planed very thin with Shaker-devised planes) for hours, until they would curve around the form without cracking, and then the finger joints were fastened with copper brads. The metal plate on the form clinched the nails behind. When the box was dry, Brothers pulled it off easily after knocking out the small wedge from between the two halves of the form. The box was bottomed and sometimes finished with a lid made the same way. Below, a handle-bender for the boxes worked on the same principle of curving steamed wood; thirty handles at a time dried in the press to a uniform curve. (Canterbury, N.H.)

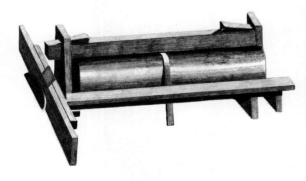

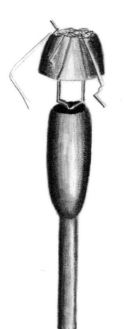

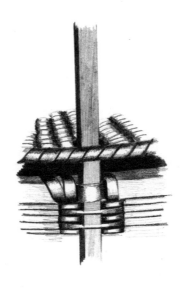

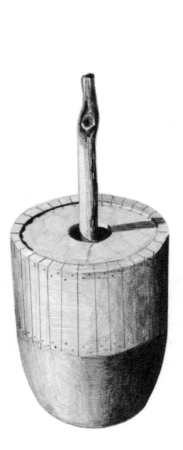

Clockwise from upper left, this page: Tiny basket form, 1 inch in diameter; detail of basket with attached lid; detail of weave; detail of bentwood handle, notched to grasp the rim, with tapered ends woven into the basket; completed basket. Wooden basket form at Canterbury, about a foot high without the handle, was inverted; the handle fit into a hole in the worktable. The form rotated so the weaver could keep his work before him. Facing page, clockwise from upper left: Detail of crown of Brother's straw hat; Sister's bonnet, woven of palm and straw and finished with a cloth neck flounce; wooden form for shaping bonnets; a "melon-bottom" basket with the bump on the bottom stood so firmly on all sides that it couldn't tip over; drainage basket used in cheesemaking.

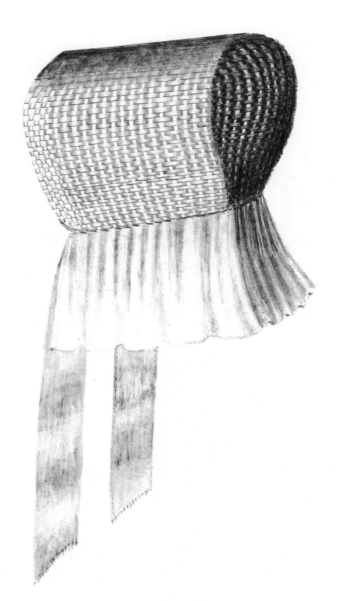

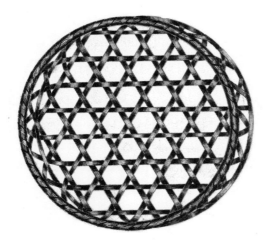

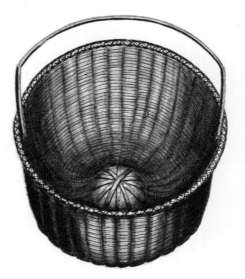

The Shaker Brothers' uniform haircut—trimmed straight across the forehead—as worn by Elder Giles Avery (1815-90). The subject of beards caused a gentle uproar in 1875. According to a printed circular sent out by the head Ministry at Mount Lebanon, clean-shaven Brothers in most of the villages "were not at all able to appreciate the virtues of beard-wearing" among young men interested in converting. The outcome was simple:

1st. Believers, at present, cannot be uniform in beard wearing.

2nd. Uniformity contributes to a oneness of spirit.

3rd. As nearly all clean shaven Brethren feel decidedly opposed to wearing the beard by requirement, therefore it is not, at present, wise to introduce beard wearing, in any style, as the uniform custom among Shakers.

The Sisters, we assume, stayed out of the debate. (From an old photograph)

ference ought to be made, between Elder or younger in things spiritual or temporal, than that which is just, and is for the peace and unity, and good of the whole.

Shaker leaders were expected to work with their hands just like any other members; they weren't paid for their extra duties; and they were far more often than not the kind of people who are great in all ways, including humility. One Brother wrote in 1853,

> They are our every day companions; who eat, sleep, work and worship ever with us; who by humility, by patience, by honesty, by goodness, have been promoted to be the servant of all—self-denying men, who hold themselves not aloof from us, but to whom we listen, whom we obey, because we believe it is the order of God that we should.

The contentment of Shaker life was due to a great extent to the absence of struggle for leadership. From the beginning, Mother Ann like any wise leader thoughtfully considered the need for order after her own death. Over and over she told each member to serve willingly where he could do most for the good of all. She was such a strong and inspiring leader that it would have been easy for the Shaker movement to collapse after her death, if her followers hadn't done what she said. The young faith continued to grow when she was gone because no one squabbled about the new leader; as Brother Nathan Tiffany testified in 1827, the Shakers simply recognized that Father James Whittaker was "evidently called of God to be her successor in the community."

The example set a precedent, and Shakers ever after chose to avoid politicking in their own villages as firmly as they refused to involve themselves in Worldly politics. Whenever a Deaconess died, for example, or an Elder became too ill to continue, there were no campaigns and no elections. The village Ministry nominated the new leader "in union with the covenant keeping members"—that is, in agreement with everyone else. New leaders were nominated according to one standard only: their fitness for the particular job. As Elder Giles Avery wrote, the leaders were "not considered infallible oracles," and were in order only if they were "for the time, the occasion and the locality, the most appropriate."

If at any time one of the leaders proved unfit for his responsibilities, proper order in the village made a new choice necessary. The Shakers had a strong sense of appropriate behavior for every member, but especially the leaders who were responsible above all else for maintaining spiritual order in the village.

The spiritual order in the community was matched by the actual layout of the village itself. The Shakers thought so much of order that they divided their villages into several different Families or "Orders"—progressive levels of commitment to the Shaker faith, as far as both spirit and possessions were concerned. The Orders of a Shaker village were as close but distinct spiritually as they were on the map.

The first or Gathering Order was usually about a half mile from the main Family, called the Church Family or Order. Usually the common name of the Gathering Order was its direction from the Church Family—at Canterbury, for example, the Gathering Order was called the North Family because it was a half mile north of the Church Family. Here a new member had a chance to find out if the Shaker life was best for him, and vice versa, with the guidance of the Gathering Order Elders and Eldresses. At this point, the member's Worldly property was his own; if he left, it went with him, although he wouldn't be paid for the work he'd done while living voluntarily with the Shakers. When the Elders and the member felt that he was ready for the next step, he signed the Novitiate Covenant and went on to the next Order.

The second or Junior Order was usually slightly closer to the Church Family. Like each Order, the Junior Order had its own workshops, Dwellinghouse, and set of leaders. Of course, the member was free to leave at any time if he felt that the Shaker life was not for him.

The final step in Shaker life—or the beginning one—was entrance into the Senior Order, often called the Church Family because the Meetinghouse was there, besides workshops and a Dwellinghouse. The Church Family Elders and Eldresses were the head leaders in the Shaker village Ministry. Church Family members entered freely and voluntarily, promising to devote their lives and their personal property to God and to each other in the Shaker way. Only at this point did the member sign the Shaker Covenant and become a full Shaker. The Shakers today still celebrate their "Shaker birthdays" as the anniversary of this date.

Beeswax cakes were found in every Sister's sewing basket; the women ran thread through the wax to coat and strengthen it when sewing on buttons. Sisters poured melted wax into a hand-carved wooden double mold. When the cakes were hard, the top part simply swiveled on its base so the cakes could be pushed out neatly from behind. (Canterbury, N.H.)

Sisters used special wooden forms to make satin strawberries stuffed with powdered emery for sharpening needles. The Canterbury Shakers still make beeswax cakes and emeries. (Canterbury, N.H.)

❋

The notion of "a place for everything and everything in its place" was also responsible for the various standard buildings in the Shaker village: the Dwellinghouse, the Meetinghouse, the Office, and so forth. Visible order was a necessity everywhere, but nowhere more vitally than in the Meetinghouse. The Shakers' notion of a place for everything made a distinct type of building for worship literally "in order." The building was intended as a place for worship and worship only. Elder Giles Avery explained in 1879 why the Meetinghouse was intended for that single purpose:

> If sacred places are abandoned to secular uses, cumbered with the truck of trade, papers, books, literature of a worldly character, or needless furniture inappropriate to a place of retirement and worship, there is unavoidably added much labor of obtaining, in those retreats, a heavenly, devotional, worshipful spirit; because of the sensitiveness of the human soul to surroundings.

As the most sacred spot in the village, it was important for the Meetinghouse to reflect spiritual order visibly in the peaceful order of its own arrangement.

Yet the building was not sacred in itself. When the Shakers at Mount Lebanon built a new, larger Meetinghouse there in 1822–4, the "ancient church edifice" built originally in 1785 became the storehouse for the Shaker garden seed industry there. Whenever the Shakers found one use more fitting than another, they had no qualms about change. The practical Shakers simply saw the fitness of the old building for a new use (despite the fact that it was revered as the first Shaker church ever built), and therefore using it as a practical workshop was entirely "in order."

Certain kinds of behavior in the Meetinghouse were considered a fitting expression of divine order. The *Millennial Laws* devoted an entire section to "Orders concerning the Spiritual Worship of God, Attending to Meetings &c.":

> All should go into meeting in the fear of God walking on their toes, and two abreast if the passage way be sufficiently wide to admit of it, keeping step together, and none should have any talking, laughing, or hanging on the railing, *while going to, or coming from meeting.*

Brethren and sisters should not allow themselves to be gaping or yawning in meeting.

Certain ways of expressing spiritual communication with God were considered more fitting than others. When Elder Daniel Boler visited the Shakers at Groveland, New York, in 1852, he noted in his travel journal that Elder Brother Jesse "spoke appropriately on the occasion. Their exercises were devotional, and well fitted to the time & place." Five years later, a reporter for *Harper's Magazine* witnessed a Shaker worship service at New Lebanon, New York, and concluded, "It can not be denied that their public worship at Lebanon is dignified, solemn, and deeply impressive.... Their movements in the dance or march, whether natural or studied, are all graceful and appropriate."

Shaker daily life outside the Meetinghouse was just as much influenced by the concept of order or fitness; the *Millennial Laws* included rules for domestic order in every part of Shaker life from housework to eating to handwork. The Deacons and Deaconesses, as overseers of daily chores, industry, and food and clothing for all the members, were responsible for keeping the village in practical order. What they needed was a solid streak of plain common sense and a knack for organization. The Deacons at Union Village, Ohio, for example, kept track of shoes for the whole Family by taking a census of the shoes in the village:

Feb. 5, 1856   Registering the shoes of each member.
Feb. 11, 1856   each member of the Church is requested to hand in a list of all their boots & shoes.

One of the most important duties was keeping the dwellings and workshops in the neatest possible order, to avoid time-wasting confusion, and to reflect the spiritual order within. When Eldress Nancy Moore of South Union, Kentucky, visited a neat workshop room at Canterbury in 1854, she was delighted if not downright reverent at the sight of such deliberate order. She wrote in her diary,

All around the walls are the sisters milking & washing dresses hung in order, and on a shelf above their bonnets are arranged, and in a tier of cupboards the shoes are all placed in good order,

Brothers kept their straw hats clean with this specially designed hatbrush. The rounded end dusted the inside, while the long row of bristles swept the brim.

This is a simple arrangement to be sure, but to me it spoke more than to see a splendid hall decorated with the richest furniture.

From the beginning, Mother Ann realized the importance of order "in the outward things" perfect enough to match divine order. She told her followers, "Go home, and take care of what you have. Provide places for all your things, so that you may know where to find them at any time, day or night." Young members in later years were taught by their *Youth's Guide* to "keep all things in order, as keeping the law of heaven; and keep the order of Zion, that heaven may protect you." As usual, the Shakers practiced what they preached. At Canterbury, for example, the Shakers numbered all the drawers and walk-in closets of their Dwellinghouse attic (circa 1795) so that every member had a place for everything and could put everything in its place. And the order of the "Medicine Room" in the Infirmary (1811) could really help heaven protect the sick—in an emergency a Shaker doctor could go immediately to the right drawer for the right equipment or medicine because all the built-in drawers were neatly labeled. Members like Sister Polly Lawrence were so convinced that outward order was a sure sign of inner spiritual order that the last thing she did before she closed her eyes and died in peace was to straighten the bedclothes and say, "All things must be made straight, in temporal as well as in spiritual things."

Even the humblest workshops were kept in the same scrupulous order. A typical example was the workroom of Brother Francis Roderick, of Union Village, Ohio, in 1873. In his tool room and woodshed "every stick of wood was exact in its place, and the face of the pile as true as if laid by a strait-edge. His little work shop exhibited the same care." Order in the village was especially important on the Sabbath: spiritual order and physical order went hand in hand. The *Millennial Laws* stated: "All of the gates should be closed on Saturday night and work rooms should be swept; the work and tools should be in order, and safely secured from thieves and fire."

The neatness of Shaker fields and gardens was just as much a reflection of divine order, as far as the Shakers were concerned. Taking the spiritual advice of the *Youth's Guide* seriously—"Say not to thy friend, there are weeds in your garden, when thy own is choked with the same; but rather look at home"—Shaker farmers made their fields and gardens a model of orderliness. A Western Shaker visiting the Harvard village in 1850 wrote with admiration and devotion about the neat gardens there: "Good Berries, Straw Berries, Raspberries Currents Mellons &c. &c. Everything was arranged in beautiful order, and seemed to invite the blessings of heavens sweet smile upon it."

The Shakers' notion of proper order and fitness also led them to follow certain rules about gardening. In a section of the *Millennial Laws* called "Concerning the Order of the Natural Creation," Shakers were not to upset the order of nature by "cultivating fruits and plants, not adapted to the climate in which they live."

Even more important, Shakers were not to violate the order of nature by unnatural breeding of plants or animals:

> Different species of trees, or plants may not be engrafted or budded upon each other, as apples upon pears, quince, etc. peaches upon cherries, or contrary wise.

> The different species of animals should also be kept distinct, each in their own order.

Regular scientific breeding for improved stock—plant and animal—was on the other hand an important part of Shaker agriculture.

The result of these efforts to keep the village in order was a neatness and orderliness so striking that almost every visitor to Shaker villages in years gone by found fit to mention it. James Fenimore

Wooden glove forms, above, were used for blocking knitted gloves to their proper shape; when not in use, the forms folded to store neatly. Gloves of hand-knit coon fur and silk, pictured here, were sold to the World. (Old Chatham, N.Y.)

"A place for everything and everything in its place"—a perfect description of the Dwellinghouse attic at Canterbury, finished c. 1795. Opposite: Built-in walk-in closets and 88 numbered drawers of beautiful old pine—pegged together and dovetailed front and back, even where no one could see them—line both sides of the room where Shakers kept their clothing.

Cooper commented in 1828 that he had never seen during his American travels "villages as neat, and so perfectly beautiful, as to order and arrangement, without, however, being picturesque or ornamented, as those of the Shakers." Elder Henry Blinn of Canterbury, on a visit to Whitewater, Ohio, in 1873, wrote simply: "There was a neatness that spread a halo over the whole place."

"A place for everything and everything in its place" was as strong an influence on the Shakers' outlook on working as it was on the neat Shaker workshops themselves. Although members were encouraged to learn as many skills as they could through job rotation, anyone with a particular gift was always encouraged to make the most of it. According to the Shaker Covenant, "We believed we were debtors to God in relation to Each other, and all men, to improve our time and Tallents in this Life, in that manner in which we might be most useful." So there were men like Brother Isaac Youngs of Mount Lebanon, the Shaker clockmaker; Elder Otis Sawyer of Sabbathday Lake, Maine, noted Shaker hymnwriter; and in the twentieth century, Sister Helena Sarle of Canterbury, well known for her oil paintings. Each of them could do many things well, but all were encouraged to use their particular gifts for the benefit of everyone.

A story written by Elder Henry Blinn of Canterbury about Brother Micajah Tucker of the same village gives us a good idea of how seriously the Shakers applied standards of fitness or order to themselves. Brother Micajah, the stonecutter at Canterbury who during his Shaker life cut and laid granite foundations and steps and over a half mile of granite sidewalk, worked at that occupation until he was in his seventies. When he reached his eighties, moving the granite chunks got to be a mite hard, so he took up carpentry instead. Unfortunately,

> on the 4th of July 1846 while using the whirl saw at the mill, he accidentally cut off two of his fingers. He felt very sad in regard to this as it was a strong admonition that a person of his age (82 years) should not be using kinds of machinery. He had learned from the first Elders and had for many years taught others that there were "no accidents in Christ," and this came home as a sorrowful lesson that he was not quite right.

It was apparent to Brother Micajah that his work in the sawmill was no longer in order, and the sorrow he felt shortened his life. (But being in such good shape after a life of hard work, it took him two years to pine away and die—he finally passed away at eighty-four!)

The Shakers also felt that the work of their hands should reflect a kind of moral order; that is, Shaker-made items were to be as simple, as honest, and as fit for their purposes as the Shakers were themselves. A visit to any Shaker tool shop would prove that they practiced what they preached. All the illustrations in this chapter show the Shakers' knack for making the right tool for the right job; even though they took a little longer to make, these tools saved time and trouble in the long run because they were fit for their purposes.

The things that the Shakers made with their tools were well known for their own good order. No matter whether the work was done for home use or for sale, the Shakers said,

> All work done, or things made in the Church for their own use ought to be faithfully and well done, but plain and without superfluity. All things ought to be made according to their order and use; and all things kept decent and in good order, according to their order and use. All things made for sale ought to be well done, and suitable for their use. . . .

The *kinds* of work done by Shakers were likewise felt to reflect a certain proper order; that is, whatever work was good for the economic and spiritual order of the Shaker village was definitely in order. Farming, carpentry, bricklaying, blacksmithing, cooking, sewing, and all the other jobs of farm and home were useful and appropriate.

What was not in order was any undertaking that required the Shakers to give up their self-sufficiency. Elder Frederick Evans said emphatically, "We ought to get on without the use of outside labor. Then we should be confined to such enterprises as are best for us." This was practical advice, from the standpoint of Shaker economy: if they didn't have to pay salaries or buy goods, so much the better for the thrifty Shakers. The savings could be impressive. According to Hervey Elkins, describing the Dwellinghouse at Enfield, New Hampshire,

> Such a dwelling, as the one I have described, could not be erected in one of our cities for less than a hundred thousand dollars; but as

Above: Shakers at Mount Lebanon were famous for their high-quality garden seeds. Colorful seed boxes like this one kept the seeds in order—Beets, Carrot, Sage and Pepper, Tomato, Flowers, Corn—and were perfect for advertising. Opposite: Shakers were among the first to put up seeds in paper packages, at top, as early as 1816; chisels with bent blades, bottom, cut the package shape quickly. (Old Chatham, N.Y.)

the quarry of stone, and forests of pine, whence its materials were extracted, are owned by the family who erected it, they probably expended in cash not more than half that sum.

But self-sufficiency was also in order from a spiritual standpoint: outside influence could easily ruin the harmony and order of the village. The Shakers believed that God would ask of them according to, but not beyond, their own efforts—

> *For God in justice will demand*
> *According to our measure*

—so that they could afford to remain self-sufficient.

No wonder it was with unease that a Shaker visitor to the Harvard Village noted the step away from self-sufficiency there in 1846. He wrote,

> Pass the dairy house, have much conversation in relations to the profits made by selling milk, & purchasing butter & cheese . . . they think it to be profitable, but I do not know—I love butter & cheese made by clean hands, not defiled with sin—not only so, but I think our Heavenly Parents will bless us if we strive to do our own work & not be idle.

For this "order of people called to rise into angelhood," the notion of a place for everything and everything in its place even helped in accepting the name "Shakers." The shaking motions that were part of the early members' worship gave them the name, originally a scornful term. Although they chose later to be called the United Society of Believers in the First and Second Appearing of Christ, they themselves accepted the name "Shakers" from the beginning. As Richard McNemar pointed out during the Western revivals around 1810, no other name could have been more in order:

> The first thing that struck me, when I heard that name, was that the universal cry in the revival had been that God would *shake the heavens and the earth! Shake out the things that were made, that those things that could not be shaken might remain.* How then was he to do it? He always works by means and instruments. . . . Then was it not reasonable for the subjects of the revival to expect that God would shake the heavens and the earth with his *Shakers?*

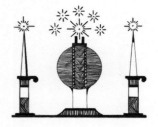

In 1842, an English visitor stopped at the Shaker village in New Lebanon and to his dismay had the worst of times. Accustomed as he was to the cozy environment of British parlors, Charles Dickens obviously found it alien and wrote accordingly, "We walked into a grim room, where several grim hats were hanging on grim pegs, and the time was grimly told by a grim clock..." Dickens came away with a distinct impression of the Shaker style—spare, relatively subdued in color (few carpets and no wallpaper at all), and entirely free of homey clutter.

Few visitors today seem to agree with Dickens. Where he found aesthetic and emotional poverty, we tend to find the spareness of a Shaker room refreshingly spacious rather than chillingly sparse. Our appreciation, of course, is just as much influenced by our own times and taste as Dickens's disapproval was of his—and just as revealing about his times and ours as it is about the Shakers.

Dickens (and he was typical of the nineteenth century on both sides of the Atlantic) felt at home in a world where *matter* was of the essence. Matter, things, bric-a-brac, knickknacks, doodads—to be displayed, to be collected, to fill a need and a nook, and most of all to afford security with their solidity, tangibility, and stability. If a little matter was good, why then a superabundance of it was superb; and the more authoritatively its mass was asserted, the better. If for no other reason than its taste in interior decorating, the nineteenth century deserves its title, the Age of Materialism.

Picture a typical Victorian home: outside, a massive pile of Gothic or Roman masonry, slit with narrow windows frequently dimmed with dark stained glass. Inside? Masses of heavy draperies, ponderous chairs, heavy gilt frames, thick patterned carpets, wallpaper jungles, curios and whatnots in every perch, and in the corner a massive gray umbrella stand, compliments of an elephant deprived of life and limb. Even the lady of the house was a formidable presence, buttressed from behind in her bustle and as monumentally forbidding as her house, in her dozen separate bulwarks of under and outer clothing.

It sounds claustrophobic and materialistic to us, as it did to the Shakers. One member wrote in 1853, "The low, dark, and heathenishly ornamented structures are not compatible with the liberal and enlightened spirit of modern times. They behoove despotism and seem the concomitants of slavery and terror."

If the last century's passion was for accumulation, ours is equally insistent on getting rid of the clutter. In the twentieth century, it is space, not matter, that counts the most. It took the twentieth century to declare, "Less is more"; to streamline the fussy detail in everything from cars to toasters; to produce the first all-white painting and the first all-glass house, and to find them both valid and satisfying. Look through the large picture window of a twentieth-century house and see how we love space: above a seemingly weightless glass-and-chrome coffee table floats the ethereal instability of an overhead mobile. Even the lady of the house has been streamlined—no more corsets, drawers, hoop skirts, or bustles.

Certainly, it took twentieth-century technology to create the first see-through plastic chair or the first glass walls: but more significantly, it took twentieth-century taste to want to make a chair or a wall that

Space was at a premium in Shaker Dwellinghouses, since a Shaker Family often numbered over a hundred. They made the most of limited space by furnishing very simply. Ideally, a Shaker dwellingroom for Brother or Sister was to contain little more than (clockwise from upper left):

one candlestand
two beds on rollers, easily movable
several large windows for light and ventilation
two straight chairs
one lamp
one table
one broom and several clothesbrushes
one small iron wood-burning stove for heating
one or more built-in cupboards and sets of drawers
one woodbox with dustbrush
one small hanging mirror
one simple carpet
. . . and of course wall pegs.

looks as if it isn't there. The nineteenth century pretended that its iron-frame skyscrapers, perfectly capable of standing under their own support, needed the mass of heavy masonry sheathing; we pretend that our skyscrapers, as well as our furniture, don't have mass at all, because we make them transparent. Only the twentieth century could take immense skyscrapers weighing millions of tons and wrap them in mirror glass to melt into the space of sky around them.

We are obsessed with space. We talk about outer space, inner space; we get "spaced out" on mind-expanding drugs. We talk about "personal space"—any stranger within two feet is an unwelcome intruder into a private zone of spatial insulation.

A hundred years ago, empty space was something to be crammed to the brim, whether it be a whatnot or a city block. Today, space is a commodity in itself, all the more desirable and expensive because it's getting scarcer all the time. The chaos of the megalopolis—flashing signs, buildings blown sky high, and highways sprawled twelve lanes across—is more claustrophobic than any parlor the most conscientious Victorian clutterer would have created. After all, isn't the intricate webbing of power lines across the landscape worse than the intricate webbing of an antimacassar on the parlor sofa?

Even the relatively open space of our rural landscape is cluttered with high-tension lines and towers, radio towers, water towers, cliff-side graffiti, underpasses, overpasses, and neon billboards. No wonder the classic twentieth-century interior is marked by the simple line, the plain surface, the simplicity of color and texture; these offer a feeling of relief with a sense of spaciousness missing from our environment. It's fitting that our century has turned its vision and its technology to the invitingly empty expanse of the moon and beyond. We too deserve our own title, the Space Age.

Our appreciation of open space is one reason for our sudden appreciation of the airiness and roominess of the Shaker style. The bare white walls and the slim tables and chairs free of knickknacks make a kind of sense that was incomprehensible to the last century. But the Shakers' reasons for valuing space for its own sake—so contrary to the feelings of their Worldly contemporaries—are different from ours. The open lands that bring high prices on the market today were, after all, still widely available when the Shakers were establishing their own homes. Shakers didn't crave wide open spaces as a

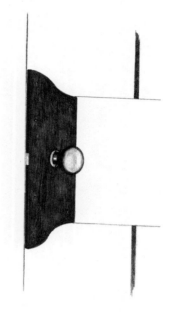

A wooden latch plate in the Dwellinghouse (1883) at Sabbathday Lake, Maine, prevented smudgy finger marks and kept the white door clean.

luxurious retreat from the crowded cities and suburbs; they demanded isolation to practice their unique form of worship and to work in peace and freedom. Their success in choosing sites far from the "great and wicked cities" is evident in that the Shaker villages that remain today are still surrounded with stretches of open land.

What, then, were the Shakers' reasons for the deliberate roominess of their architecture and village planning? Why did the Shakers develop a genius for saving space with their distinctive wall pegboards and built-in cupboard systems?

It was a uniquely Shaker blend of practicality and spiritual idealism that produced their space-saving ways. The most obvious answer lies in the fact that Shakerism was a way of life designed to bring many people together into one home, to live as one Family under Christ. Very often fifty or more people lived under a single roof. It was simply the most practical solution to eliminate as completely as possible any unnecessary furnishings that would take up valuable living space, as well as valuable funds, work time, and cleaning time.

The practical necessity of economizing space was backed up spiritually as early as 1841, when Sister Anna Dodgson received the following instructions on interior decorating while under divine inspiration. According to the spirit of Father Joseph Meacham (one of Mother Ann's most important successors), via the "Holy Angel of the Lord," dwelling rooms were ideally to contain nothing more than:

> Green painted bed steads, plain chairs, with splint bottoms are preferable to any other kind, because they can be mended when they break. One rocking Chair, in a room, except where the aged reside. One table, or more, if necessary according to the number of inmates and size of the room. One stand.
>
> One good looking glass, which ought not to exceed eighteen inches in length, and twelve or fourteen in width, with a frame one inch and a half wide. . . . If another glass is really necessary, have a smaller one, and hang it in the closet. . . .
>
> Carpets are admissable but they ought to be used with discretion and plain. Mother Lucy [Wright, another revered early Shaker and Father Joseph's counterpart] says two colours are sufficient for one carpet. Make one stripe of red and green, another of drab and grey, another of butternut and grey. . . .

Shaker furniture often had drawers on two or three sides, like this pine sewing chest (c. 1830) from Enfield, Connecticut. Shakers had the space to use these chests, which had to stand where drawers on all sides were easily reachable. The space they saved made work and movement more convenient. (Old Chatham, N.Y.)

One good glass Lamp to be provided for every room, if more are needful, as often is the case, let them be provided in order for the room. . . .

Three good clothes brushes, I think are sufficient, for any room, and if there are any held in possession by individuals, they ought to be given up to supply places where more are needed.

No drawers, chests, nor cupboards, ought to be put in the lower halls of the dwelling house. But they may be placed in the other halls if necessary. . . .

The *Millennial Laws* incorporated much of Sister Anna's heavenly advice, with the added specifications that the "carpets in one room should be as near alike as can consistently be provided and these the Deaconesses should provide." Also, "No maps, Charts, and no pictures or paintings, shall ever be hung up in your dwelling rooms, shops, or Office." (The ever practical Shakers did, however, see fit to allow "modest advertisements" in the Trustees' business Office "when necessary.")

The Shakers practiced what they preached. In 1853, an observer described a Shaker room in almost exactly the same way as prescribed by the *Millennial Laws,* with the addition of

plain chairs, bottomed with rattan or rush, and light so as to be easily portable . . . an elegant but plain stove . . . one candle-stick, and a smoker or tin funnel to convey to the chimney the smoke and gas evolved from the lights; and 2 or 3 bibles and all the religious works edited by the Society, a concordance, grammar, dictionary, etc.

The result of the Shakers' deliberate steps to limit the amount of furnishings in their rooms was a spaciousness and airiness that immediately impressed most nineteenth-century visitors as a contrast to their own homes. Some, more appreciative than Dickens, found the effect odd but pleasant. In 1869, William Hepworth Dixon described the room he visited at Mount Lebanon like this:

A bed stands in the corner, with sheets and pillows of spotless white. A table on which lie an English Bible, some few Shaker tracts, an inkstand, a paper-knife; four cane chairs, arranged in angles; a piece of carpet by the bedside; a spittoon in one corner,

Another way Shakers saved space was by making single pieces of furniture do double duty, like this table-desk (c. 1840) from Shirley, Massachusetts. The pull-out writing board not only saved space, but protected the table top from marks.
(Fruitlands Museum, Mass.)

Above: A low-backed dining chair slid under the table after the meal, out of the way of the Sisters clearing up.

Opposite: A typical Shaker dining hall. Underbraces on long dining tables usually ran directly below the trestle top, leaving plenty of space for Shaker legs—and for the low-backed dining chairs. Chairs also hung from wall pegs, saving floor space. At Canterbury, seasonings hung from the ceiling to save space on the table top; built-in serving tables folded out of the way. Sturdy wooden placemats hung in racks from the pegboard. In the kitchen behind, a Sister works near a flight of shelves.

complete the furniture. A closet on one side of the room contains a second bed, a wash-stand, a jug of water, towels; and the whole apartment is light and airy, even for a frame house.

Besides the obvious practical reasons for light and spacious rooms, however, lay other reasons rooted in the spiritual nature of the Shaker way of life. After all, the Shaker way was a religion; the main emphasis was always on the realm of the spirit, not the material World. The things that they used were of less importance to the Shakers than the Brothers and Sisters who used them and the good uses to which they were put. The few possessions that a Shaker family did have taught the members to share willingly among themselves—to see themselves as part of a Family, not as a group of selfish individuals. Sister Anna's spirit message warned that while several lamps might be provided for each dwelling room, "I hope I shall never hereafter see any of my brethren or Sisters carrying a lamp, from room to room, or hear the word spoken, 'My glass Lamp'!"

If the Shakers succeeded in eliminating totally all unnecessary clutter from their homes, they also succeeded ingeniously well in their efforts to design the furnishings that were absolutely necessary to take up as little space as possible. They were quick to incorporate several basic space-saving ideas into the things that they made. To conserve space, Shaker furnishings were designed to hang from or be built into the walls; to fold or collapse when not in use; to satisfy several needs in a single article; or to be easily portable.

The Shaker wall pegboard, usually 6 feet from the floor and a feature of nearly every Shaker room in every workshop or dwelling, was one of the single most important space-saving developments in the Shaker way of life, because it often eliminated the need for free-standing furniture that used up valuable floor space. For example, candlestands, wardrobes, and even standing shelves and cupboards were mostly unnecessary because candlesticks, clothing, and portable shelves and cupboards were designed to hang from the pegs. Even chairs that were not in use were hung up from the pegs off the floor. In the Meetinghouse, two rows of pegs held coats, cloaks, hats, and bonnets.

Other areas of the village provided their own ingenious opportunities for hanging items to save space. A visitor to Canterbury in

1893 described how the vinegar cruets and other seasonings in the dining hall hung from the ceiling over the tables, easily within reach and yet saving space on the tabletop for the food. If he had gone into the food cellar, he would have seen a screened shelf hanging from the ceiling; besides saving floor space, it protected the food from mice. He continued, "In the large family diningroom, ample for seating sixty persons, is a long table . . . and low-backed chairs—low enough to stand clear under the table when not in use." This type of low-backed dining chair was a standard feature of Shaker villages from Maine to Kentucky.

The visitor might also have mentioned the built-in serving tables in the Canterbury dining room, that folded up into the wall when not in use. Collapsibility was a significant space-saving feature of all kinds of Shaker items, from table swifts to telescoping metal pens to folding shutters to the folding stereoscope—all designed with the idea of decreasing storage space. Shaker carpenters didn't economize to save space for its own sake, however, like other nineteenth-century inventors famous (or notorious) for dreaming up "space-saving" creations that often worked better on paper than in the living room. In the general U.S. Patent records are folding contraptions from wardrobes that unfolded into bathtubs to one wonderfully useless invention which received its patent in 1866: a piano that folded out

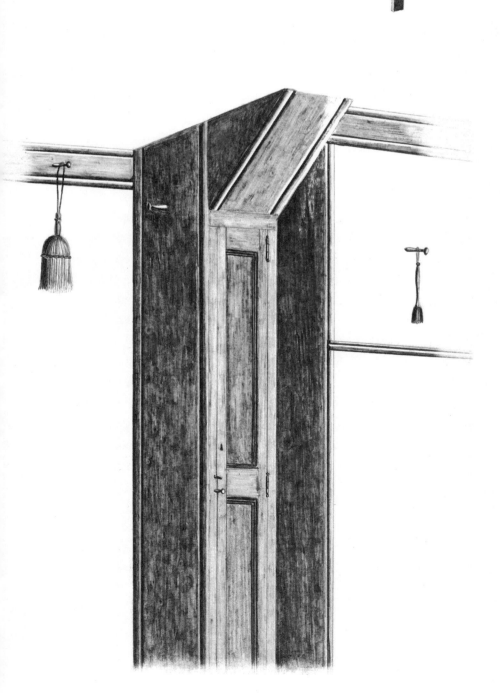

Above: A folding child's bed from South Union, Kentucky (at the Shaker Museum in Auburn, Kentucky); when folded, it forms a hutch seat with open storage space beneath. Left, a wall beam in the Dwellinghouse attic at Canterbury made a closet just big enough for brooms and brushes.

Opposite: top, Shakers didn't waste a slanted attic space—rows of pegs hang from the ceiling in the Ministry Shop (1848) at Canterbury; below, a built-in ladder at Canterbury was easily lowered when needed and raised out of the way when not in use. A wooden catch fastened it to the ceiling, saving floor space.

into a bed, a bureau, two cupboards, and a wash basin with pitcher and towel! The piano stool opened for use as a lady's toilet with mirror and a fold-out writing surface. Rube Goldberg would have loved it—the piano even played. When the Shakers designed collapsible and built-in features, on the other hand, they tried to let common sense be their guide.

The same visitor observed with admiration another space-saving feature at Canterbury: "In every room where a fire is needed, a woodbox, built into the wall, with a trap door near the stove, so that no wood or dirt is to be seen, is a feature characteristic of the Shakers." Not only wood boxes but entire sets of drawers, shelves, and cupboards found their places built into the walls between rooms. The result—greatly increased individual room space. The Shakers at Enfield, New Hampshire, showed exceptional devotion to the built-in storage wall. A Shaker visiting from the West recorded that in the Dwellinghouse (built 1837) there were "800 drawers in the house on a side of their dining wall which is set full of door cupboards & drawers. Elder Orville said there was not a box or chest in the house."

The notion of building in, when applied directly to furniture, usually resulted in a practical versatility of purpose. Sewing stands featured pull-out surfaces that sufficed for writing or cutting; the kindling drawers built into wood boxes eliminated the need for separate containers. Even the portable steps the Shakers used to reach the upper levels of their built-in wall cupboards were often fitted as storage compartments themselves. In Enfield, long low work tables doubled as cupboards below for cooking utensils.

The easy mobility of Shaker furnishings was another space-saving feature, nowhere more evident than in the Meetinghouse where Shakers sat on portable benches rather than fixed pews. One reason for this, of course, was that the Shakers needed room and plenty of it to express their worship in dancing. They also needed plenty of room to seat the spectators who came to watch and sometimes to be inspired.

Besides these practical reasons, another more spiritual reason may have prompted the Shakers to build their dwellings, workshops, and Meetinghouses exceptionally large and light inside. The Shakers saw their homes as the nearest thing to heaven here on earth, which meant primarily that their conduct was to imitate heavenly perfection as

Above: The Shaker table swift, used for winding skeins of yarn into balls, collapsed like a folding umbrella when not in service. It fastened to any flat surface and expanded to the right size for any skein by means of wooden screws which held it in place. In 1869 Elder Thomas Damon of Hancock, Massachusetts, the maker of these swifts, was constructing "machinery for cutting out and dressing up the various parts of the kind of swifts that are screwed to a Table for use" and turning out an order for 20,000 at the wholesale price of 50 cents each. Left: A sewing desk from South Union, Kentucky (at the Shaker Museum in Auburn, Kentucky), with a pull-out cutting board and a vertical spool drawer at the back. Right: "Chase's FOLDING STEREOSCOPE, IMPROVED, Patented July 16, 1872" was a space-saver by Brother Nelson Chase of Enfield, New Hampshire. Folded, it fitted into a pocket; the view from underneath shows all the hinges that make it collapsible. Stereoscopic views of Shaker villages were popular in the nineteenth century. One (decidedly non-Shaker) view the author has seen shows a fin de siècle *can-can dancer with, of all things, two Mount Lebanon Shaker rockers as props!*

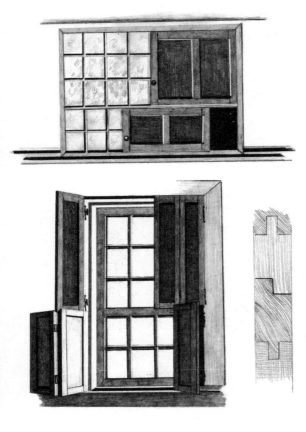

Top: Called "Indian shutters" in colonial homes, at Canterbury these shutters slid across to keep out drafts in the Infirmary and Girls' House. Folding shutters, also pictured, used as well in the Infirmary (1811), took up less wall space, leaving more room for hanging utensils. For as much light as possible, Shakers used simple curtains. According to the Millennial Laws, white, green, or blue curtains were allowed, but not "red, checked, striped or flowered."

nearly as possible. But it also often meant that the actual physical environment of the Shaker village was shaped to some heavenly ideal: lines were perfectly straight, not crooked; angles were exactly right; deceitful workmanship was forbidden; and all was kept pure, clean, and orderly.

If the concepts of perfection, honesty, and purity—all qualities associated with heaven—affected the way the Shaker village looked to such an extent, it makes sense that another traditional concept of heaven, as the realm of infinite light and space, could just as much have influenced the Shakers' homes. If God's heaven were boundless, it was only natural for the Shaker to build his home as spaciously as possible.

A visitor to Watervliet, New York, received the impression there in the mid-nineteenth century that heaven was "a Shaker community on a very large scale." In the Shaker notion of heaven, he continued, "The buildings are large and splendid, being all of white marble. There are large orchards with all kinds of fruit. There are also very large gardens laid out in splendid style, with beautiful rivers flowing through them, but all is spiritual." How clearly the Shakers identified spaciousness as a divine ideal. Another visitor wrote in 1848 that, like the infinite space of heaven, "Their buildings were made capacious with a view to receive the world when they shall be converted to Shakerism." God, and the Shakers, had plenty of room for anyone with faith.

Similarly, light was a characteristic feature of Shaker buildings, for practical and spiritual reasons. Shaker appreciation of space and light was expressed sensitively by Hervey Elkins, describing the Enfield, New Hampshire, Dwellinghouse in 1853. He wrote,

> The interior of the edifice is finished with beautiful white pine, and not a knot, blemish, or nail head was visible, *before painting,* from the cupola to the cellar. The finish is painted white, and varnished, and shines with the brilliancy of reflected light. The house contains about two hundred windows of twenty large panes of glass each, with an inside finish, around each, of thirty dollars cost.

The Shakers thought enough of light to spend thousands of dollars for it and consider them well spent. The result was what Elkins called "a combination of space, beauty, symmetry and the light and splendor of a summer's day."

Daylight streamed in through the many windows that typify Shaker architecture, reflecting off the white plaster walls to lighten the rooms even more. Windows in interior walls of large buildings like the Dwellinghouse let daylight into even the innermost rooms. A cupboard in the South Kitchen of the Canterbury Trustees' Office (added in 1867) has a window in the side to let in light, the easier to see and clean inside. In 1873, a Shaker housekeeper visiting a typical Victorian townhouse concluded,

> to preserve the carpets and the accompanying furniture in their beauty, carefully exclude all the light; and to exclude the dust, keep the windows closed; and to preserve the health of the family, let them live in other rooms, with no carpets, plenty of air, and floods of sunshine.

Good natural light was practical for working and cleaning. Yet the Shakers' love of windows and light also reflected their love of spiritual light. Eldress Aurelia Mace (1835–1910) of Sabbathday Lake, Maine, who spent her life writing about the meaning of the Shaker way of life, explained their spiritual notion of light in terms of just how they built their rooms: "Good and evil are typified by light and darkness. Therefore, if we bring light into a dark room, the darkness disappears, and inasmuch as a soul is filled with good, evil will disappear." The way they thought of heaven could as well have suited the humble Shaker workshop or Meetinghouse:

> *A robe that is spotless,*
> *A crown that is bright,*
> *For you is preparing,*
> *In mansions of light.*

Since the Meetinghouse was the most sacred place in the Shaker village, it was natural that this large hall was as roomy and as light as heaven itself. The New Lebanon Meetinghouse (1824) was one of the largest. In 1828 an observer described "the immensity of size and arch" there and recorded the dimensions, obviously impressed: 80 by 65 feet for the Meetinghouse and 27 by 34 feet for the porch. Four years later, another visitor wrote admiringly of "their place of worship, which is

The spacious Meetinghouse at Mount Lebanon was built in 1824 to accommodate hundreds of Shakers and visitors (the original Meetinghouse, much smaller, became a herb shop). Its airiness, light, and arching roof—all traditional notions of heaven—suggested the Shakers' desire to imitate these ideals in their homes and places of worship.
(From an old print)

one of the neatest buildings, both inside and out," that he had ever seen. The floor was "perfectly smooth, except a single seam in the middle of it, which seems to be the line of demarcation between the men and the women. On this floor there are movable benches, which are brought in, both for the accommodation of visitors when the galleries are filled, as well as for themselves." (He judged that about 250 Shakers and 400 visitors could be comfortably accommodated.)

The Shakers wanted to have their worship halls as spacious as possible, without pillars to interrupt the open space. In 1853, a Shaker described the worship hall of the Dwellinghouse at Enfield, New Hampshire; the dining hall immediately below it was supported by four columns, but the worship hall was not. He wrote, "It is fifty-eight by forty feet, and is lighted by twelve large windows. Not a post, or support of any kind, interrupts, in this place, the felicity of space." *The felicity of space*—in the place of worship, an ideal put into practice.

The effect of this heavenlike place on worship was noted by a Sister in 1837, who entered in her diary, "Sab. 11 June   We assemble this forenoon in meeting with hearts and souls devoted to God. It felt as if the windows of heaven were open and showers of blessings descended upon us, yea more than we had room to receive." A vision of the Meetinghouse as a bit of heaven on earth made all the more sense since the Shakers chose to paint the wooden trim inside all their Meetinghouses blue—"*Sky Blue* for New Meetinghouse. Watervliet 1849. Inside Work," according to a Shaker paint formula book dated 1849. (It took "10 lbs. White Lead, 1 lb. Prussian Blue, mixed in Linseed Oil and drying Materials" to duplicate the color of the heavens on the beams of the Meetinghouse.)

Inside their large and light Meetinghouses, the Shakers sang,

> *My Mother is a Joiner wise*
> *She builds her spacious dome*
> *And all that trace her sacred ways*
> *Will find a happy home.*

Mother Ann's "spacious dome"—Shakerism—had plenty of room for anyone who came with faith: literally, in the spaciousness of the homes the Shakers built; and spiritually, in the generous welcome they gave to the homeless.

Thrifty Shakers felt that writing five lines of music wasted time and space, so they wrote just one. Letter names of the notes were written in a single line, with varying dots and dashes to indicate different lengths. One approving member said of this style in 1834 that it was "the more speedy manner of noting, or writing tunes in a straight line, and takes up less room" in the hymnal. (From an old hymnal)

When a World's Fair was held several years ago in Japan, one of the most popular features was an exhibit of Shaker furniture. Chairs without carving, tables without knickknacks, the simplicity of Shaker stoves and baskets, even the white walls and the bare wood floors—all these made sense to the Japanese, who recognized and appreciated the same simplicity based on spiritual principles that characterizes traditional Japanese culture. An exhibit of Shaker design a few years later in Germany met with the same reaction from admirers of the Bauhaus design, who found in Shakerism a similar embracing of simple functional solutions based on social and economic principles. Opposite sides of the world—spiritual reasons versus practical reasons—no matter. What people saw and appreciated was the total simplicity of the Shaker spirit.

The simple chairs, the simple clothing, the complete absence of showy decoration, all these are mute evidence of a people of simple tastes. And yet there are subtle signs—the graceful turning of a finial or leg, the gloss and sinuous curves of banisters, the bird's-eye maple panel in a desk—which indicate that simplicity did not mean rusticity or crudeness to these people. The feeling many get when they enter a Shaker room is of a way of life well summed up in a passage describing an Elder at the Harvard village about a century and a half ago. Commented the observer, he was "dignified without being proud, simple without being disgusting, and familiar without being offensive, and in a few words, is like a capable Redeemed Man of God." Dignified; capable; and especially, simple—the marks of a man, a sect, and a life style.

And "familiar": in many ways we feel at home in Shaker rooms because our century has seen fit to rid itself of the fussy ornament that dripped from Victorian eaves or perched on turn-of-the-century whatnots. A description of the International Style in architecture and design, which played the most influential role in eliminating fuss and feathers from the characteristic design of the twentieth century, is relevant here:

> . . . the design was based upon such nonaesthetic factors as social utility or simplicity and economy of construction . . . additionally emphasized by two aesthetic decisions—the rejection of all extraneous ornament and a preference for the neutral surfaces of glass

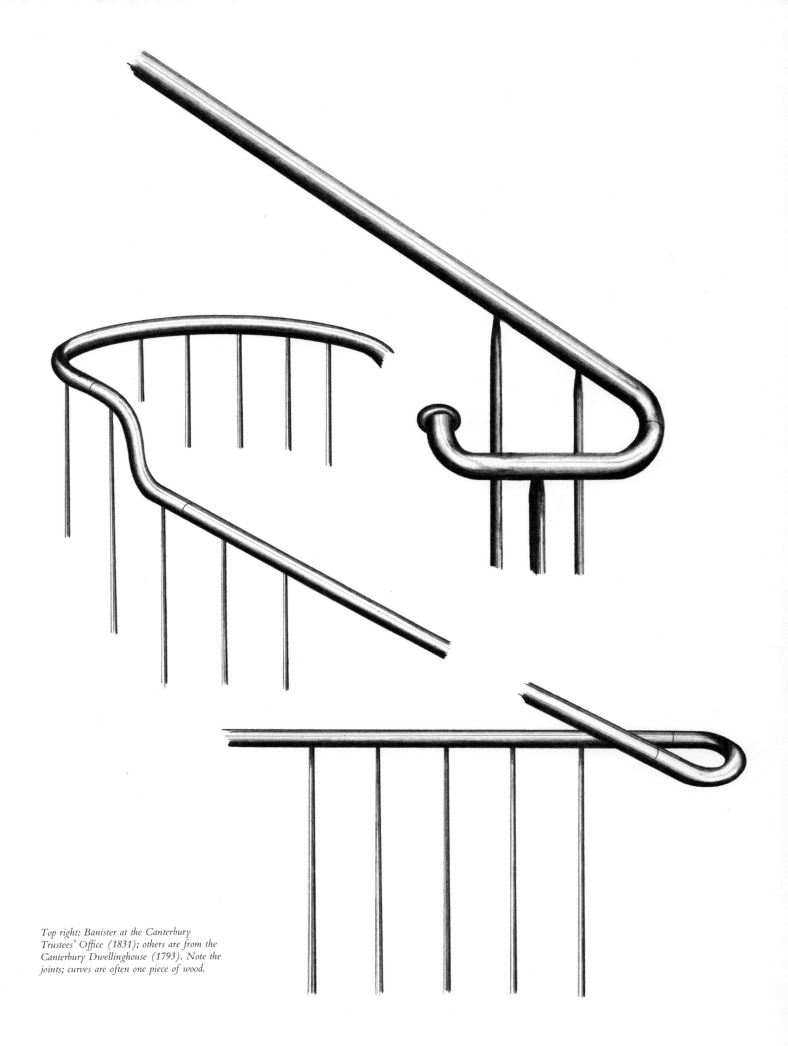

Top right: Banister at the Canterbury Trustees' Office (1831); others are from the Canterbury Dwellinghouse (1793). Note the joints; curves are often one piece of wood.

and of flat, smoothly finished stucco . . . white or near-white surfaces were more usual.

No wonder that the twentieth century appreciates Shaker simplicity as the nineteenth century never could.

But the reasons we appreciate the Shaker style, and their reasons for creating it, are very different. Twentieth-century simplicity is machine-made, out of man-made materials, and the result of a movement in design; the Shaker kind of simplicity was made by hand, of wood or wool or stone by Shaker craftsmen, and the result of a religious movement to create a simple and perfect way of life. Twentieth-century simplicity is more often than not the manufacturer's demand since it means a faster rate of production. But to the Shaker who took all the time he needed to make his work perfect, simplicity was a gift of the spirit. He sang in his Meetinghouse,

> *Tis the gift to be simple*
> *Tis the gift to be free*
> *Tis the gift to come down*
> *Where we ought to be . . .*

and thanked God with all his heart for the happiness that comes with simple needs and simple pleasures.

The Shakers felt that the village they saw was a true reflection of the spiritual world within. When they built their simple homes and made their simple goods, they were confident that they were on the right spiritual track. Nineteenth-century Shakers would probably feel a sharp sense of irony in the fact that we admire them for the things that mattered the least to them, their material goods. We imitate their chairs, while ignoring their charity; we reproduce their tables and oval boxes, and reject their celibacy. How much more the Shaker valued the simplicity and humility of his spirit than the chair he used or the box he made.

There were practical and spiritual reasons for the Shakers' choice of the simple life as an ideal to put into daily practice. It wasn't hard for the earliest Shakers to live simple lives—if anything, it was difficult for them to do otherwise, even had they so desired. Mother Ann and nearly all of her early followers were humble members of the working class, accustomed to simple manners and means. It was hardly likely

The cherry candlestand made at Hancock, Massachusetts (c. 1830), is a classic of Shaker simplicity. The Shaker faith forbade ornament, so its beauty lies in its form, not in carving or painting.

Simplicity in ironwork: right and center, handwrought latches in the Canterbury Meetinghouse (1792); bottom, latch on a Canterbury gate.

that these simple people would have wasted their time and effort on unnecessary frills, when simply building homes was enough of a problem.

Spiritual simplicity was, instead, the Shakers' main concern. Above all else, Mother Ann and her followers wanted to pattern their lives after the humility and spiritual simplicity of Christ and the early Christians. In 1848, a Shaker wrote, "We all ought to be simple, and plain in our intercourse, and conduct. . . . Our Savior is an example to us of perfect simplicity. He was always simple, and always dignified; but never silly. . . . He told the simple truth in the most simple and intelligible manner!"

Deliberate simplicity marked every part of the Shaker's daily life, from the food he ate to the way he spoke to the rooms where he lived and worked. The Shakers felt that it was wrong to waste time on fancy furniture or fancy manners when the result could so easily be pride or envy, disastrous to Family harmony.

The ideal of simplicity that Shakers practiced was nowhere more evident or appropriate than in their faith itself. They did not believe in long formal creeds and ritualized prayer; communication with God through dancing, singing, or praying was simple, direct, and spontaneous. The basic beliefs of the faith were simple enough to be understood by anyone: celibacy, common property, freedom from debt and disease, pacifism, independence, honesty, charity, and separation from Worldly politics.

The Shaker Meetinghouse was just as simple as the faith itself. Shakers put their hearts to God in plain white clapboard buildings without stained glass, altars, tapestries, or gold candelabra. Instead, they danced and sang in praise of God on bare wooden floors, under plain white plastered walls and simple blue beams and pegboards. The "Sunday best" of Shaker Brothers and Sisters was hardly fancier than their everyday work clothes.

The utterly simple room was a suitable setting for the simple service of inspired prayer and singing and dancing. When a Shaker visited the worship service at Mount Lebanon in 1869, he commented with feeling: "The deliberate simplicity with which they expressed their faith and feelings, giving effect to their words by appropriate actions, bowing their [heads] before us & their Elders, asking a blessing and strength &c. was truly beautiful and affecting."

The hymns that the visitor might have heard were just as simple and often asked God to send them more simplicity. The Shakers at Watervliet, Ohio, sang:

> *I love to feel simple, I love to feel low,*
> *I love to be kept in the path where*
>   *I should go;*
> *I love to be taught by my heavenly lead,*
> *That I may be holy and perfect indeed.*

A simple pierced tin skimmer lifted eggs or vegetables from hot water. (Canterbury, N.H.)

Simple behavior was just as important outside the Meetinghouse as it was inside. What the Shakers sang on Sunday—

> *I will be simple as a child;*
> *I'll labor to be meek and mild;*
> *In this good work my time I'll spend,*
> *And with my tongue I'll not offend*

—was put into practice on Monday. Mother Ann had said that "little children are simple and innocent; they should be brought up in simplicity, and then they would receive good as easily as they would evil."

Young Shakers were instructed by the *Youth's Guide,* "Simplicity is needful in conversation; it forbids high flown words, and guides the tongue in wisdom, to speak in simple language." An observer wrote in 1781 that the Shakers "use no compliments, and their language is, *yea* and *nay.*" Fancy manners were dismissed along with fancy language: "Simplicity scorneth pride, and is far from mincing steps and stiffened joints."

Fancy manners were also discouraged at mealtime. About fifteen minutes before the meal, all the Family gathered in their rooms or in the sitting rooms to rest and quietly wait for the bell. Led in by the Elders and Eldresses, the Brothers and Sisters sat at separate tables, kneeling in silent prayer before and after the meal. Mealtime was simply for eating; idle talk was strictly forbidden in the early years of Shakerism. The *Millennial Laws* stated that "no talking, laughing or playing" was allowed in the dining hall. Everything put on the Shaker plate was expected to be eaten.

The food was as simple as the manners. Shaker Sisters used common ingredients to make good plain food like bread, soup, stew, cake, and drink—the tastiness of the food came from careful cooking and the herbs and spices that the Shakers grew in their gardens. In 1854 a typical dinner menu included "Rye Indian bread, Mutton, Irish potatoes, Corn, Apple Pie, Cranberry Tarts & turnovers, pound cake, White Bread."

Accustomed as they were to simple, substantial food like this, no wonder Shakers traveling and forced to eat hotel food sighed wistfully as they sat down to fancy dishes. One member visiting the New England coast in 1846 wrote in his diary: "What a dish is Lobster! An animal cooked with all its contents—Too much for my stomach." Elder Henry Blinn of Canterbury, on the road to Kentucky in 1873, wrote with something less than divine patience during a bout with Worldly indigestion: "O dear! it would require a stomach made of cast iron to endure all the indigestible compounds that active minded cooks are led to invent. . . . Many of these varieties are about as indigestible as shingle nails."

Shaker tables themselves were set in the simplest manner, without cloths, centerpieces, or fancy china, and with everything convenient to a small group so that passing could be done without talking. Shaker tables looked like this from the earliest days, when Mother Ann told her followers: "Never put on silver spoons for me nor tablecloths, but let your tables be clean enough to eat on without cloths; and if you do not know what to do with them, give them to the poor."

Visitors to the Canterbury tables in the mid-nineteenth century were passed printed copies of a table etiquette monitor in verse, written by Sister Hannah Bronson, which neatly summed up in two of its lines the deliberate simplicity of Shaker mealtime:

To customs and fashions we make no pretense,
Yet think we can tell what belongs to good sense.

In their style of dress, the Shakers were equally determined not to be slaves of Worldly fashion. From the earliest days, Shakers dressed in simple clothes and wore simple hats and bonnets. Mother Ann strictly forbade jewelry and other vanities—"gold beads, jewels, silver buckles and other ornaments"—that wasted money and caused pride and envy, saying, "You may let the moles and bats have them; that is, the children of this world; for they set their hearts upon such things; but the people of God do not want them."

Although Shaker dress changed slightly now and then throughout the years, styles remained remarkably consistent and always simple. In 1848, for example, Brothers wore broad-brimmed hats; straight coats; a vest, "very deep, or long waisted . . . and without a collar; and butter-nut-colored pantaloons." Even the style of their hair was consistent: "their hair, and beards, all combed and trimmed precisely alike, according to the divine order." Shakers knew that fine clothes did not make the man. In spite of his simple manners and clothes, Brother Daniel Goodrich of Hancock replied to a young man who asked if he thought himself a gentleman, "Certainly . . . if I understand what constitutes a gentleman. It is the man who respects the feelings of his neighbors and do [sic] unto others as he would be done by."

Following Mother Ann's example (she said, "You ought not to dress yourselves in rich apparel; but dress in that which is decent and modest, as becomes holy women of God"), Shaker Sisters dressed as simply as their Brothers. Again, the styles changed a little over the years; but the Sisters always wore long skirts, either pleated or gored, "of various colors," and always some kind of covering over the shoulders and bust for reasons of modesty. In the early nineteenth century, Sisters wore a large silk kerchief tied in the front; later, the Kentucky and Ohio Shakers wove fine iridescent silk kerchiefs that were sent to other communities. By the end of the nineteenth century, the style was an oval cape in back and front—the same style the Sisters still wear today.

On their heads the Sisters wore "long sugar-scoopshaped, palm-leaf bonnets, with silk, or cambric capes to them of various colors"—the same flounced palm bonnets that Canterbury Sisters wear today. The hair style is also unchanged since 1848: "The sisters are required to comb their hair clean, and straight back from the forepart of the head, and fasten it in a knot upon the back part with a pin made for that purpose. And to wear a straight plain muslin cap, which shall come so closely over the face as to conceal the hair entirely." Today, the caps are net, but still a traditional part of the Shaker costume. Symbolic of purity, they were given to young sisters at the time each signed the covenant.

Not for Shaker women the elaborate Victorian bonnets; not only were they of course much too fancy, but the Shakers thought it

Each of the large windows in the Sisters' Shop (1816) at Canterbury has seven miniature pegs below it—for dustpans, brushes, or short Shakers.

Above: Shakers dressed simply in warm woolens for winter and cool linens for summer, all hand-spun, -woven, and -sewn. Brothers wore hats and long vests; Sisters wore caps inside, bonnets outside, and a shoulder kerchief or oval cape that concealed the bustline for modesty's sake.
(From an old print)

Opposite: Shaker spinning wheels were light and simple in line. Note the graceful legs in this wool wheel from New Lebanon; the spokes flare to turn the wheel better. The "snap winder" in back, from Sabbathday Lake, wound yarn into skeins. Every forty turns, it "clicked" to measure yardage. When the large basket was filled with knit sweater bodies, the Canterbury Sisters would finish their well-known "Shaker knit" sweaters with collars and sleeves.

inhumane to kill birds just for their feathers to suit some hatmaker's fancy. One Sister from Mount Lebanon summed up her Sisters' attitude toward Worldly bonnets when she wrote in 1895:

> *A woman whom fashion long held in her sway,*
> *Whose vanity naught could embarrass,*
> *Was decked in rich silks and velvets all gay,*
> *And a beautiful bonnet from Paris.*
> *A head-dress, you know to the feminine mind*
> *Is the principal point of attraction,*
> *A part of adornment we frequently find*
> *That causes mental distraction.*

The things that the Shakers made and used were as simple as the workers themselves. The Shaker carpenter didn't waste his time on carving or stenciling; instead, he used beautiful woods like bird's-eye maple and curly maple in forms simple enough to show off their natural beauty. The respect that Shakers had for their tools and utility pieces is evident when you see tiger maple butterworkers, bird's-eye maple planes and spatulas, or a bird's-eye maple towelrack. The "dignity of work" suddenly becomes meaningful.

Most Shaker cupboards and drawers have simple round wooden pulls or plain white porcelain knobs, even when the members could afford fancy brass hardware. In 1840, Brother David Bowley was "employed for several days in taking out Brass knobs, and putting in their stead wood knobs or buttons (on furniture)." The reason? Brass ones were "considered superfluous, through spiritual communication." Simplicity for Shakers like Brother David was not an abstract ideal—it was a daily part of life and work, a matter of choice. It wasn't the material cost of the brass knobs that decided the Shakers to remove them; it was the spiritual cost of pride.

The things that the Shakers made for sale were just as simple as the things they used at home. As "the people of God," Shakers felt it was wrong for them to add more to the sins of the World; according to the *Millennial Laws*, they could not "in any case, manufacture for sale, any article or articles, which are superfluously wrought, and which would have a tendency to feed the pride and vanity of man, or such as would not be admissible to use among themselves, on account of their superfluity."

On the one hand, Shakers refused to add to the temptation of the vainglorious; on the other, they freed themselves from the tyranny of Worldly fashion. Considering the Shakers' determination to separate themselves from the World, merely doing business with outsiders was hazard enough in the early days. If the Shakers had tried to suit what they made to every passing fancy, they would eventually have found themselves helpless before the whims of fashion and more dependent on the World than ever.

When the Shakers did buy things, they chose the plainest items for the village. One member wrote in 1853, "No image or portrait of anything upon the earth, or under the earth, is suffered in this holy place. Consequently clocks and such articles, purchased of the world, go through the process of having all their superficial decorations erased from their surfaces." The Shakers valued simplicity so much that they were even willing to pay more for it. According to the *Millennial Laws,* "The purchase of needful articles that appear substantial and good, and are suitable for believers to use, should not be neglected, to purchase those which are needlessly adorned because they are a little cheaper."

Every part of the Shaker's world reflected the simplicity of his spirit; everything he saw reminded him that his goal was humility. The very rooms in which he spent his day were as simple as possible. The *Millennial Laws* stated: "Odd or fanciful styles of architecture may not be used among the Believers.... Beadings, mouldings and cornices, which are merely for fancy may not be made by Believers." In the early days he didn't even hang pictures on his walls. No wonder the Shakers could say of their homes,

> *Our Zion home is not adorned*
> *With pictured walls, or gold;*
> *Nor in a glittering chain or pearls*
> *Is all her glory told.*

Whatever glory belonged to the humble Shaker village was not of an earthly kind; in simple manner, and surrounded with the work of simple faith, the Shakers found all the glory they needed in the kingdom above.

These hanging shelves were made at Hancock, Massachusetts. On the bottom shelf, a paper carton of Shaker baked beans, prepared in Canterbury's famous revolving oven and popular for years; also a box of candy made by the Sabbathday Lake Shakers. Note the Meetinghouse design on the box.

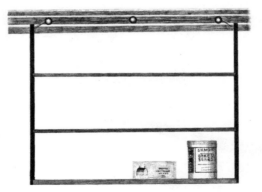

Perfection

More than anything else, what shaped the Shaker way of life was their desire to be perfect in all ways—in their union of brotherly love; in their thoughts and acts; and because they believed in practicing what they preached, in the works of their hands, too. When a Shaker carpenter built a desk, he made sure that each drawer fit perfectly because he used properly seasoned wood and patiently dovetailed each one. Often you can find the number of the drawer marked on the bottom to indicate its place—and if you switch the drawers, they won't work as well. Mrs. Grover Cleveland knew that Shaker Sisters were just as much perfectionists. When she ordered a Shaker-made "Dorothy cloak" to wear to her husband's inaugural ball in 1893, the Mount Lebanon Sisters made her a second cloak because they found a flaw in the original one—an imperfection so minute that no one today can find it in the one they didn't send.

The reasons for the Shakers' demand for perfection were both practical and spiritual. Certainly, drawers that don't stick are useful and cloaks that are perfectly sewn satisfy a customer. But most of all, desks or cloaks or anything else made perfectly by Shaker hands satisfied the Shakers because they satisfied the pattern of perfection that God had set before men in His son, Christ.

Since the Shakers believed that the world they saw in their villages was a true reflection of the inner spirit, they equated perfection in their works and daily deeds with spiritual perfection. A Sister who took care to keep perfect the pattern of a chair seat she was weaving would also take care to pattern her life to perfection. If a Brother wanted to be perfect, he would want to make boxes whose lids fit perfectly, and vice versa. Why else would a Brother write of his tape measure, "I can go no further in my work without it, for positive exactness is required not only in the inches, but in the sixteenths and thirty-seconds of an inch"? Why bother with a few insignificant fractions of an inch? The Shakers had a saying to sum it all up: "Trifles make perfection, but perfection itself is no trifle." No trifle, for sure, when the result was salvation.

Precision in all things was necessary for perfection. One way the Shakers achieved precision was by using patterns, in their work and in their faith. Patterns also helped achieve uniformity, another Shaker ideal. The Shaker village was literally patterned right after heaven. God was of course the master pattern-setter, with Christ and Mother

Ann each "a perfect 'pattern' or specimen of genuine Christianity." Mother Ann was remembered by those who had known her as "a perfect pattern of godliness, both in word and deed"—"a perfect pattern of piety to all who saw her"—"a pattern of godliness to all Christians"—and "a perfect pattern of righteousness, in every good word and work."

The Shaker's belief in divine patterns made it natural for him to believe that fashioning a precisely dovetailed joint, for instance, was also a form of worship, since in doing perfect works he was following God's example. Elder Benjamin H. Smith of Canterbury was "so conscientious that all his handwork should keep close to the perfect pattern of the Master Workman,—who drew his affection in early days."

Mother Ann was also termed by some a kind of carpenter, who straightened things out and squared them away. According to an old Shaker song,

Shaker Sisters wove different patterns into the seats of chairs they used and sold with homespun, home-dyed, and home-woven fabric tapes they called "listing." Striped and solid tapes in colors from "pomegranate" to "peacock" made precise designs like checkerboard, basket weave, and herringbone. Later in the nineteenth century, canvas listing was used.

Opposite: Until about 1876, chairs that Mount Lebanon Shakers sold to the World were uniformly identified with a stamp showing a typical Shaker chair; note that each chair was numbered. After that, gold stencils marked the chairs. (Old Chatham, N.Y.)

My Mother is a carpenter
She hews the crooked stick
And she will have it strait and squair
Altho it cuts the quick.

The Shaker carpenter took the metaphors of moral perfection (straight, upright, foursquare) literally and made them a part of his daily work. Chairs stood straight and perfect—as straight and perfect as the Gospel, which to the Shaker was "without fault . . . as straight as straightness." The Mount Lebanon Shakers were so precise that they even numbered the chairs they made and sold according to size—from #7 (the largest) to #0 (the smallest). When they sent Abraham Lincoln a chair in 1864, no doubt they sent him a size 7, because according to the thank-you note of this long-legged President, it was a "very comfortable chair."

Since the Shakers were deliberately intent on patterning their homes to heavenly ideals of love, charity, truth, perfection, and so on, it was natural for some of them to assume now and then that every detail of the community was an exact counterpart of a heavenly pattern. One Sister, convinced that the Shakers were such good people that they were like angels without the wings, was sure that the angels she saw in a vision were dressed in suits "like that of the brethren. That is, they wore the Shaker habiliments." Well, why not? After all, the Shakers felt that they were "called to live after the manner of the angels, in heaven," so no wonder she assumed they dressed alike, too.

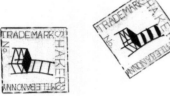

On a grander scale, the whole village was sometimes imagined as a literal copy of a heavenly pattern of precision and perfection. In 1843, a spirit drawing called *Explanation of the Holy City with its Various Parts and Appendixes pointed Out* was a remarkable example of city planning that represented the "perfect pattern" for the layout of the village at Hancock, Massachusetts, and the surrounding twelve square miles. According to the drawing, Hancock's walks and workshops were a direct copy of "the High City" in the heavens, "right over this the Holy City on Earth." It was clear to the artist and receiver of the vision which inspired the map that the streets and buildings of the village where he lived were a precise twin of a divine pattern from above—literally above, right over the spot in Massachusetts.

A traveler familiar with several of the Shaker villages wrote in 1844, "Each of these communities is a well-built, handsome village, with wide streets laid out regularly at right angles"; and the *Millennial Laws* found it "good order" to "lay out, and fence all kinds of lots, fields and gardens, in a square form, where it is practicable." Shakers would settle for nothing less than the perfect squareness they thought was a heavenly ideal. When Eldress Nancy Moore of South Union, Kentucky, traveled through Boston on her trip to the Eastern Shaker villages in 1854, it is not surprising that this Shaker accustomed to precision found "the waves of the Ocean, the long parallel lines which reached farther than our vision could see" more admirable than the *"narrow crooked & irregular"* streets of Boston!

Even mealtime was regarded as an opportunity to follow a divine pattern. The "table monitor" written by Sister Hannah Bronson of Canterbury and handed out at the table to visitors during the 1860s began:

"Gather up the fragments that remain, that nothing may be lost."
—Christ

Here, then, is the pattern which Jesus has set,
And his good example we can not forget;
With thanks for his blessings, his word we'll obey,
But on this occasion we've somewhat to say.

Patterns were an important part of the Shaker workshops, too. A visitor to the Shaker village at Niskeyuna (later Watervliet, New York) wrote in the early nineteenth century that "the Shakers believe that their furniture was originally designed in heaven, and that the patterns have been transmitted to them by angels." Visitors to any Shaker museum or collection can see patterns for tinware, for furniture parts, for boxes, for trousers, cloaks, and bonnets, for baskets, and so forth. Everyone knows the satisfaction of a job well done; but imagine how much greater was the contentment that Shakers felt at their work, convinced that the perfect finished product was not just an end in itself but a means to spiritual perfection, too. Putting "hands to work and hearts to God" at the same time came naturally.

Another important reason for using patterns was the Shakers' belief in uniformity. They realized that the more people have in common, the easier it is for them to feel like a brotherhood of man. The *Youth's Guide* encouraged young Shakers: "Never try to run on

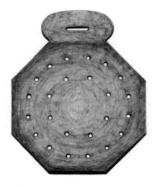

Shaker Sisters were such perfectionists that they used tin gauges to measure needles for the right size. This one is about 1½ inches in diameter; infinitely small variations in the holes illustrate how Shakers took to heart their motto of "perfection in the details."

ahead, before the main body of good believers, and above all, never fall back; but keep close up & be in the gift."

To make this sense of unity a part of everyday life, Shakers believed in keeping all the members and even all the villages as precisely close to common standards as they could. The nineteen Shaker villages differed somewhat in layout and occupations, of course, but on the whole a Maine Shaker visiting Kentucky villages would have felt right at home: the members would have been wearing much the same clothing, living with the same simple furniture and buildings, and following the same kind of worship in the same kind of Meetinghouse.

Rules specified uniform clothing styles for each of the sexes; children dressed just like the adults. One visitor to Mount Lebanon in 1845 noted that "the women all had on white caps even the young girls of 10 in fact all the Ladies were dressed precisely alike and all the men also." At one time it was even "contrary to order to wear hats above the height given by the Elders," simply to "preserve a uniformity of apparel, which the Shakers deem almost a point of faith."

There were rules for what colors should be painted on the woodwork trim indoors of all the standard buildings found in the villages (Meetinghouse Blue, Ministry Green, and Trustee Brown). The gambrel-roofed Meetinghouses in many of the communities were virtually identical (Hancock; Canterbury; Sabbathday Lake; Shirley, Massachusetts; Alfred, Maine; Enfield, New Hampshire; and Mount Lebanon) because they were deliberately designed after one pattern to symbolize the uniformity of the Shaker worship of Christ in all the villages.

The rooms inside were as uniform as possible, too, in some cases. According to one member, the retiring rooms in the Dwellinghouse at Enfield, New Hampshire, were "all exactly twenty feet square, nine feet high, and of identical furniture and finish, rendering it difficult to determine, but by the number, one room from another."

One reason for the Shakers' success at achieving uniformity was their custom of travel and note-taking, an efficient communication of spiritual and practical ideas. In 1854, for example, Shakers visiting from the Western villages liked a certain kind of work stand made in Canterbury and took home the designs. One visitor wrote, "The Ministry here work at Tayloring. They sit on chairs at their work

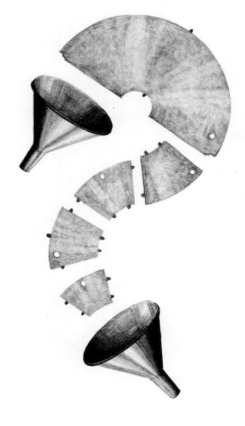

Funnels constructed in Canterbury are shown with the tin patterns used to make them. (Old Chatham, N.Y.)

stand such as the Sisters have here. We Sisters were much taken with their work stands and are anxious to have some made at home like them. We got Brother Urban to take the dimensions and description of them."

Rules even demanded uniformity in the manner of sitting. According to Elder Henry Blinn's *Gentle Manners* of 1899, "If you are privileged to sit in a rocking chair, you should endeavor to conform to the general custom of the company,—but chairs without rockers should always rest their four posts on the floor." At one time, the *Millennial Laws* even stated rules for a uniform way of folding hands: "When we clasp our hands, our right thumbs and fingers should be above our left, as uniformity is comely."

Rules for uniformity served as guidelines for every part of Shaker life from worship to work. In business dealings, excellence and uniformity of the product went hand in hand. Shakers were praised for "keeping the top, middle, and bottom layers equally good in every basket or barrel of fruit or vegetable" sent to market under their name.

With all the rules for uniformity, it's not so surprising that when Elder Henry Blinn from New Hampshire visited the Shaker villages in Kentucky and Ohio in 1873, one of the biggest differences he found was the way the Brothers wore their caps: the Kentucky Shakers wore theirs pushed back on their heads instead of low on the forehead.

The Canterbury Meetinghouse (1792) was one of several nearly identical Meetinghouses designed by Brother Moses Johnson. All had gambrel (or "barn") roofs and double doors—left for Brothers, right for Sisters. Interior woodwork pegs and trim were painted a uniform "Meetinghouse blue." Inside, a visitor, after watching the Shakers dance in worship, noted in 1875: "All the movements are performed with much precision and in exact order."

That villages separated by a thousand miles and different backgrounds, sharing little communication but letters and visits, could be so much alike shows just how successful was the Shakers' ideal of uniformity in practice.

Another way the Shakers achieved perfection was by using exactly precise measurements. The Shakers even defined "perfection" in terms including precise measurement:

> Anything may, with strict propriety, be called perfect, which perfectly answers the purpose for which it was designed. A circle may be called a perfect circle, when it is perfectly round; an apple may be called perfect, when it is perfectly sound, having no defect in it; and so of a thousand other things.

The only way to make a perfect circle was to use a precision instrument, like a compass. Likewise, rulers, yardsticks, and T squares were very highly regarded as precision means to precise ends—so much so that Shakers made simple rulers from beautiful pieces of fine wood like tiger maple. Ralph Waldo Emerson seemed to catch this spirit of perfection when he visited the Shakers and found a "spirit-level" used by one of the carpenters *"a very good emblem for the Society."* Boys who were raised in Shaker villages were taught by the Brothers to make their own precise rulers and squares as their first tools in the carpenters' shop.

Shaker tailors and seamstresses, working according to systematic principles from 1825 on, were careful to lay the patterns so as to waste as little cloth as possible and used special curved yardsticks to take more precise measurements of the human body. A tailor's notebook from New Lebanon, circa 1840, contained charts with the name of the individual and all his measurements, from "Size around the entire Neck" to "Length of garment," for every article of clothing he wore. The measurements were even dated and could be changed if necessary.

As a typical example of the Shakers' knack for anticipating progressive trends, the Shakers at Sabbathday Lake were adapting in 1877 to the use of the metric system, which appealed to them because it was more logical and precise (about one hundred years before their time, since the U.S. is just now making the switch to metric). In February

Carpenters used a hardware compass, about 18 inches long, to scribe circles; the screw arrangement allowed for fine adjustments in the radius. (Canterbury, N.H.)

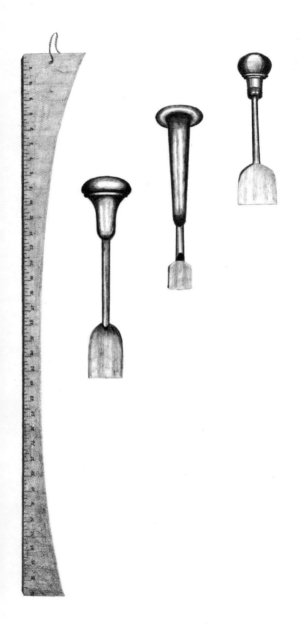

Straight yardsticks were fine for straight measurements, but a Shaker curved tailor's yardstick, left, measured more precisely the rounded human body. Shakers made buttonhole cutters with steel blades, right, because they were faster and easier to use than scissors; buttonholes were always straight and precisely the same size, too. Note the graceful wooden handles.
(Canterbury, N.H.)

1877, Brother Hewitt Chandler put in the Schoolhouse "a chart explaining the Metric System of Weights and Measures—the first of the kind introduced into any school in town." By the end of March of that year, the Shaker carpenters were making wooden dry measures in the metric system.

Shaker Sisters in the kitchens quickly found out that cooking for several hundred people demanded some measurements more precise than a pinch-of-this and a dab-of-that. One old kitchen journal read, "Your proportions must always be right in cake mixing, therefore it is always wise to use carefully worked out rules and measure all your materials with great exactness." A recipe from Canterbury for squash biscuits gives a good idea of their precise measuring and the size of a Shaker batch of biscuits. The recipe was marked "all right for family":

> *6 cups sifted squash.*
> *3 cups sugar.*
> *2 tsp. salt.*
> *2½ yeast cakes dissolved in 1 pt. lukewarm water.*
> *12 tblsp. melted shortening.*
> *3 cups milk, scalded & cooled.*
> *16 cups flour.*
>
> *Mix like any biscuit dough, rather limber.*

Sisters made perfect biscuits in the kitchens and sang in the Meetinghouse about "Mother's love measured, Heap'd up, heap'd up, Press'd down, press'd down." How typical that precise measuring should be a part of their work and their worship.

Loving straightness and precision as they did, the Shakers were especially fond of the metaphor of the precisely straight and narrow path. It was mentioned on spirit drawings during the 1840s and 1850s, and even used as the title of a dance in 1841, which they exercised to a hymn called "Precept and Line":

> *Precept on precept and line upon line,*
> *We'll walk in the path our Mother has trod,*
> *Yea straight and clear straightness, the pure way of God.*

This symbol for spiritual discipline was not just an ideal to sing about, however. The stone paths in Shaker villages were in fact literally straight and narrow. In 1882, Elder Otis Sawyer of Sabbathday Lake decided that the stone walk from the Ministry's dwelling across the road was "very crooked," and ordered it "taken up and laid straight." Not just for practical reasons; he felt that according to the revelation of God, as taught to the Shakers by Father Joseph Meacham, "all walks must be laid straight, fields laid out square and fences built straight."

In typical Shaker fashion, the symbol of the straight and narrow path was put into practice for practical and spiritual reasons. A straight walk is safer to use and easier to shovel in winter. And when the Shaker sang in worship about keeping to that straight and narrow path, it made sense to him to practice what he preached—Shakers walked on the stone paths and did not stray into the lawn. Certainly, Elder Otis wouldn't abide any "crooked winding paths that lead unto the devil" (from a hymn written at Sabbathday Lake), and visitors today can walk the same straight paths ordered by him there.

If you're beginning to get the feeling that the average Shaker was like a fussbudget great-aunt, stalking the house in pursuit of pictures to straighten, don't be misled. Precision was not an end in itself, and precise measurements weren't made pointlessly just to have every last thing straight. When the Shakers put ideals like precision and uniformity into practice, the practicality and good common sense that resulted in their everyday world convinced them that they were on God's right track. As one member wrote in his diary, "A Man can Show his religion as much in measureing onions as he can in singing Glory halalua." The dovetailed drawers that to this day neither stick nor jam, the squash biscuits made right, the straight stone walks, the shoes that fit because the cobbler carved each last from an individual set of precise measurements—all these "perfectly answer the purpose for which they are designed," and therefore were perfect and pleasing to God. It was as simple as that.

The Shakers' love of patterns, precision, and precise measurement affected every part of the Shakers' daily world. For one thing, they tried to adopt a general pattern of perfect neatness in the village. One visitor writing home to his family may not have appreciated anything else about the Shakers, but he had to admit that they were neat:

Canterbury Shakers made over 2 tons of maple sugar a season in the 1860s; Sisters turned out small cakes of sugar by the hundreds in these fluted tin molds, only 1½ inches across. (Canterbury, N.H.)

Brothers sowing rows used a wooden plant spacer about 7 feet long, rolling it along to set out their seeds precisely the same distance apart. (Old Chatham, N.Y.)

March 12, 1852 . . . went to a Shaker meeting 6 mile distant, and that was a great treat since, there was 100 of those animals I call them for they do not resemble the human family, their heads are shaped like a sugar loaf and their brains are all shook down into their heels. Their church is a perfect pattern of neatness, as well as themselves and that is the only redeeming trait in Shakerism.

For another thing, the patterns of daily life were decidedly affected by the concepts of straightness, squareness, and uprightness. To illustrate the influence these ideals had on everyday life, let us pick a hypothetical member—call him Brother Ebenezer—and follow him through a typical day.

Brother Ebenezer wakes at 4:30 A.M., prays, washes up, goes to the barn to help with the chores, and by 6:00 is more than ready for breakfast with the Family.

They kneel for a silent grace, then pull out their chairs, each with the right hand, and as soon as all are seated the meal begins. Each table holds sixteen persons, but the unit of the dining room is a "square" or four people, two on each side of the table. Every square forms an independent colony, with its own butter, salt, pepper, cream, bread and sugar; in the center of the square is a board on which are placed the oatmeal, potatoes and codfish which form the usual breakfast, for in a Shaker Village both courses are put upon the table at once.

The square, then, influences the whole dining custom of the community. Brother Ebenezer finishes his last piece of bread, one of a sixty-loaf batch.

Before he starts his day's work of making yardsticks, however, Ebenezer gets his hair cut according to the *Laws in relation to cutting the Hair and trimming the Beard:*

The hair shall not be left unnecessarily long before, nor behind. It shall be cut square across the forehead, and thence in a line with the bottom of the ear. . . . The ear locks [whiskers] shall be cut square with the bottom of the ear.

Suitably squared away and straightened up, our Brother puts on his hat and leaves for the carpentry shop. His hat is by order precisely 4½ inches high at the crown, and the rim "from four to five inches in width according to the wearer's breadth of shoulders."

As he works, he tries to pattern his own work after the amazingly precise skill of the Shaker Meetinghouse architect Moses Johnson, who "excelled in those early days in the skill of hewing to a line." Brother Moses could hew a log with an adze "nearly as smoothe as though trimmed by a Jack plane."

When the dinner bell rings fifteen minutes before noon, Ebenezer returns to a large dining hall. A printed table monitor hanging on the wall reminds him to "sit upright at the table." He is also cautioned to be careful to have his feet straight in front of his own chair, never in the way of others. When he takes the meat, Brother Ebenezer is always reminded of a little jingle he learned as a boy:

> *But cut your meat both neat and square,*
> *And take of [fat] an equal share*
>
> *And butter, which you must cut nice*
> *Both square and true as polish'd dice.*

Sighing appreciatively after another square meal, Ebenezer returns to the Brethren's shop and works until the supper bell.

From seven-thirty until eight is "retiring time," after which the Brothers and Sisters go directly to the Meetinghouse for a dancing and singing worship meeting. Ebenezer enters through the Brothers' door on the left and sits on a bench on the Brothers' side of the room. When Brother Ebenezer was younger it was considered "contrary to order to go into meeting without sleeve strings"—blue or green ribbons tied around the arm to prevent the Brothers' shirt sleeves from being too loose—to present a "uniformity of appearance."

For a while all sit in silent prayer. Then one of the Elders urges each Shaker "to pattern your life by the Christian model" and "to square your life by him whose life was without blemish." Another Elder reports a heavenly vision he has received of the souls of the Mount Lebanon Ministry. He says, "I can yet remember the order that they were placed in, they were in a perfect square."

When the leaders are finished speaking, all the members rise and stand in long rows while the benches are taken away. There are small marking pegs in the Meetinghouse floor "to aid the Brethren and Sisters in the forming of straight ranks, as they stand to sing and to

Shakers used tin stencils for quick and uniform labeling of crates of medicines, such as their famous Sarsaparilla Syrup, shipped for sale to the World. (Old Chatham, N.Y.)

speak." It is of the highest importance that the ranks be straight, according to the *Millennial Laws*, "not only to the right and left, but also forward and back; forward ranks should always be as long as the rest, and by no means should there be vacancies in the ranks, it has a tendency to excite disunion."

The singers get their precise pitch from a tone-ometer, a one-stringed device marked to produce any pitch desired and the invention of the Shaker clockmaker Brother Isaac Youngs. When the dancing begins, the members arrange themselves in ranks about 10 feet apart at the top and 4 feet apart at the bottom, all the Brothers and Sisters on opposite sides of the room. The first marching dance they do is called the *Square Order*.

After the first dance, they perform *One, Two, Three Steps:*

> *One, two, three steps, foot straight at the turn,*
> *One, two, three steps, equal length, solid pats,*
> *Strike the shuffle, little back, make the solid sound,*
> *Keep the body right erect with ev'ry joint unbound.*

Brother Ebenezer agrees with a fellow Brother, who writes later in his diary that "more than a score of new dances were performed with an attitude of grace and with the precision of a machine." He meant Shaker dances like the *Lively Line*, the *Double Square*, the *Moving Square*, or the *Square and Compass*.

Finally at nine the day is over and Brother Ebenezer goes to his bed, made for him every morning by a Sister when he is out at work. Straight after prayers, our Brother climbs into bed, remembering the rule to "retire to rest in the fear of God, without any playing, or boisterous laughing," and to "lie straight." The rules of precision and perfection which demand squareness, straightness, and uniformity will affect him until and including the day he dies. Then to the burying ground, where the "graves are laid out in regular order & the headstones uniform."

Patterns for Shaker dances were as precise as their patterns for clothing or furniture. In this view of a dance form called the "hollow square," members in straight ranks marched to the center, opposite sides at a time, then back again with a shuffle step. Singers stood in a square on the side. Pegs in the floor helped in forming straight ranks for other dances. (From an old journal)

Long before the Chicago architect Louis Sullivan said: "Form ever follows function," and so changed the way American architects and designers thought about the environment they created, a small and relatively obscure religious sect was quietly putting this standard into every practice of their daily lives. The Shakers worded their proverb slightly differently, but the ideal was the same: "Every force evolves a form." Nearly a century after the heyday of Sullivan and Shakerism, the demand for functionalism has become a part of the twentieth-century way of life. The impact of the German Bauhaus designers on our way of life was even more important. "Functional" no longer means merely useful; it means well designed, people-oriented, and convenient.

Now that "functional" has become a term of approval, we can appreciate the unadorned usefulness of Shaker architecture, furnishings, and utensils as the nineteenth century could not. The Shaker Dwellinghouses of one hundred seventy years ago and more were wonderfully efficient facilities for feeding, sheltering, and maintaining the health and privacy standards of large numbers of people; yet for many people of the last century they suggested nothing more admirable than "mere factories or human hives," remarkable only for their "homeliness." It took the twentieth century to produce an architect proclaiming that a house should be a "machine for living," as Le Corbusier was to show in his designs; and only now are we coming to appreciate the Shaker Dwellinghouses for being just that, almost a century and a half before their time.

Utility as an ideal of the Shaker way of life is evident in the furnishings, utensils, clothing, and buildings that remain for us to see and admire. What is less obvious, but no less remarkable, is the way the Shakers applied their standard of utility to every part of their life, from education to manners to rules for working to the Shaker faith itself. The nineteenth-century observer was not exaggerating when he commented: "These people are strict utilitarians. In all they do, the first enquiry is, 'will it be useful?' Everything therefore about their buildings, fences, &c., is plain."

The Shaker demand for utility was partly a result of practical reasons. Whether in the form of fancy dress, fancy furniture, or fancy manners, frills cost time and money—commodities the early Shakers found scarce. When the followers of Mother Ann began to establish

This seed-sorting stand made c. 1840 at New Lebanon had a rim notched on one side so workers could easily push seeds into containers after sorting them. (Hancock, Mass.)

their own communities at the end of the eighteenth century and the first few years of the nineteenth, what resources were available were essential for food, clothing, shelter, and charity.

The really significant point is that when later Shakers could well have afforded fancy luxuries, they still chose, for the most part, to make their goods, their homes, and themselves as useful as possible, without frills. If the Shakers had more of everything by this time, it was still judged by the yardstick of utility. Anything called "superfluous" was guaranteed short shrift in a Shaker home.

Just as important as the Shakers' practical reasons for utility, however, were their spiritual reasons. Anything kept for show and not for use was considered wrong because it encouraged the sin of pride—pride which threatened to turn the Shakers' thoughts from worship to Worldly possessions. One member wrote in 1853, "An arbitrary inhibition rests upon statuary, paintings, watches, jewelry of all kinds, knives of more than two blades, sofas, divans, musical instruments, and whatever gorgeous appendage would serve to feed vanity and pride, more than subserve the practical utility of civilized life."

Utility became so much a yardstick by which the Shakers judged their world that they even defined beauty in terms of usefulness: "Beauty rests on utility. That which has in itself the highest use possesses the greatest beauty." The reaction of Elder Frederick Evans of Mount Lebanon to the question put to him by a visitor in 1875 shows typically that the Shakers practiced what they preached. When the visitor asked whether, "if they were to build anew, they would not aim at some architectural effect, some beauty of design," Elder Frederick replied emphatically, "No, the beautiful, as you call it, is absurd and abnormal. It has no business with us. The divine man has no right to waste money upon what you would call beauty, in his house or his daily life, while there are people living in misery."

Elder Frederick went on to explain what improvements he *would* plan if building anew, all of them completely utilitarian: "more light, a more equal distribution of heat, and a more general care for protection and comfort, because these things tend to health and long life." A machine for living, indeed. "But," as the visitor concluded, "no beauty."

Well, times changed and so did tastes; now most of us think that the Shakers' homes and furniture are beautiful in their functionalism.

But we see only part of the picture if we don't appreciate the Shaker concern for utility in all parts of their way of life—in Shaker education, for example. Mother Ann herself, raised in an eighteenth-century English working-class family, never had the opportunity to learn to read or write. Her main concern was with work and worship, not with theology, and she said simply, "Put your hands to work, and your hearts to God." It's evident that her followers put their minds to work, too, considering the ingenuity they put into their work.

Very soon, however, the Shakers thought it best to match their practical wisdom with a more bookish kind and considered a sound education a useful investment. As early as 1793—the year after they built their Meetinghouse and the same year they put up the Dwellinghouse—the Canterbury Shakers were sparing what time they could to teach reading and spelling. The utilitarian approach taken by the Canterbury Shakers a few years later, in 1806, typical in its matter-of-factness, was described by Elder Henry Blinn in his history of the village:

> . . . Hannah Bronson had charge of the school, which was kept in a barn at the North Family. The children had to sit on the floor, or provide themselves with a block or box. Lessons in reading and spelling, only, were given. Webster's spelling books, primers and the New Testament, were books read.

Arithmetic was soon added when pupils began to use kernels of corn or beans to learn addition and subtraction. Shaker girls and boys confined their book-learning in these early years to the three R's and spent most of their time learning practical skills that would serve them usefully in later life, Shaker or not. Even free time in school was put to good use. "When tired of study," Elder Henry continued, "the boys were employed in learning to set card-teeth, used in carders for carding wool and cotton, in the preparation for thread; and the girls spent the time in learning to knit."

As practical and utilitarian as Shaker schools were, however, they had nothing of the grimness of Dickens's Gradgrindian "fact factories." Elder Henry added that the "time for recreation was during the intermission at noon," and that the Shaker teachers spent the considerable sum of one dollar in the early years to buy peppermints to treat the children.

This six-seater school desk, also from New Lebanon, was as utilitarian as Shaker education: it saved space as well as work for the carpenters since two benches took the place of six chairs. Each place had a flip-over writing surface that doubled as a lid for the storage wells, each of which had a pen tray and a built-in inkstand holder.

In 1898 a Sister at Mt. Lebanon wrote:

*Should any one care
For a good Shaker chair,
At Mount Lebanon, N.Y. let them call,
We have them just right,
Cherry color and white,
And can suit both the great and the small.*

*Left, a high-seated weaving chair from
South Union, Kentucky (at the Shaker
Museum in Auburn, Kentucky); right,
spindle-bender for pressing curved spindles for
chairs (on facing page), detail of shawl bar;
below, chair finials, useful as handles for
lifting. The cone-shaped finial, center,
was a characteristic Mount Lebanon design.*

Above, a sewing rocker at Old Chatham, New York; the drawer for supplies stayed put no matter how lively the rocking because stops prevented it from falling out. Above right, a Mount Lebanon bentwood rocker (c. 1870), influenced by Thonet's Art Nouveau rocker, but simpler and easier to dust; right, a short-legged apple-sorting chair at Canterbury eliminated stooping; below, spindle-backed chair with solid pine seat; below right, the bar of a Mount Lebanon "shawl-bar" rocker supported a soft cushion hung on cloth loops or a shawl to keep drafts off the back. This and the bentwood were sold to the World.

A small lap stand from Harvard, Massachusetts (at Fruitlands Museum), was designed as a portable work surface to fit over the lap of a seated member.

Since later Shakers felt that a simple life did not have to mean a narrow life, education in all the communities grew progressively broader during the nineteenth century. By mid-century, according to the *Millennial Laws,* Shaker children were studying "Spelling, Reading, Writing, Composition, English Grammar, Arithmetic, Mensuration, The Science of Agriculture, Agricultural Chemistry, a small portion of History and Geography, Architecture, Moral Science, Good Manners, and True Religion"—these were "sufficient as general studies for children among Believers."

By the 1870s, Canterbury pupils were studying botany, physiology, music, drawing, algebra, and even "Elocution" in their nine years of schooling. Yet in spite of this change in the Shaker practice, the Shaker ideal of practical utility never changed. Young people still learned to bake bread and build barns, whether the skill for counting and measuring came from beans or geometry charts. What was more, a visitor to the school at New Lebanon realized, the satisfaction of feeling useful was an added lesson not taught in most other schools. As he found out, the Shakers thought "it will avail nothing for children to spend their time in acquiring a knowledge of the higher branches of literature, and especially of what is called classical learning, unless they can apply their knowledge to some useful purpose."

Shaker rules for manners and proper behavior were also greatly influenced by the standard of utility. The *Millennial Laws,* by which the Shakers ordered their lives, was on the whole simply a useful set of common sense guidelines geared to maintaining the safety and ideals of a large group of people sharing work and worship in a celibate community. Sections of the laws with headings like these give a good idea of the practical and functional nature of the rules:

Orders to Prevent Loss by Fire
Orders concerning Clothing
Of Prudence Neatness and Good Economy
Orders concerning Attending to Meals, Eating, &c. &c.
Orders concerning rising in the Morning and retiring to Rest at
    Night

Orders "Concerning Superfluities not Owned" were in effect a catalogue of fancy items unfit for Shaker use because of their uselessness. On the forbidden list were:

Silver pencils, silver tooth picks, gold pencils, or pens, silver spoons, silver thimbles, (but thimbles may be lined with silver,) gold or silver watches, brass knobs or handles of any size or kind. Three bladed knives, knife handles with writing or picturing on them, bone or horn handled knives, except for pocket knives, bone or horn spools, superfluous whips, marbled tin ware, superfluous paper boxes of any kind.... Superfluously finished, or flowery painted clocks, Bureaus, and Looking glasses, also superfluously painted or fancy shaped sleighs, or carriages, superfluously trimmed Harness, and many other articles too numerous to mention.

According to another section, "Order concerning Beasts, &c.," Shakers were not to keep any "kinds of beasts, birds, fowls, or fishes" if they were "merely for the sake of show, or fancy." Until the twentieth century the Shakers kept no pets because animals were considered fit according to their utility just like anything else in a Shaker village. A good illustration of how seriously the Shakers considered the usefulness of anything before making a decision to accept it happened in 1831 at Mount Lebanon when the Believers there decided to post birdhouses for the martins which flocked to the area. According to a journal,

> In years past, there has been a religious scruple against keeping martins, on account of their being rather an object of pride, than of usefulness. But being a report lately that they were useful in keeping off the hawks & preserving the poultry, it was considered and agreed that a trial might be made.

Whether the martins proved themselves useful enough to become Shaker martins was not recorded, but the importance of utility certainly was.

The same rules of utility applied in the earlier years of Shakerism to plants of all kinds. In 1906, Sister Marcia Bullard remembered how in her youth roses were grown strictly for their usefulness as rosewater—a flavoring for apple pies and a soothing lotion for fevered foreheads. According to Sister Marcia,

> The rose bushes were planted along the sides of the road which

A utility stand at Old Chatham, New York, was as useful as it was simple: a candlestand, a nightstand, or . . .

ran through our village and were greatly admired by the passerby, but it was strongly impressed upon us that a rose was useful, not ornamental. It was not intended to please us by its color or its odor, its mission was to be made into rose-water, and if we thought of it in any other way we were making an idol of it and thereby imperiling our souls.

She added, "In order that we might not be tempted to fasten a rose upon a dress or to put it into water to keep, the rule was that the flower should be plucked with no stem at all."

Within Sister Marcia's lifetime the rule changed, of course, and Shakers began to appreciate the beauty of a rose as the work of God just as fully as the beauty of a loving soul. But even when Shaker gardens bloomed with flowers good for the soul, there were always beds of lavender for scenting linens and useful herbs for the kitchen. Utility was not given up; it was just joined with beauty as an ideal.

If the birds and flowers that lived in a Shaker village had to prove themselves useful, we can imagine the demands of utility the Shakers made of themselves. Members felt they must be as useful as the things they made and the ways they followed. For sure, there was no place in a Shaker village for a plane that didn't shave right or an education that didn't teach common sense. But after all, any use is merely potential; it remains to someone to see that use *is* made, and made in the right way. Far worse than a plane that didn't work or an impractical education was a useful plane neglected or a useful education wasted. The Shakers were doers, not dreamers; for all their heavenly visions, no one was more down-to-earth. Elder Daniel Fraser's biographer spoke for all Shakers when she wrote that "whatever of truth he might possess as an ideal, would be far more potent for good when exemplified in practical life."

The demand for utility reached far beyond the tools and furniture the Shakers made. Said Father James Whittaker, "We have given you the gospel;—see to it, that you keep it, and make a good use of it." Utility was an ideal. The Shaker's greatest responsibility of all was to make good use of the lessons of God.

Cleanliness

The Shakers believed in good clean living, in every way. The pursuit of cleanliness shaped the Shakers' daily routine, their homes, and the distinctive design of their furnishings and utensils: in short, their way of life as a whole. It is no accident that we speak of the "clean" lines of Shaker furniture; without unnecessary carving or ornament, there was no place for dust to collect.

The reasons for their determination to banish dust and dirt lay in the Shaker conviction that the village they saw was a true reflection of the inner spiritual world. Mother Ann had told her followers, "Be neat and clean: for no unclean thing can enter heaven." For the Shaker, spiritual purity and physical cleanliness went hand in hand.

Mother Ann also said, "Clean your rooms well; for good spirits will not live where there is dirt. There is no dirt in heaven." Since the Shakers aimed to pattern their communities in every way according to their notion of heaven, there was no dirt in Shaker rooms, either. Mother Ann's advice was taken to heart by Shakers ever after. Eldress Harriet Bullard of Mount Lebanon, who lived on into the twentieth century, liked to recount a lesson she learned about cleanliness when she was a little Shaker girl:

> She had at one time the care of a dark corner closet, into which people seldom looked. One day, being in haste, she brushed it carelessly, thinking, "It does not matter if it is not clean, no one ever looks in here." Just then, as she looked, an eye appeared. It came to her at once as a lesson and a token that the angels saw all that she did, whether in the dark or in the light, and from that time it became her fixed practice to do all her work, even in the dark, well enough for the angels to see.

Evidently Mother Ann's "good spirits," accustomed as they were to the spotlessness of heaven, weren't very tolerant houseguests!

The connection between cleanliness and godliness that seemed so evident to the Shakers was responsible for a fascinating and uniquely Shaker form of worship—the "sweeping gift" and the "scrubbing gift," both symbolic pantomimes of cleaning motions accompanied with appropriate hymns. A Sunday visitor to Shaker worship services in the 1840s might have seen rows of reverent Shaker Brothers and Sisters sweeping heartily away at the Meetinghouse floor with imaginary "spiritual" brooms or bending down to scrub out the stains of sin.

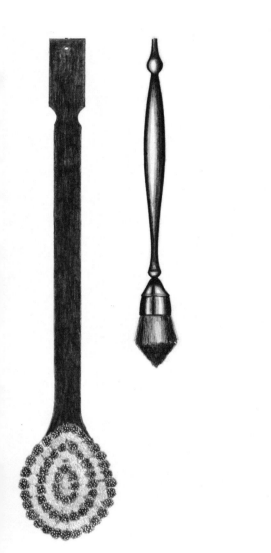

The origin of the sweeping gift lay in the explanation that Mother Ann gave to her follower Hannah Goodrich about the meaning of the Lord's command to "sweep clean." According to Mother Ann, the spiritual meaning of this command was to sweep clean "the floor of the heart." For a Shaker, the act of sweeping and the concept of a pure heart were meant to suggest each other as naturally as "hands to work" suggested "hearts to God." With the refreshing simplicity of their attitude, born of the confidence that heaven was just the flip side of everyday life, the Shakers made sweeping a part of their worship and sang hymns to suit, like this one by Sister Elizabeth Potter of Mount Lebanon in 1839:

> *Sweep sweep & cleanse your floor*
> *Mother's standing at the door . . .*

Another vigorous example was called "Decisive Work," written in 1845:

> *I have come,*
> *And I've not come in vain.*
> *I have come to sweep*
> *The house of the Lord*
> *Clean, clean, for I've come*
> *And I've not come in vain.*
> *With my broom in my hand,*
> *With my fan and my flail,*
> *This work I will do*
> *And I will not fail.*
> *For lo! I have come*
> *And I've not come in vain.*

Left: A long-handled back brush with black and white bristles in a pleasing pattern. The beautifully tapered horsehair corner brush, right, swept away hard-to-reach dust. Its knobbed end isn't just decorative—work brushes hung by the knob from a tin holder on the wall. (Canterbury, N.H.)

Scrubbing motions accompanied a hymn that required a back as willing to bend as a contrite spirit:

> *Bow down low, bow down low,*
> *Wash, wash, clean, clean, clean, clean, scour and scrub,*
> *Scour and scrub from this floor*
> *The stains of sin.*

Besides the spiritual reasons for cleanliness, however, were such practical reasons as health. In 1828, an observer commented, "They are remarkably neat and clean in their houses and door yards. Their

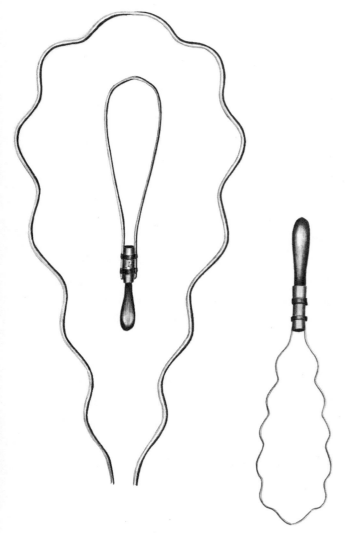

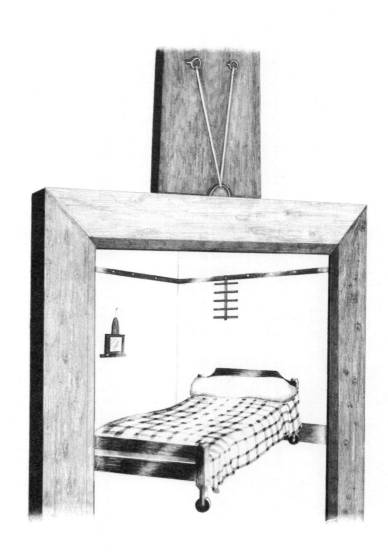

Top left: Rugbeaters to clean woven, braided, or knitted Shaker rugs. Wooden ones, patented in 1898, were made for sale; the wiggly wire types were lighter. Top right: The first daily task a Believer faced was stripping and airing the bed, shown reflected in a tilting mirror. Beds on wheels were easy to move for making or sweeping underneath. Right: A corner of the Canterbury Dwellinghouse attic (c. 1795) shows handy built-in numbered drawers and brushes hanging just where needed. (Canterbury, N.H.)

circumstances force them to it. Disease would be the effect of un-cleanliness in their dwellings, as many are the inhabitants of them."

Another practical reason for cleanliness was fire prevention. The workshops of the Brothers and Sisters were as clean as their dwelling rooms. Every evening, Brothers in the carpentry shop swept up all the shavings and sawdust from the day's work. This was not only sensible from the standpoint of order, it eliminated a dangerous fire hazard; the shavings were saved and burned in the small cast-iron stoves that heated Shaker rooms.

The spinning, weaving, and printing shops all received the same careful sweeping—even the farm buildings. Old photographs of the Canterbury cow barn (1858) show floors swept and polished so clean that it's hard to believe a hundred cows occupied the stalls when the pictures were taken.

With good reasons like these for cleanliness, it's easy to see why cleaning was an important part of the everyday routine for all Shakers. For the Sisters, cleaning was the first job of the day, even before breakfast. They dusted, swept the floors, and stripped the beds to air them out in their quarters in the Dwellinghouse and then did the same in the Brothers' rooms as soon as the men left for their morning chores in the barns. Cleaning the gathering rooms, halls, and stairways of the Dwellinghouse was another regular chore. The size of the job might have been overwhelming (the Canterbury Dwelling-house had fifty-six rooms, for example) if there hadn't been so many Sisters ready to put their hands to the job.

As relentless as daily cleaning was, from time to time the Shakers attacked dirt with even more vigor: traditional spring and fall house-cleaning was an important part of the yearly schedule. The *Millennial Laws* specified that "shopcleaning" was also a semiannual event: "Sisters shall clean brethren's shops twice a year, and brethren sweep them every day when used and clean the spit boxes."

There were also occasional days set aside "for general purifica-tion," as much for spiritual cleansing as for practical scrubbing. On such days, according to a visitor to Watervliet, New York, in the early nineteenth century,

The brothers must clean their respective work-shops, by sweeping the walls, and removing every cobweb from the corners and under

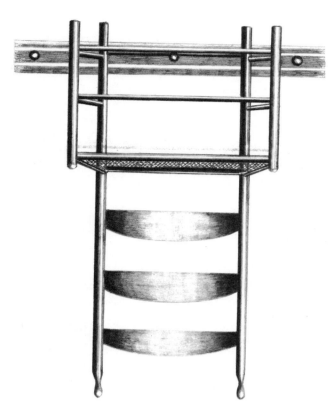

Above: Shaker chairs hung on the wall to clear the floor for sweeping; Canterbury Shakers hung their chairs upside down so dust would fall on the bottom of the seat and not dirty the top. Above right: Brothers at Enfield, New Hampshire, designed this workbench (at Fruitlands Museum) to be as simple to clean as the furniture they made on it: lidded drawers kept sawdust out. Right: A large double desk from New Lebanon, probably designed for two Deacons or two Trustees, was easy to clean and saved space too.

Canterbury Schoolhouse windows, above, were ingeniously simple to clean or mend. Wooden strips, fastened with easily removable wooden screws (detail), allowed the window-washer to bring the window inside for safe, thorough cleaning. The upper window slid down and out too.

their workbenches, and wash the floors clean by scrubbing them with sand. By doing this they would remove all the devils and wicked spirits that might be lodging in the different buildings; for where cobwebs and dust were permitted to accumulate, there the evil spirits hide themselves.

Mother Ann would have been pleased at the way her followers cleared out the dust to make the good spirits feel at home.

Since Shakers put so much emphasis on cleaning, naturally they wanted to do it as quickly and efficiently as possible. It was in this way that the demands of cleanliness helped to shape Shaker furniture and architecture. If you had to dust every chair in every room every day, chances are that you too would eventually come to despise every ornamental detail as a home for wayward dust. And if you had to move those chairs every day to sweep the floors, you would gradually realize that unnecessary ornament means unnecessary weight, too.

No wonder a distinctively Shaker style in chairs and all other furniture developed in response to the demands of cleaning. Pieces were as light as possible if they had to be moved. Frequently, large heavy pieces rolled easily on wheels. Otherwise, pieces like cupboards, shelves, drawers, and even tables were built into the walls of the room itself, so there were no tops, backs, or sides to dust. Most importantly, all the furniture was as simple in style as possible. Fancy furnishings did not impress the Shakers, except as dust-collectors. The reaction of Elder Frederick Evans of Mount Lebanon to a "costly New York dwelling" in the Victorian era was typical. He saw carpets nailed down to the floor, "of course with piles of dust beneath, never swept away, and of which I had to breathe," and heavy picture frames, also "the receptacles of dust."

The architecture of the Shakers, especially their interior design, was as simple and uncluttered as possible. Simple braided or woven rugs were small and light enough to take up and clean regularly, never nailed down. In 1873, an article on housecleaning in the Shaker newspaper advised against tacking down carpets—not just because dirt collected under them, but because the dust was "injurious to health, so far as the lungs are concerned!"

From small pegs in strategic spots hung brushes, dustpans, and other cleaning aids. The Shaker flat broom was not hidden in a closet:

it was readily and matter-of-factly available hanging from the pegs on the wall of every room.

The wall pegboard itself was the single most important Shaker contribution to the cause of efficient cleanliness and neatness. Virtually every room, in every building, in every Shaker village, had its pegboard fastened across the walls about 6 feet from the floor and punctuated every 18 inches or so with the distinctive wooden pegs. Even Shaker Meetinghouses had two rows of pegs, for the Brothers' hats and coats and the Sisters' bonnets and cloaks.

The initial work of turning all these pegs was staggering—each village probably contained between five and ten thousand pegs—but they proved to be one of the most valuable investments of time and labor in all of Shaker history. Anything and everything—clothing, mirrors, brushes, even pieces of furniture like cupboards—could be hung neatly on the walls. The pegboards also allowed a unique flexibility in room arrangement: rearranging a room to make it more efficient or to adapt it to a new use often meant simply moving mirrors, shelves, and candleholders to a different peg—as much flexibility as the continuous electrical outlet provides us today. More than anything else, this ingeniously simple idea provided the convenience that let the Shakers make their ideals of perpetual cleanliness and neatness a part of their daily life.

The success the Shakers had in maintaining their ideals of cleanliness is clear from the impressions that visitors had of Shaker rooms. Charles Nordhoff, a journalist who studied communal societies in America a century ago, described the Mount Lebanon Shakers' rooms in 1874:

> . . . if there is a stove in the room, a small broom and dust-pan hang near it, and a wood-box stands by it; scrapers and mats at the door invite you to make clean your shoes; and if the roads are muddy or snowy, a broom hung up outside the outer door mutely requests you to brush off all the mud or snow. The strips of carpet are easily lifted, and the floor beneath is as clean as though it were a table to be eaten from. The walls are bare of pictures; not only because all ornament is wrong, but because frames are places where dust will lodge. The bedstead is a cot, covered with the bedclothing, and easily moved away to allow of

Hidden shutters built into the Trustees' Office (1831) at Canterbury took up no space inside the room; when down they were absolutely sealed from dust. During New Hampshire winters, both panels slid up to cover the window.

dusting and sweeping. Mats meet you at the outer door and at every inner door. The floors of the halls and dining-room are polished until they shine.

Nordhoff's appreciation of Shaker cleanliness—and his awareness of what the tools were for—no doubt made him a welcome guest in any Shaker village.

Another noted visitor, William Dean Howells, reported his first impression of Shaker cleanliness in 1876 in the *Atlantic Monthly*:

> In each village is an edifice known as the Dwelling-house, which is separate from the office and the other buildings. In this are the rooms of the brothers and sisters, the kitchen and dining-room, and a large room for family meetings. The first impression of all is cleanliness, with a suggestion of bareness which is not inconsistent, however, with comfort, and which comes chiefly from the aspect of unpapered walls, the scrubbed floors hidden only by rugs and strips of carpeting, and the plain, flat finish of the woodwork.

The Shakers must have been gratified by reports like these. Confident of the immaculate outward appearance of their simple homes and certain that it reflected a similar purity of spirit within, the Shakers found contentment in obeying the commands of their *Holy Laws of Zion*:

> Do not be expensive and extravagant in your buildings; but modest and neat. For a lowly cottage, in order and cleanliness, is far more beautiful than a grand dwelling, made or inhabited by that which is unclean.

Health

For a group of people who willingly gave up bodily pleasure to ensure salvation for their souls, the Shakers put what can seem like a surprising amount of effort into keeping their bodies healthy. If what really counted was cleanliness of thought, word, and deed, then why did the Shakers make such a point of bathtubs and regular bathing? And if it was the word of God that healed, why did nearly every Shaker village have a fully equipped Infirmary, and why were Shakers well known throughout the Eastern states a hundred years ago for their medicinal industry? Schoolchildren at Canterbury and other villages were studying the body and its organs from detailed physiology charts in the mid-nineteenth century and being told to get enough fresh air daily. Last but certainly not least, Shakers enjoyed an excellent diet—positively ruinous to the waistlines of those who didn't match Shaker dinners with Shaker hard work—and slept comfortably on corn-husk mattresses at night.

The answer was simple, to the Shakers. They drew parallels so naturally between their heavenly ideals and their daily practice that for them good health reflected a healthy spirit. If the body was in perfect working order, then so was the soul, and vice versa. Health was one part of the total perfection they sought.

A Shaker poem entitled "Health" written in 1895 says it best:

> *A pearly brow that tells of holy thought;*
> *A ruddy cheek, and eye with sparkling light;*
> *Strong, well knit arms that love to do the right;*
> *A heart that times life's motion as it ought,*
> *And crimson blood from healthful substance wrought.*
> *Free lungs that heave with pure air day and night,*
> *These make of mortal life a sweet delight.*

If man were made in God's image, then man was certainly meant to be strong and whole. Good health was practical—it took hard work to maintain the village—but it served spiritual ends, too, since the Shaker felt he should follow God's example in every way. In 1875, a visitor found that as far as the Shakers were concerned, disease was "an offense to God," and that it was "in the power of men to be healthful, if they will." Health was a gift and deserved thankful care like any other. The work of God demanded strength of body and soul; ideally, the flesh *was* as willing as the spirit.

Hancock Shakers designed adjustable wooden transoms, above, for inside doors to let fresh air flow through the Dwellinghouse (1830).

The Shakers had a saying, "It takes a whole man or woman to be a Shaker." Brother Ezekiel Stevens of Canterbury had the right idea, even if he seemed too willing a worker now and then. When he died in 1836 at the age of sixty, his obituary read:

> His faithfulness in temporal duties, like many others, of that class has become proverbial. By many of the Brethren it was thought that he was not so prudent of his health and strength as he should have been. But Ezekiel had given his soul and body to the service of the Lord, and he would say, "It is better to wear out, than to rust out."

To keep themselves healthy, the Shakers used wisely all four earthly elements for their heavenly goal—air, fire, water, and earth. Translated into health terms, that meant good ventilation; the use of static electricity as the latest in rheumatism treatment; extensive and progressive plumbing systems; and a sensible diet, herbal medicines, and for the most part no liquor or tobacco. Besides these measures, Shakers slept at least seven hours nightly and exercised not only at their work but at their worship, too. Shaker dances like the *Lively Line* were meant to work up a healthy sweat as the worshippers sang,

> *I need not think of gaining much,*
> *To give the floor an easy touch,*
> *Or labor in some handsome form,*
> *That scarce will keep my ancles warm,*
> *For I have not so far increased,*
> *That I can manage such a beast,*
> *Without my blood is nicely heat,*
> *And my whole body flows with sweat.*

Fresh air was so important to the Shakers that they built efficient ventilation systems into their dwellings and shops that make our present-day hermetically sealed glass boxes seem like tombs. They thought so much of proper ventilation that, according to a visitor, "Fresh air is the Shaker medicine." The fact that Shakers valued fresh air day and night is all the more progressive at a time when the nineteenth century was blaming half its ills, including consumption, on the evening dews and damps. While contemporary Victorian America snored genteelly in airless rooms behind heavy draperies, the

Mount Lebanon Shakers were inviting lecturers like "Doctor Griscomb of New York" in 1869 to speak on "the subject of free ventilation and fresh air, to preserve health."

What the Shakers there learned, they put into practice. When Charles Nordhoff visited Mount Lebanon in 1875, among the first things he admired was the ventilation system in his visitors' room window:

> the sash was fitted with screws, by means of which the windows could be so secured as not to rattle in stormy weather; while the lower sash of one window was raised three or four inches, and a strip of neatly fitted plank was inserted into the opening—this allowed ventilation between the upper and lower sashes, thus preventing a direct draught, while securing fresh air.

Several years later, in 1880, the newly published periodical *The Plumber & Sanitary Engineer* sent a reporter to the North Family at Mount Lebanon to report on Shaker sanitation systems. Obviously impressed, he included a report on ventilation: "The latter is a constant study. Slats are placed in every window to make an opening between the two sashes, so that there shall always be an influx of atmospheric air." (That sounds redundant, until you consider how many city dwellers today prefer inhaling the nice conditioned stuff in their glass boxes to the real thing outside.) The report continued, "Small holes along the baseboard in all of the halls aid this end. In the gathering rooms there are round openings from out-doors, just below steam radiators, to supply fresh air, and the central (student) lamps have vent pipes to carry off the products of combustion; in addition, all beds are stripped and windows kept open to insure an ample circulation of air." Incidentally, the Sisters always stripped and aired the beds for several hours before making them up again in the morning. Some Shaker beds were designed with high footboards purposely for laying the bedclothes over to air.

Fresh air was just as good for Shaker animals as it was for Shakers. The Shaker cow barn at Canterbury (1858), for example, had specially angled windows to let fresh air but not drafts into the stalls. Elder Henry Blinn of Canterbury even ventilated his beehives with adjustable wind vents. When he noticed on a hot day that certain bees had to sit by the hive entrance and fan it cool with their wings, he was

This door, in the Trustees' Office (1831) at Canterbury, was fitted with small windowpanes, lowered for ventilation or raised to prevent drafts.

Ventilation-minded Shakers hung tin vent pipes over their oil lamps to carry off unhealthy fumes.

so concerned that he "air conditioned" the hives with the wind vents—leaving the bees confident that the honey wouldn't melt (and free to do more work!).

The large Dwellinghouse (1830) at Hancock, Massachusetts, had the same ventilation feature as the Canterbury Dwellinghouse (1793)—regular windows built into the inner walls and closets to let natural light and fresh air into the inner recesses of a large building.

The two-storey Schoolhouse at Canterbury (built in 1823 and enlarged in 1862) had a different but equally simple method of circulating air. A trap door built into the ceiling of the downstairs room opened with a rope pull to let warm air rise out of the room in the summer when the girls studied there, cooling it off. In the three winter months, when the boys attended, the rising warm air would help heat the upstairs room, used as a place for quiet study.

Insulation also had its place in Shaker villages like Canterbury. The space between the inner plaster ceiling and the exterior shingles was stuffed with birch bark and moss to keep temperatures down in summer and higher in winter. Most of the buildings there were insulated, including the first one built, the Meetinghouse, in 1792.

Shakers so appreciated the fresh air they inhaled that they tried to keep it that way when they exhaled it—at least, that was one benefit of their general abstinence from tobacco. In the earliest years of the nineteenth century, Shakers like other early Americans saw no harm in pipes or a chaw of tobacco now and then. Many converts brought the habit with them. Early Shakers who smoked made their own pipes, planing off short sections of willow twig, burning out the pith with a hot wire, then fitting on clay pipe bowls of their own molding. Spit boxes—round wooden containers filled with shavings or sawdust—were found everywhere, two to a room, for chewers of the weed. To prevent dirt and disease, the Shakers had strict rules about using the spit boxes: spitting "on floors, or stairs, or in sinks in the kitchens" or "out of the window" was considered very rude indeed.

However, the Shakers began to realize that tobacco was neither spiritually necessary nor physically healthy, so by the 1870s the official word was out: tobacco had to go. Whoever was in charge of announcing the official disapproval of the "pernicious practice" of chewing tobacco must have realized that a sense of humor would go a long way in getting the message across. The "vile weed" received the following "obituary" in an 1873 issue of the Shaker newspaper:

> On Tuesday, Feb. 20th, 1873, Died by the power of truth and for the cause of human Redemption, at the Young Believers' Order, Mount Lebanon, in much beloved Brethren, the Tobacco Chewing Habit. . . . No funeral ceremonies, no mourners, no graveyard; but an honorable Record thereof made in the Court above.

. . . And no resurrection.

Besides being healthier for the young chewers themselves, this cold turkey *en masse* was also better for the community as a whole: the spitting habit was a good way of communicating disease. And, of course, smoking was always dangerous because of fire, another reason for discouraging the practice. It was "contrary to order" to smoke "in the woodhouse, barn, or carding machine factory," or to empty a pipe into the spit box or out of the window.

Bans on tobacco were not just the result of practical health or safety reasons, though. Other reasons, based on Shaker faith, were the actual driving force behind the decision to discourage the use of tobacco. In 1842, the Elders at New Lebanon were receiving spiritual messages against tobacco by the dozens:

> There has been now within a year or two past, a great deal handed down from the Heavens. . . . Laws given in relation to using Tobacco, and all such like, unnecessary habits. Or, more properly such things as have been in constant use in times past, but now they are considered unnecessary and useless.

Since spiritual communications like these were taken seriously by the Shakers, who based their faith on divine revelation from the days of Mother Ann's visions, it was clear to them that tobacco was *spiritually* wrong. If tobacco was just another pleasurable but nonessential indulgence, it had to go. The young Shakers who gave up chewing tobacco were serious when they said it was for the "cause of human Redemption." More than anything, the Shakers wanted freedom—including freedom from sickness, bad habit, and artificial stimulants.

Spiritual messages in the 1840s also resulted in the discontinuance of "stimulants" like coffee and tea. However, this ban was only temporary. When in 1856 it was thought all right to resume these habits,

Elder Henry Blinn of Canterbury thought so much of fresh air and ventilation that he "air conditioned" all his beehives with adjustable wind vents. Round wooden covers swiveled to open or shut the air holes. (Canterbury, N.H.)

the members of Union Village, Ohio, were understandably "somewhat astonished" to again find "*green tea* for their drink at breakfast, it & coffee alternately."

Like tea and coffee, smoking was never entirely or permanently banned, and there were Believers who never gave up the habit, mainly elderly members whose small pleasures were tolerated. A journal account from January 1880 indicated that for those who wanted it, a half-pound of tobacco per person would be distributed the first day of every month. In 1873, the Sabbathday Lake Shakers recorded with satisfaction that only five members there still used the "filthy weed," namely:

Elder Joseph Brackett	aged 76 years	Chews
Josiah Noyes	aged 71 years	Smokes
Thomas Noyes	aged 80 years	Smokes
Lydia Littlefield	aged 80 years	Smokes
Celia Saunders	aged 63 years	Smokes

and that they were eagerly awaiting the day when not a single member would maintain the "pernicious practice." (Elder Joseph, according to a further note, began his chewing habit at the ripe old age of four years when "his Father gave him the first piece of Tobacco that he ever put in his mouth and it tasted as sweet as the nicest sugarplum he ever ate, not making him sick.")

All in all, the main emphasis was on sense and moderation. Good-natured but pointed rhymes poked fun at the self-indulgent, nicknamed "Old Slugs":

> *Men of sound reason use their pipes*
> *For colics, pains, and windy gripes;*
> *And smoking's useful, we will own,*
> *To give the nerves and fluids tone;*
> *But poor old Slug has to confess*
> *He uses it to great excess,*
> *And will indulge his appetite*
> *Beyond his reason and his light.*

The beesmoker, opposite, that Elder Henry used burned oily rags in the tin cone; leather bellows pumped smoke into the hives to quiet the swarm. The beesmoker was not Shaker-made.

It's amusing to realize that tobacco was considered fit for medicinal purposes. It is hard to imagine a modern doctor prescribing tobacco for anyone with "windy gripes."

❋

Old Shaker diaries can turn up plenty of hints on health matters, from the humorous to the puzzling. A Deaconess at Watervliet, New York, wrote in 1866, "Chauncey has a boil on his eye brow. it has kept him home all the week. but it has not kept his tongue still." Another Sister wrote so often in her daily journal that she'd been "shocked" again that day that anyone reading it would have thought she was somewhat easily alarmed—until he realized that she meant she was receiving static electricity treatment for arthritis. She always added how much better she felt afterward.

The ever-progressive Shakers, like most of the nineteenth-century medical world, were fascinated with the stimulating powers of electric shock. According to a Mount Lebanon journal, the first electrical "cure" was introduced in 1808 there. Brother Thomas Corbett (1780–1857) of Canterbury was one of the first to experiment with static electricity when he developed an electrostatic machine in 1810 as a "cure" for rheumatism. The principle of the device, which was a sort of Leyden jar, was simple: the sufferer held onto metal balls on the top while Brother Thomas cranked the handle until the shock that built up either "cured" his pains or at least took his mind off his aching joints for the moment.

Sister Elizabeth Lovegrove of New Lebanon recorded such a shock session, which if outmoded by modern technology at least did not kill the elderly patient. On March 31, 1837, "Elder Sister" remained feeble but was "relieved some of her cough by the vapor bath and electricity." It may not have cured Elder Sister, but it did make her feel better—and that was important, too.

Sister Elizabeth's account brings up the matter of bathing, whether for specialized health treatment like Elder Sister's vapor bath or for ordinary personal cleanliness. In 1846, the Shakers at Harvard, Massachusetts, were paying close attention to "lectures on the water cure system &c," while other Shaker villages were practicing regular bathing for the members.

The Shakers' belief in bathing for health and cleanliness was as advanced for the time as their belief in the benefits of fresh air. Most Americans readily accepted Monday as washday for their clothes, but Saturday as bath day for themselves was another proposition alto-

A water-powered wind fan from Canterbury typified Shaker enthusiasm for ventilation and progress. The remarkable contraption not only circulated fresh air, but provided fresh water from the spigot on the side. The simplicity of the idea was not matched by the fancy Victorian base. (Shelburne Museum, Vt.)

gether. In the first place, it was inconvenient without running water. Secondly, bathing was generally suspected as a good way to get sick. Third, most homes had large families and certainly no separate inside bathroom. Consequently, the privacy we take for granted today was just not available.

As usual, there were strong practical and spiritual reasons for the Shakers' attitude on bathing. The fact that a large number of people lived in close quarters in a single building certainly made frequent bathing an appealing idea. As for privacy, the laundries that were such an important part of the Shaker village provided not only that but the facilities for plenty of running water. Shaker villages usually had competent running water systems earlier than neighboring farms because community living meant that there were shared resources to afford it and men enough to spare to dig the system. Running water was worth the time and trouble to Shakers anyway, since it saved much more time and trouble in the long run.

The Shakers at Mount Lebanon had hot and cold running water aplenty, after the Brothers laid the steam and waterworks system just before the turn of this century. Always confident of their common sense ability, the self-sufficient Brothers decided to do the job themselves. One of the Sisters patiently recorded their progress during the summer; in 1895 she wrote:

> It seemed to uninstructed minds
> that brethren must be playing
> With instruments of various kinds,
> but lo! they were surveying.
> Well then they figured, scored and planned
> on horseblock and on gate-post,
> And always brought their board in hand
> when they to meals came, late most.

Day by day she followed their ups and downs:

> But there's a problem in this theme,
> the Deacons might unlock it,
> In digging drains, do men begin
> in earth or in the pocket?

applauding their noble efforts at trench warfare:

They said with Grant, "We'll take this line,"
and not employ a plumber,
But we will lay the pipes ourselves
if it should take all summer.

and valiantly holding her tongue when they tracked through her clean hallway:

If man was made of dust, as said,
we judge he must have floated,
But his descendants firmly tread
when they with mud are coated.

Never once did her confidence in them falter:

And if the dooryard was cut up
with tunnels and with trenches,
The hills were heaped with loads of boards,
pipes, tools, and workmen's benches.
And what we saw was but a tithe
of what they knew who did it,
But when they were the most perplexed
they smiled and kindly hid it.

. . . and when they finally won success, no doubt she heaved a huge sigh of relief and thanked God for the Brothers, the water, and most of all the return to peace and quiet!

The main purpose of all the labor was apparently to put in a bath, since she ended her account in verse this way:

The bath we know will henceforth keep
the vital tide in motion,
Its home significance is deep
as level waves of ocean.

Only a spiritual reason could account for significance as deep as that. Sure enough, Shakers saw a parallel between the symbolic cleansing of the soul and the actual bathing of the body, as have Christians since the time of John the Baptist. Father James Whittaker, one of Mother Ann's followers from England, was the first Shaker to put this notion into words. On preaching a sermon from the text *Cleanse your hands, ye sinners,* he explained: "What is cleansing the hands . . . but the confession of sin?"

A symbolic emblem from a Shaker spirit drawing, this Tree of Life *from the Book of Revelations was captioned: "And the leaves of the Tree is for the healing of the nations of the Earth." For healing in a Shaker village, faith was backed by competent medical know-how, herbal medicines, and well-stocked village Infirmaries.*

Potty chairs were convenient equipment in the Infirmaries. The lid on the seat lifted to reveal a chamber pot inside, easily removed through the small door on the front. The chair itself, top, is of a typical Shaker style. Also pictured, an apparently unique cherry potty chair from New Lebanon. To eliminate odor, the crosspiece on the base was raised with the lever to hold a tin pot snugly against the seat, lined underneath with coarse fabric. Removing the pot (not shown) was a simple matter of moving the lever and lowering the crosspiece again.

Later Shakers reasoned that if clean hands were symbolic of a sinless nature, then a clean body was no doubt sure sign of a spirit as clean and pure within. One Shaker writer summed up this general notion by saying, "As water washes and cleanses the body from outward pollution, so the true baptism of the water of life washes and cleanses the soul from all the pollutions of sin. . . . As water is used to cleanse and refresh the body, so the water of life will cleanse and refresh the soul." No wonder the Shakers climbed so readily into bathtubs, when they felt that cleanliness of body and soul went hand in hand.

The connection was taken quite literally by some Shakers. A Shaker visiting the Harvard village in 1854 reported that the Elders there "said there was a large spiritual Pool of water in their room and Mother [Ann] invited us to drink and wash and bathe in it. Which we did very heartily." A hymn written in 1838 by Sister Eliza Sharpe called "Wash & Be Clean" urged Shakers in the Meetinghouse to symbolically

> *Come, Come, Come to the fountain*
> *all ye that are poor and needy;*
> *and strip off your garment that's old*
> *and wash and be clean pure and holy.*
> *Then you shall be Mother's children.*

According to one Believer, the Hancock Shakers in the 1840s even had a spiritual "exercise" of pantomimed bathing as a part of their worship service, complete with spiritual towels, sponges, and water.

With spiritual and practical reasons behind them all the way, no wonder the Shakers encouraged bathing. *The Gospel Monitor*, written in 1843 under divine inspiration, advised the children's Caretakers to see that their charges were scrubbed:

Watch my little ones, closely, and see that they are punctual to dress themselves neatly and tidily; and above all, to wash clean their faces and hands, and they never ought to pass over a week, except in the coldest weather, without washing their bodies more or less, or having it done for them.

One Sister relished bathing so much that when she visited Canterbury in 1854, she devoted a whole page in her journal to the experience:

About 5 oclock P.M. we were invited to take a bath. This is one of the great luxuries we have been blest with since we left home. It is truly a blessing to be introduced to a bath of 10 inches deep and the vessel spacious enough to lie down your whole length, fed by a teem [team?] cock at the foot of the bath, and warm water enough to make it pleasant to the feel. O! it is too good to be rightly appreciated.

How typical it was of the Shakers to pantomime bathing in the Meetinghouse and to feel reverence in the bathtub—so completely did they make their spiritual ideals a part of their everyday practice. They preached that cleanliness was next to godliness, and they practiced what they preached.

If bathing was highly desirable in a Family of several hundred people, adequate toilet facilities were essential. The article on Shaker sanitation in the 1880 issue of *The Plumber & Sanitary Engineer* reported on Mount Lebanon's facilities, noting with approval the water closets in every building and the outdoor privies which were most frequently used, according to the correspondent. The Shakers' basis for such careful sanitation measures struck the reporter enough to write, "The Elders informed me that their careful attention to hygiene has a theological basis, they believing that science and religion ... are one and the same."

The Sabbathday Lake community in Maine had one of the most practical privies of all—it was two storeys tall. Since it handily adjoined the laundry (1821), the upstairs and downstairs seats were each accessible from the adjoining floor, so each level was sanitarily and privately separate. Boxes on each floor contained sawdust which was tossed down by the handful to absorb moisture. The success of the Shakers' scrupulously sanitary plumbing arrangements is evident in the freedom of Shaker villages from few epidemics more serious than measles.

Such advanced developments in sanitation required two things: a ready supply of water and often ingenious methods of getting it to where it was needed. Good water supplies were always an important factor in choosing the site of a Shaker settlement. Some chose to settle near lakes, like the Sabbathday Lake Shakers; others, like Mount

On September 21, 1878, Sabbathday Lake Shakers proudly announced: "A Bathing Tub, the first one ever introduced into this Society was brought home today and put into the new laundry." With that tin tub—designed for sitting, not stretching out—members could literally obey their spiritual command:

> *Come o ye children of the living God*
> *Come bow down low and wash and bathe*
> *And shower in the holy fountain of*
> *The Lord your God.*
>
> *(Sabbathday Lake, Maine)*

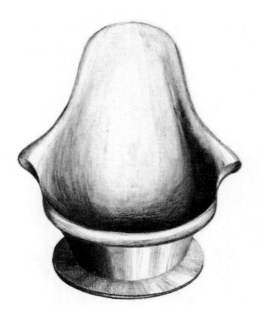

Lebanon in New York, settled in an area known for its abundant springs of good water. Still other places, like Canterbury, New Hampshire, and North Union, Ohio, converted swampy areas into functional pond systems by digging or damming.

The Canterbury Shakers' water system provided fresh running water in the village as early as 1797—only five years after the community was established. The members thought running water so important that they willingly spared their workmen from building and farming to drill by hand through at least a half mile of wooden water pipes to bring spring water down from the North Family into the Center Family. Some of the original log pipes and the iron auger can still be seen there.

Other communities showed equal imagination and hard work. Some villages were faced with the problem of raising water from a source lower than the village. Pleasant Hill, Kentucky, solved the problem with a horse-operated pump, which kept a large cistern filled with spring water. In 1837 a visitor wrote, "This Cistern is in the upper part of a small two story building and from this Cistern all the buildings in the Church [Family] (where water is needed) are supplied by means of lead pipes &c." An account written in 1852 described just how this operation worked: it consisted of a "force pump attached to a strong cast-iron pipe, carried by horse power, and occupied the time and labor of a horse about 6 hours each day, in order to give a sufficient supply to their buildings wash places &c."

The Union Village, Ohio, Shakers rigged up a "hydraulic Ram" which forced water from a spring 700 feet up into the cistern of the Gathering Order, enough to supply all the buildings. This operation was working before the 1850s. In 1869, according to the account of a visiting Shaker, the Harvard Shakers had similar "hydraulic pipes" which brought the spring water three quarters of a mile across the valley.

Other villages got their water from above rather than below. At Mount Lebanon, for example, a visitor found that "Water is conducted from the mountain in pipes, and every story [five in the Dwellinghouse] is abundantly supplied with both hot and cold water at all times, for drinking washing and bathing." All that in 1869. The Shakers at North Union, Ohio, used a double-filter cistern for rainwater as part of their supply. George Budinger, one of the last chil-

This garden design, from an 1854 spirit drawing, suggests the extensive botanic gardens where Shakers raised herbs for their kitchens and medicines.

dren raised at North Union before it closed in 1889, recalled in later years how it worked. The underground cisterns were bricked and cemented, and "rainwater drained off from the roof of the family residence, and down into the first cistern which was filled with charcoal." After it filtered into the second cistern, "it was pumped up by hand into the kitchen for cooking, drinking, and washing dishes."

The Shakers were as careful to choose and develop good land as they were their water sources. Extensive orchards and gardens provided the villages with fruit and vegetables, while "physics' gardens" or botanic herb gardens and the surrounding fields and forests provided the basis for the dozens of patent medicines they made, used, and sold. Chickens supplied meat and eggs, ponds produced fish, and pasture lands fed beef and lamb on the hoof.

This raises the question of meat-eating in Shaker villages. Were they vegetarians? The general answer is no, which may seem surprising since the pacifistic Believers did not like the thought of killing. Yet they were also completely down-to-earth, practical people who recognized the value of their animals for meat and leather. Remember, too, that the early Shakers lived and worked when leather was indispensable for boots, saddles, and harnesses—essentials for life and work in a time when these things could not be made of plastics. In fact, the first industry at Canterbury was a tannery; since killing the animals for leather was unavoidable, the thrifty Shakers naturally ate the meat, too.

What the Shakers wouldn't tolerate was cruelty to animals:

> A man of kindness, to his beast is kind.
> Brutal actions show a brutal mind.
> Remember: He who made the brute,
> Who gave thee speech and reason, formed him mute;
> He can't complain; but GOD's omniscient eye
> Beholds thy cruelty. He hears his cry.
> He was destined thy servant and thy drudge,
> BUT KNOW THIS: HIS CREATOR IS THY JUDGE.

The Canterbury Shakers even treated their pests with consideration: the "humane mousetraps" didn't injure the mice in their barn.

The Shakers never believed in hunting for sport, either, and the

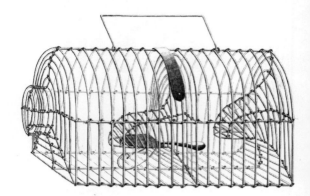

Even pests like mice were treated humanely by Canterbury Shakers with traps like these (purchased from the World). Mice crawled in on the right and fell through the weighted trap door into the left side, but weren't injured by the trap. The practical Shakers disposed of them through the door on the left. Who knows? Maybe they went out the back door or off to the nearest "great and wicked city"! (Canterbury, N.H.)

Elder Frederick Evans (1808–93), an outstanding leader at Mount Lebanon during the nineteenth century. In 1875 a visitor described this vegetarian "with a hobby for science as applied to health, comfort, and the prolongation of life" as looking fifteen years younger than his age of sixty-seven. A strong advocate of fresh air, he believed: "Every house should breathe as really as does a human being." (From an old print)

Millennial Laws revealed the Shakers' reluctance to kill: "Boys under fifteen years of age, may not go a hunting with guns, and the longer they let guns alone the better." While they did periodically slaughter, they relied on the quickest and least painful methods they knew.

Elder Frederick Evans (1808–93) of Mount Lebanon, one of the influential Shaker leaders of the nineteenth century, didn't approve of eating meat himself. A strict vegetarian, he traveled to England in the 1870s, lecturing on the health benefits of a meatless diet, as well as hygiene and brotherly love. Elder Frederick's example at Mount Lebanon was followed by two other noted members there, Elder Daniel Fraser (1804–89) and Elder Daniel Offord (1844–1911), noted chemist and inventor respectively. These men were both strict vegetarians, whose study of dietetics led them to experiment with a milk diet. Let the life spans of these men speak for their success: Evans, 84; Offord, 67; and Fraser, 85. The influence of men like these was evident in Shaker kitchens. Many Shaker recipe books included sections on such meatless dishes as Chestnut Omelet or Lentil Loaf, as well as cheese, egg, and rice dishes.

None of these men felt it was his right to impose his own preference on any other Shaker, however. Even during the time when some chose a vegetable diet, there were tables set for meat eaters along with tables for the abstainers. For example, in 1873 three young Brethren at Sabbathday Lake "commenced to live on a vegetable diet. Abstinence from all flesh meats butter cheese and grease. Tea coffee and all stimulating drinks. So the Elders permit them to occupy a square by themselves at the table." (One of the young Brothers, William Dumont, later became an Elder there and lived to the ripe old age of seventy-eight—no doubt thanks in part to his healthful diet.)

The only meat really entirely banned from 1848 to the 1870s was pork, a sensible health measure since pork improperly prepared can be a dangerous source of disease. Elder Daniel Fraser was also ahead of his time in stressing that grinding the whole wheat grain produced flour superior in nutritional value to superfine white flour. He disapproved of using white flour, an "ignorant and very wasteful habit," because it wasted most of the grain, and the nutritionally important part at that.

No matter what the diet, however, the food was delicious and simple. Shakers were emphatically not bread-and-water ascetics. In fact, the food was so good and so plentiful that members who liked to eat were in danger of blackening their souls with gluttony while filling their middles with the tempting stuff. Anyone who has ever fought the battle of the bulge will look with awe on Brother Abijah Worster, whose strength of will enabled him to control his appetite successfully for thirty years. When he was eighty-one, he wrote with justifiable satisfaction,

> And considering a gluttonous appetite as a voracious propensity of nature, which ought not to be indulged, I set out to crucify it, by taking as much food as in my judgment was sufficient for a laboring man, and no more.... And tho I have not felt the sensation of hunger for more than thirty years; yet my food relishes well, and I never feel straitened in eating and drinking whatever I find needful for my health, strength or comfort; nor do I feel the least temptation to go beyond. This is my victory in this one point; and this victory neither men nor devils can take from me.

Nor even Shaker cooks! Brother Abijah's victory would be admirable in any case, but his ability to resist good Shaker cooking should have made him eligible for sainthood.

For those with less determination than Brother Abijah, little jingles served as gentle reminders for moderation:

> *The glutton's a seat in which evil can work,*
> *And in hoggish nature diseases will lurk:*
> *By faith and good works we can all overcome,*
> *And starve the old glutton until he is done.*

The Gospel Monitor, the Shaker guide for raising children, written in 1843, advised the children's Caretakers to "not stuff them with victuals. They had much better leave the table hungry, than to eat one mouthful more than is needful." The Shakers also had a rule that members had to clean their plates; in some parts of the country "Shaker your plate" still means "finish the contents." Those with eyes bigger than their stomachs learned soon enough to be moderate.

Moderation and abstinence were also key words as far as alcohol was concerned. The Shakers' disapproval of strong drink reflected the attitude of their founder. Sister Hannah Cogswell and other early Shakers who had known Mother Ann personally swore that she made

Kitchen Sisters made dough in enormous batches every morning for their daily bread, measuring flour according to a precise recipe. Dough for forty loaves could rise in this tin dough box, nearly a yard long. Shakers were quick to disapprove of superfine white flour, preferring whole grain flours. (Canterbury, N.H.)

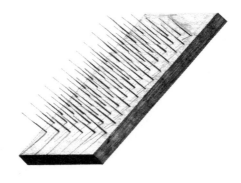

Shakers were among the first to develop the pill form of medicine, more convenient than old-fashioned powders. A few large pins and a piece of wood were the simple requirements for this "pill dryer." Six dozen laxative pills at a time were dipped into a coating solution and then dried on the spikes.

"but very little use of spirituous liquors, and that only as a medicine." Shakers ever after followed the lead of their Mother—medicinal purposes were the only justifiable reasons for making whiskey or wine in a Shaker village. Old medical recipe journals included concoctions that called for any amount from a gill of gin (a gill is a quarter of a pint) in a cure for dropsy, to a recipe beginning, "To thirty gallons of whiskey add three lbs. of barks" et cetera. (This "tonic," as it was called, was "to be given in any debilitated state when there is a general weakness of the system and weak nerves, it is also good for poison &c." It must have worked wonders, since the recipe made a barrel at a time.) If other safe pain relievers or anaesthetics had been available at the time, no doubt Shakers would gladly have given up spirits altogether.

As the nineteenth century passed, the Shakers' disapproval of rum, brandy, whiskey, and so on, grew as Americans in general began to brandish Bibles (or hatchets, like Carrie Nation) in the war against the Devil and his drink. The Kentucky Shakers, who had been distilling whiskey, put away their stills when it became clear that their spirits would be better off if they stopped making spirits of the liquid sort. Even cider was treated with caution, in the days before chemical preservatives. Its tendency to "improve" with age made it one of the rare things Shakers felt necessary to lock up, mostly to prevent hired help or outsiders from enjoying it too freely. Said the *Millennial Laws,* "Cider if it is kept at all, should be secured by locks; and kept under the charge of the Deacon, or some trusty person appointed for that purpose."

As usual, the Shakers made exceptions for elderly Shakers who appreciated a little homemade wine now and then for health reasons. One of the dangers of alcohol that was most feared was less likely to affect the older members, anyway:

> *Inebriation, we allow,*
> *First paved the way for am'rous deeds;*
> *Then why should poisonous spirits now*
> *Be ranked among our common needs?*

For ordinary members, however, who might suffer temptation, carelessness, or sluggishness as a result of imbibing, the "pernicious stuff" was strictly discouraged:

Why, then, should any soul insist
On such pernicious, pois'nous stuff?
Malignant spirits, you're dismissed!
You have possessed us long enough.

The Shakers were as self-sufficient as they could be in medicine as in all other occupations. Their success was impressive, but not really surprising. The converts who made up a Shaker village came from all professions and brought all manner of skills with them. There were stonecutters, carpenters, weavers—and doctors and dentists. Besides, doctoring in the last century was much more a matter of the common sense home remedy than years of study in medical schools. The materials for making medicines were nearly all available on the Shakers' own property, and Shakers were always encouraged to experiment with new ideas.

Their famous patent medicine industry began in the 1820s and continued successfully for nearly a century with nothing but commendation for their well-known preparations such as Healolene, which was made from quinces at Mount Lebanon and used as a hand lotion. Villages like Mount Lebanon, Canterbury, and Union Village, Ohio, had extensive botanic gardens for their industries.

Many of the original Shaker settlers got valuable herbal lore from the local Indians. One such mixture, a "Diet drink or Medical Beer" (nonalcoholic) called for "Meadow fern, White pine bark, Balsam bark, Evan root, Yellow Dock, Burdock, Comfrey Wintergreen, Balm of Gilead, Hemlock boughs, Spruce, Smellage, and Rheubarb." To their store of information about the medicinal properties of wild plants, Shakers added common wisdom about the benefits of cultivated herbs.

One of the most successful Shaker pharmacists was Brother Thomas Corbett (1780–1857) of Canterbury, mentioned earlier as the designer of the electrostatic rheumatism cure. (He was a particularly gifted Shaker who also built clocks and, in 1822, the village fire engine—with a twenty-four-man crew, it could throw a stream of water 60 feet.) One of his contributions to the medical world was the "Re-Improved Rocking Truss," single, double, or umbilical, and "adapted to all ages and sexes; for the relief and permanent cure of Hernia, or Rupture."

This beautifully grained wooden mortar and pestle ground dried herbs into powdered medicinal ingredients. The first commercially available Shaker remedies dated as early as the 1820s. (Canterbury, N.H.)

Another was Corbett's Shakers' Sarsaparilla, a well-known commercially sold panacea, which according to the label soothed the pangs of "Diseases of the Kidneys, Liver, Bladder, Skin and Blood, Scrofula or King's Evil, Scrofulous Swellings or Sores, Cancerous Ulcers, Canker and Canker Humor, Salt Rheum, Syphilitic Humors, Erypsipelas, Dropsy, Scurvy, White Swellings, Gout, Gravel, Rheumatism, Neuralgia, Palpitation of the Heart, Female Weakness, General Debility, Fever and Ague, Loss of Appetite, Nervousness and Emaciation." Claims like this often represented in later years the optimistic outlook of city business agents, who were perhaps carried away a little by their enthusiasm for the Shaker product. Contemporary Worldly remedies were even more extravagantly touted, while often depending to a dangerous extent on opiates to deaden pains and cares.

The Shakers' herbal medicines, made from many natural ingredients with the traditional standards of perfection and precision, were certainly highly recommended by leading physicians and pharmacists. According to countless testimonies by satisfied customers, Shaker medicines—the common sense remedies of the folk tradition raised a giant step in scientific and scrupulously hygienic preparation—worked. Food and Drug Act standards, which forced plenty of quacks out of the business, approved Shaker remedies like Shakers' Toothache Pills in 1906 wholeheartedly. The consistently healthy appearance of the Shakers themselves testifies as well as anything to the quality of their medicines.

The extent and importance of this business to the Shaker livelihood was evident in their large and professionally equipped herb shops. In 1869, the herb shop at Mount Lebanon—one of the largest and most important—was

an extensive establishment conducted on scientific principles. The Machinery is driven by an oscillating Engine, the exhaust steam being used for drying herbs, warming the house and heating water &c. They use coal for fuel and have a patent drying kiln for drying herbs, and a hydraulic press for pressing them. Altogether it is a valuable Institution.

The Infirmary, staffed by the most knowledgeable Sisters and Brothers, was another valuable institution and standard feature of

Opposite: A typical Shaker Infirmary was efficient and neat. The hospital bed from Mount Lebanon could tilt the patient to a comfortable angle with wooden cams at feet and head. An electrostatic "cure," on the right, was also from Mount Lebanon; when not in use, its domed lid kept out dust and prevented shocks. In back, a Sister carries a porcelain "feeder" (not Shaker-made) to an elderly patient in the adult cradle from Harvard, Massachusetts. Brother Thomas Corbett of Canterbury stands before the beautifully organized built-in drawers of the Medicine Room in his Infirmary (1811).

almost every Shaker community. The confidence that one Brother felt in the Shaker Infirmary when he visited Mount Lebanon in 1869 is typical. He wrote, "The Infirmary came next, and that is the most perfect model of neatness and convenience for the comfort and restoration of patients that I have ever seen. It would seem like a mere entrance into this heartsome place, might render a patient convalescent." He certainly had good reason for his enthusiasm.

The Infirmary was well stocked with medicines, beds, instruments, and know-how, so that most ailments could be handled successfully by the self-sufficient Shakers themselves. The Shakers even performed surgery on occasion. In 1852, at Watervliet, Ohio, one Brother

> witnessed a surgical operation performed upon a young man for stone in the bladder. He was put under the influence of Chloriform so he was not concious of the operation, or of suffering any pain, quite a successful performance. The stone was about the size of a small walnut and as hard as a limestone. He came to conciousness in about 10 minutes after the performance.

The patient made a full recovery.

Shaker dentists like Elder Henry Blinn of Canterbury and Brother Nelson Chase of Enfield, New Hampshire, pulled teeth in their fully equipped "Dentist shops" and were successful in making false teeth. (Brother Nelson was also the inventor of the folding pocket stereoscope.)

When very serious ailments occurred, however, the Shaker physicians did not value self-sufficiency above life itself, and other doctors were called in if the Shakers felt they had done all they could. Elder Daniel Boler recorded that this is what happened in Whitewater, Ohio, when "Elder Rufus" took very sick there in 1852. Shaker physicians cared for him for the first day; but when it was evident that he grew no better, "it was generally thot best to call in a neighboring physician a friendly man."

Elder Rufus died very soon anyway, despite the care. Some Shaker communities were self-sufficient to the point of doing their own undertaking, like the Shakers at Canterbury. In the third floor of the Infirmary there still remain built-in drawers and cupboards labeled neatly, "Home Undertaking." The plain wooden coffins were made next door in the upper floor of the Carriage House.

Besides being a place of rest and rehabilitation for the ill, the Infirmary also housed feeble or elderly members who found it too difficult to move around the village. With help and a loving hand always nearby, and with special menus prepared and served to them there, some members spent their last days in the Infirmary, assured of quiet and the continual care they might need. Special potty chairs were installed to prevent long walks or chills. Some of the communities even had adult-sized cradles to rock the extremely weak to comfortable rest. The Canterbury Infirmary had another convenient piece of equipment, "a splendid Rocking Chair of exquisite arrangement . . . you can lie down, or sit up just as you feel to; It is turned into a bed or a chair at pleasure by the aid of a little Machinery."

In general, the Infirmary was so well run and so conducive to health that members were warned against mistaking ordinary doldrums for real illness. Those tempted by treatment like breakfast in bed or the rocking chair-bed were warned not to be "Old Slugs":

A little cold or aching head
Will send him grunting to his bed,
And he'll pretend he's sick or sore,

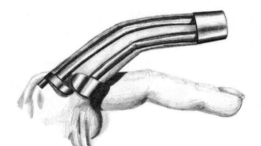

Top left: Tin bedpan, easily emptied through the handle-spout when the cork stopper was pulled. Top right: A regulated funnel could measure precise amounts of powdered ingredients because a long screw turned into the hole to diminish its diameter. Pharmacists could use both hands for their work, since the funnel hung on the container by its hook. Above: A heat-retaining soapstone bedwarmer, wrapped in cloth, forerunner of our hot-water bottle. Center: A finger splint slipped over a bandaged finger, protecting it and holding it rigid. Right: The dentist's chair from Enfield, New Hampshire, was as beautiful as it was useful—finely constructed with wooden pegs, its wooden screw knob (detail) suited the headrest to each patient.

Just that he may indulge the more.
Nor would it feel much like a crime
If he should sleep one half his time.

Despite the respect and care the Shakers had for their bodies, in the final analysis the flesh was still a force to be overcome in the battle for salvation. Mother Ann, astonished when two prospective converts told her that they believed in the immortality of the body, told them:

Look at yourselves; you carry about you all the marks of mortality that are on other people. Your skins are wrinkled; your hair is turning white and falling from your heads; your eye-sight is failing; you are losing your teeth, and your bodies are growing decrepid. How inconsistent it is for you to think you shall never die! These natural bodies must all die and turn to dust.

Shakers had no interest in physical resurrection, either. It seemed neither possible, reasonable, nor fair to their practical minds:

Shall the humpback, and the cripple,
And the dwarf, diseased and lame,
Take their bodies, somewhat bettered,
But essentially the same?

They could not believe in a return to the flesh that they had battled so hard to overcome on the way to salvation.

A healthy body for its own sake was not the goal of the Shakers; it was simply the means to a spiritual goal:

Health, priceless health, a boon from heaven wrought.
In sacred writ, we learn that God made man
In his unblemished image, strong and whole,
But sin, usurping power, has marred the plan,
Destroying even beauty of the soul.
But God has yet dominion, and we can
Through righteousness, regain the perfect goal.

People who think of Shakerism as a dusty relic of the nineteenth century—quaint and interesting, like a velocipede, and about as relevant to twentieth-century life—might have second thoughts when they begin to understand how the Shakers operated their economy. The remarkable success story of the American Shakers would have made Horatio Alger himself sit up and take notes. For so long the Shakers have typified good old-fashioned American success with their magnificent farms and large comfortable homes that it's difficult to imagine a time when being a Shaker meant hardship, uncertainty, and even hunger. The nine immigrants who brought their faith to America had no neat, prosperous communities to settle into; early converts were not moved to join by the prospects of a secure, comfortable existence. Far from it—Mother Ann and her followers endured miserable squalor; she worked as a washerwoman who at one point had nothing in her cupboard but vinegar, the story goes. The early members in most of the villages proved that man does not live by bread alone, since they went for days without it.

They were cramped, they were hungry—and they were determined to match the spiritual bounty of their faith with homes that provided their simple needs in comfort and security.

The Shakers' success in rising permanently from the lean years of the 1770s to the 1790s was evident in the huge barns they built and the beautiful lands they tilled. But even more important, a century later in the 1870s and 1880s, Shakers kept their heads and maintained a level of simple comfort when contemporary Victorians were smitten with guilt in our nation's first love affair with conspicuous consumption. That they continued with prudence when they could have afforded a grander way of life is still more impressive.

Of course, it would be silly to suggest that a nation of several hundred million dyed-in-the-wool capitalists should run its economy like communities of several hundred people who believed in sharing everything in common ownership. But in our age of shortages of fuel, ore, and even land, clean air, and water, it would do us all good to see how a group of thrifty people based a successful economy for two hundred years on a simple but valuable bit of advice: Waste not, want not. If we all, like the Shakers, had consistently felt it necessary to "observe good economy; to use the things of the world as not abusing them; to be prudent and saving, and let nothing be lost or

A small wooden tool with metal teeth split long planed shavings of poplar into even strips which Sisters wove on hand looms into "poplar cloth" for covering boxes. In the 1870s, Granville Merrill of Sabbathday Lake, a progressive Brother, invented a small steam-powered splitter.

wasted through carelessness or neglect," we might not now be faced with such a long trip back to prudence.

The Shakers felt it was wrong to waste anything—be it time, space, talent, or anything they raised, picked, made, or used. They appreciated the value of seemingly trivial things, taking care of the pence and sensibly letting the pounds take care of themselves, as the saying goes. Shakers were also ingenious at getting as much use from anything—a field, a building, or a man—as possible, by recycling or adapting to a new use.

The Shakers' reasons for thrift weren't just practical ones, however. They appreciated their homes and their bodies, but realized that these were just temporarily theirs. A Shaker didn't feel he had the right to treat anything as if it were made just for his own use or abuse; as one member put it, "We ought not to call our own, a brute, bird, tree, or plant, that God has created; for he never intended his creation should be devoted to selfish and mean purposes." He also felt that he had no right to waste what was really not his, be it his health, his time, or the food on his plate. The Shaker didn't waste a thing because it was contrary to God's purpose. Waste was not just impractical, it was spiritually wrong. The Shakers were "only stewards upon God's heritage," wrote one Elder. He continued, "Therefore, if we were extravagant or wasted any useful thing, it was a loss to the Consecrated interest and in proportion to its value would prove a spiritual loss to our souls."

The Shaker's appreciation of the value of little things was summed up best in his motto, "Trifles make perfection, but perfection itself is no trifle." Since perfection was his goal, he valued every small thing, no matter how insignificant it might seem. He taught the children he raised, "Never pass carelessly by a pin, needle, nail, bits of thread, cloth, pewter, tin, iron or any thing of the like, without picking it up and saving it, or putting it in some suitable place to be used."

He based his daily behavior, his manners, his work, and even his attitude toward the aged according to this principle. In typical Shaker fashion, he practiced down-to-earth thrift for practical and spiritual reasons. Whatever was good for his soul was bound to be good for his way of life all around: according to the *Millennial Laws,* "No one should carelessly pass over small things, as a pin, a kernel of grain, etc.

thinking it too small to pick up, for if we do, our Heavenly Father will consider us too small for him to bestow his blessing upon."

Mother Ann's words of wisdom, as usual, provided the Shakers with their spiritual and practical reasons for choosing thrift as an ideal. She urged her followers to recognize the worth of even a single kernel of grain, saying, "You must be prudent and saving of every good thing that God blesses you with, that you may give it to the needy. You could not make either a kernel of grain or a spear of grass grow, if you knew you must die for the want of it . . . without the blessing of God." A careful effort to save grain made good farming sense to the first generation of Shakers, who faced real hunger during the difficult early years. The reason it continued to make sense when the Shakers became prosperous was because it made spiritual sense just as clearly, when the result of thrift was a profit which could be given charitably. Advice from the *Youth's Guide* (1842) shows that Mother Ann's words were never forgotten: "Prudence provides stores for charity to give to the poor, clothes to cover them, and food to sustain them." Even the children were taught by *The Gospel Monitor:* "Never throw any thing into the fire that has the least morsel of nourishment in it, or that is good for any creature to eat."

Father James Whittaker, who succeeded Mother Ann as the leader of the faith, likewise told the Shakers to appreciate the value of seemingly insignificant or useless growing things. He said, "God has caused it to grow, and you ought to be careful to save it." The Shakers, who practiced what they preached, did just that when they found a use for the poplar tree. Most woodworkers thought that poplar was inferior as a furniture wood because it splits and warps so easily; it doesn't even make good firewood. But the Shakers felt that since God had seen fit to plant so much of the stuff in Maine and New Hampshire, He must have had some good reason in mind. So they found that they could make it into useful workboxes. Brothers shaved and shredded the wood when it was frozen in the winter; then Sisters wove the poplar strips into "cloth" to cover sewing and utility boxes. Everyone knows that the best way to show thanks for a gift is to use it; the Shakers thought that God who gave all gifts deserved that kind of thanks, too.

The same spirit for using "useless" plants resulted in the small sweet-grass baskets that the Canterbury Shakers learned how to make

Poplar sewing baskets—made of a "useless" wood—were a favorite sales item in the nineteenth and twentieth centuries. Satin-lined and kid-bound boxes came in sizes from 6 inches by 4 inches (at $1.40) to 10 inches by 7 inches (at $2.50)—1908 prices, that is. Bows weren't just for "fancy"—tied inside the box were a tomato-shaped pincushion, poplar needlebook, beeswax cake, and strawberry emery. (Canterbury, N.H.)

Shaker applesauce, made from dried apples cooked in boiled-down cider, sold by the buckets at Canterbury in the nineteenth century. Sisters prepared the sauce; Brothers made wooden tubs and printed labels. Unlike today's disposable containers, the sturdy tubs had many uses when the applesauce was gone. (Canterbury, N.H.)

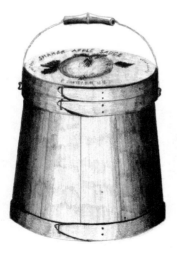

from local Indians, or the medicines from the barks of evergreen trees. The ability to look at anything and dream up a use for it takes considerable imagination and effort, but how much easier it is when you're convinced that even a weed has a definite purpose since God thought it fit to put on earth. With their hearts put to God and their hands put to work, Shakers put everything else under the sun to good use.

Feeling as they did that perfection was the result of attention to trifles, the Shakers refused to make, use, or sell anything that had any flaw, no matter how slight. One Shaker oval box was never finished because of a tiny crack in the end of one "finger" joint. In spite of all the work that had already gone into it, the Shaker who made it felt that it was more of a waste to make an imperfect box than it was to abandon it.

Shaker-raised and packaged seeds were so highly regarded that they were guaranteed not to be adulterated with even a single non-Shaker seed. Shaker apple pickers snapped each apple off at the stem, then gently lowered it into the basket. If a large perfect apple dropped just once, it was no good; although the bruise was invisible, in time it would rot and waste the whole barrel. Even Shaker cider was better because the Shakers refused to use anything but perfect apples.

The Shaker didn't waste any small opportunity to make his work perfect, and he felt just as strongly that any small job done right was a blessing to the community. One reason that aged members continued to lead happy and useful lives was that their efforts, no matter how slight, were deeply appreciated by the rest of the Family. Elderly members didn't sit uselessly; they simply adapted from hard work to hand work. Brother Josiah Corbett of Canterbury, who died in 1833 at the age of seventy-five, was praised for his devotion to such "trifles" as common household pins: "When he was quite aged and unable to be employed in laborious work, he would do little household chores for the Sisters, even to the repointing of needles, and making servicable, with pliers, the headless pins." He renewed his ability to serve the Family while he renewed the life of the pins—neither the man's willingness to work, nor the pins, were wasted. Brother Josiah never knew what it was like to be old and "useless"; quite literally, he took to heart the Shaker motto, "You must give all to them, to a pin's value."

The Shakers refused to use assembly-line methods for the same reason that Brother Josiah's efforts were appreciated: quality counted more than quantity, were it in chair production or a man's ability to produce. A Shaker carpenter built the whole desk or chair, he didn't just turn out spindles or knobs all day.

In every way, the Shakers appreciated quality over quantity; they measured a man by the stature of his soul, not the length of his legs. Brother David Bowley of New Lebanon was little in size, but his worth was as great as his soul:

> *With satisfaction I will state*
> *To you his statue [sic] and his weight*
> *Four feet & eleven inches; found*
> *Was his higth, and eighty six pounds*
> *In heft was all that he excelled*
> *Is truly strange for one to tell*
> *Tho small, he was a kind brother*
> *We can't forget him Nay never*
> *With ease I could say much in praise*
> *For he was faithful all his days.*

The Shakers didn't waste a chance to do a good deed, no matter how slight, any more than they wasted a chance to make something right. Guidebooks of rules for good manners and proper behavior were popular and encouraged them to appreciate any kindness done by following the example set by Mother Ann and the earliest Shakers. After the persecution they had suffered in England and America, no wonder Mother Ann and her followers "would show respect and gratitude for the smallest favors. For instance, if any one picked up a pocket handkerchief for them, or the like, they would turn around and thank the person, in a very respectful manner."

The Shakers knew how important even minor actions could be. Elder Henry Blinn of Canterbury wrote in a guide to "gentle manners," "As the loss of a small pin in a machine may render the whole useless, so the neglect of a small duty may prove our ruin!" If prudent, a Shaker would take care to avoid "the small beginnings" of crime and sin, since those "who would steal from an orchard, cheat their companions, or make false returns when sent on errands," were bound to wind up at best as "pilfering clerks in pecuniary want and

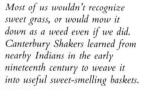

Most of us wouldn't recognize sweet grass, or would mow it down as a weed even if we did. Canterbury Shakers learned from nearby Indians in the early nineteenth century to weave it into useful sweet-smelling baskets.

One of America's beloved institutions, the rocking chair, was often created when some handyman added rockers to a plain straight chair. Chairs with short runners are called "suicide rockers"—if you don't teeter gently like a Shaker, you can land on your head! Short runners were practical in Shaker rooms, since the chairs could still hang from wall pegs. This rare tiger maple chair of majestic proportions was adapted from a "suicide" model to a standard one, with finely beveled extension rockers.

with a ruined reputation!" Let us hope the lesson was as memorable as Elder Henry's alliteration. The whole purpose of such advice was the same for everyday manners as it was for everyday work. If waste and loss were sins, then the waste and loss of human souls were the greatest sins of all.

Another general way of avoiding waste was to get as much out of anything as possible. A look at the efforts of these early believers in recycling could teach us a few lessons in economizing. God said, "Behold, I make all things new"; Shakers took Him at His word and tried to do the same, never throwing out what could possibly be put to continued use.

As usual, the Shakers' reasons were a blend of ordinary common sense and a feeling of spiritual fitness. Father James Whittaker always told the Shakers to "remember this thing and lay it up: don't ever throw yourselves away, though you be fallen ever so low,—it is never too late to cry to God." It was of the highest importance to the Shakers that a human being could be saved from destruction and restored by accepting the godly life. The spiritual renewal of Shaker souls was reflected in the practical renewal through recycling of the things they made and used.

One way they recycled was by replacing worn parts instead of throwing out the whole. In a chair, for example, the seat often wears out first. One of a flurry of inspirational messages in the 1840s (which the Shakers considered to be direct communication from heaven) advised that "plain chairs, with splint bottoms are preferable to any other kind, because they can be mended when they break." If the decision to use splint seats, practical in itself, furthermore came on such good heavenly authority, so much the better reason for using them.

Another way the Shakers recycled was to adapt something from one outmoded use to another, better one. Take again the example of a chair. If a low-backed chair did not suit, Shakers added a special two-slat device which could be attached to make an "instant" high-backed chair. All kinds of furniture were adapted from one use to another; sometimes a chest or chair was even adapted to suit a particular member. In 1840, Brother Henry DeWitt of New Lebanon noted in his journal that "it was thought best for me to leave South garret and go down below in Levi's shop, and take the wheel business accordingly I did, and fix over Levi's old work bench and put some drawers under it."

Buildings were also adapted for changing uses. At New Lebanon in 1839, Daniel Boler and several hired men worked "at the underpining of the old hatters shop, intending it for a school house." As reverent as the Shakers felt toward the old Meetinghouse at New Lebanon, which had been raised by Brother Moses Johnson in 1785, it nevertheless became a herb house when the newer Meetinghouse was built in 1822–4.

The Shakers at Canterbury enlarged their Schoolhouse in 1862 from a one-room to a full two-storey building, in a remarkable kind of recycling. Most people add the second storey to a one-floor building by raising the roof and adding it above ... but not the Canterbury Shakers! The Schoolhouse is one of the few buildings in New England with a second storey older (by about forty years) than the bottom storey. In 1823, when it was built originally, a one-room building was big enough. By 1862, however, it was too small and considered to be too far from the Church Family. The Shakers moved it closer to the village; then felt that as long as the room was up off its foundation, it was less trouble to jack up the building and add four walls below than it was to raise the roof and build another gable end. When we outgrow our schools, we tear them down and build anew ... maybe we can all still learn a lesson about thrift in the Canterbury Schoolhouse.

Often buildings were moved to a different part of the village if they could be more useful there; this happened frequently as membership in the villages declined. One sister remarked that the buildings ought to have been on wheels, they were moved so often. Even the buildings that the Shakers tore down were not simply destroyed, however. Rather than let them stand and decay, the Shakers carefully dismantled them and made good use of the nails, glass, and lumber. The Sabbathday Lake Shakers took down "two old Barns" in 1873 and then recycled the timbers into a "shed to put Lumber in at the Mill."

The opportunities for recycling and adaptive use were everywhere in any New England or frontier village; it was only the fact that the Shakers took extraordinarily imaginative advantage of these oppor-

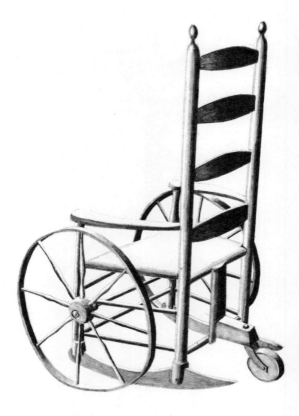

This early rocking chair from Watervliet, New York, was given new life and use as a wheelchair by the addition of side wheels and a small wheel behind that allowed the chair to adjust to different angles. (Old Chatham, N.Y.)

Shakers adapted an old yarn reel into a mop winder by cutting down the spokes. Sisters wound loops of yarn around the top reel to make distinctive Shaker "looped" mops. A clock dial on the side originally measured skein yardage; graceful finial atop resembles chair finials, and was useful as a handle. (Canterbury, N.H.)

Opposite: Built originally in 1823 as a one-room Schoolhouse, the Canterbury Schoolhouse was moved closer to the Church Family in 1862. Shakers then raised the whole building 12 feet and added four walls underneath to make a second room—one of few "upside down" buildings in New England. At right, they added stairs, a woodshed, a cloakroom, and an indoor three-holer privy. The school remained in use until 1934—proof that "waste not" measures saved time and cost.

tunities which makes their Yankee ingenuity legendary. As illustrations in all these chapters show, living together as an independent community provided quick-witted Brothers and Sisters with unlimited chances to practice thrift. They brought as converts all the skills they had learned in the World; when they freed themselves spiritually from the World, however, they also freed themselves from the World's conventional methods and experimented with ways that could and did turn out to be more efficient and more thrifty.

The kitchen was, naturally, where the Sisters' thrifty ways made the leftover a thing to be carefully rescued and resurrected into a glorious new life; a good example was a dish from Shirley, Massachusetts, honestly called "Second Day Chicken." Saving that chicken meant avoiding waste—and that meant saving their souls. Sisters cooked leftover meat and vegetables into hearty soups and stews. An old recipe from North Union, Ohio, showed how even stale bread scraps could lead a new life under the more glamorous guise of "scalloping crumbs":

> Put all bread crusts and fragments of stale bread in the oven until they are thoroughly dry. Then roll them to a coarse powder with the rolling pin. This crumb is far better in scalloping foods than cracker crumbs which are tasteless and too floury.

Even the water used to boil vegetables was carefully saved and used as nutritious "pot-likker" in soups.

Shaker dining habits were likewise opposed to waste. No one is more frugal than a New Englander, but to Mother Ann even these saving folks could stand room for improvement. She told them, "You New-England people are very wasteful; you ought to pick your bones clean, and be more saving and prudent; you must save all, and let nothing be lost through your carelessness, that you may have something to give to the needy."

Those who shared food with the Shakers were expected to observe the same rules. Because visitors often shared meals with the Shaker Family, "table monitors" in verse were hung right on the dining room wall:

> *What we deem good order,*
> *We're willing to state—*

> *Eat hearty and decent,*
> *And clear out our plate.*

Visitors to Canterbury were even handed a printed reminder by Sister Hannah Bronson during the nineteenth century:

> *We find of those bounties which heaven does give,*
> *That some live to eat, and that some eat to live.*
> *That some think of nothing but pleasing the taste,*
> *And care very little how much they do waste.*

No doubt advice like this meant that the guests Shakered their plates, too, although Shaker cooking was so good it's hard to imagine anyone being prompted to finish it up!

The Brothers were just as thrifty in their farm work as the Sisters were in the kitchens. They adapted the corn crop, for instance, to every possible use. Kernels were used as food or dried and fed to the stock; husks were used to stuff mattresses; and cobs were burned as fuel or used for smoking meats. When the Shakers began making flat brooms for sale in the earliest years of the nineteenth century, the broom corn crop did double duty. The fibers were good for brooms, and the grain was good for flour. In fact, there was only one use for corn that the Shakers didn't put to advantage—that was whiskey. A

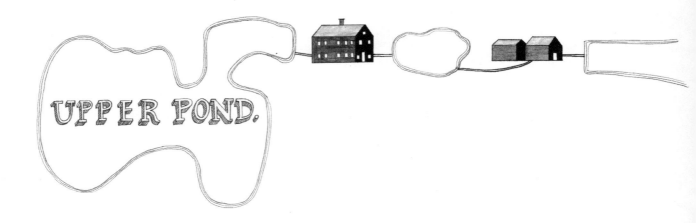

Shaker Brother traveling through Ohio in 1837 was disgusted when he saw a good corn crop going to waste in the stuff: "Three of these cribs were full of ears of corn, perhaps 200 waggon loads in each. This of course is all to be made into whiskey, to gratify the worse than beastly appetite of the intemperate, while thousands are suffering for the want of food. This is surely an incontestable evidence of the depravity of the human race," he concluded.

Farm animals were not only productive in their own right, they also used up anything that might have gone to waste. Pigs ate the whey from the dairies; the Shakers had "a sow for every cow" to eat up anything left. On his visit to Ohio in 1873, Elder Henry Blinn of Canterbury approved of the thrifty feeding time there: "Elder Cephas took time to give the horses their dinner. For this purpose he had brought a bag full of corn on the cob." Elder Henry watched with interest as Elder Cephas poured out a half bushel of cobs onto the ground and concluded that giving the horses "the privilege to shell their own corn," as he put it, was a mighty smart timesaver. The only thing that bothered him was that the horses were not able to eat all the kernels—until he saw that "four or five little pigs were on hand to secure their share of the corn. These little scavengers were ready to secure every kernel that was left by the horses." Satisfied that nothing went to waste, Elder Henry concluded that "in Ohio economy is studied as well so they think only in another form."

One of the greatest recycling achievements of the Shakers was the way they made the most of their water sources. The pond system at Canterbury, developed from a swampy stretch of ground good for nothing but raising mosquitoes, was a marvel of environmental engi-

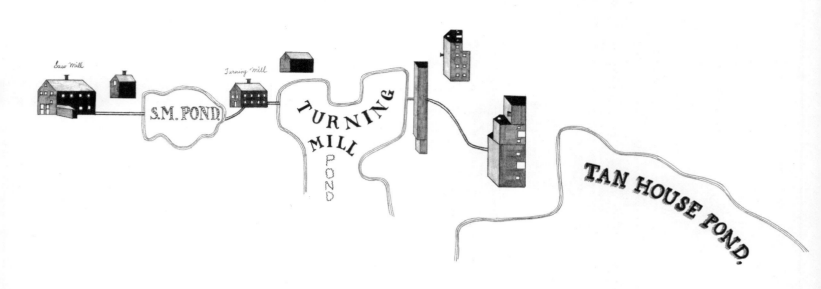

Canterbury Shakers ingeniously and thriftily cycled one stream through five man-made ponds to turn the wheels of five different mills. (From an 1848 map by Elder Henry Blinn)

neering. Before 1840 the Brothers had dug out five manmade ponds, connected with a stream, and built a mill on each pond; the same water flowed down and turned the wheels of the five different mills. In 1847 a visitor wrote, "There is a small stream of water on the east side of the village, the Church [Family] have 5 ponds on it and a building at each pond. The first pond,—Tan works and cloth dressing. 2^d wood sawing. 3^d Mashine Shop; 4th Grist mill and Saw Mill. 5th carding and grinding herbs."

A Shaker visitor marveled in 1850 that at the Canterbury cloth mill, "Spool, warp weave, double and twist, quill and knit" were all run by water power. Shaker use of water was so efficient that other farmers in the area said Shaker water wasn't any good when they were done with it because it was all worn out. The Shakers at nearby Enfield were even more thrifty with the use of water power. Hervey Elkins wrote in 1853,

No where do the elements assist more in the performance of labor than among the Shakers. The sisters weave, wash, press and iron their clothes, churn, knit shirts and drawers and sew by water; and when I left, a brother was making a machine for rolling pastry. The brethren saw and plane lumber, thresh grain, shell garden seeds and corn, saw fire-wood, &c., by the same power.

The Shakers' rightful appreciation of the usefulness of water was so great that we can almost hear the wistful tone of Brother William Deming, who visited Ohio in 1810 and wrote, "Went to a Cave which was 40 feet deep & water enough Running through it at the bottom to turn any kind of mill." Obviously the thought of all that water power wasted at the bottom of a cave tugged at his thrifty Shaker heart.

Not only were buildings, crops, and streams adapted to many uses—so were the Shakers themselves. On an average of every four weeks or so Brothers would alternate turns at different jobs—for example, smithing, farming, tailoring, and carpentry—while Sisters shared turns in the laundry, kitchen, gardens, sewing shop, and so on. Brother Henry DeWitt of New Lebanon wrote in 1827,

Jan. 31   My work is so often changed; it is hard to give a true statement of it.

> *Sometimes a fixing spinning wheels,*
> *At other times to work at reels;—*
> *If I should mention all I do,*
> *My time and paper would be few.*

Brother Isaac Youngs, whose "history in verse" provided colorful insight in the chapter on Time, had his own opinion of job rotation:

> *I've always found enough to do*
> *Some pleasant times, some grievous too*
> *Of various kinds of work I've had*
> *Enough to make me sour or sad,*
> *Of tayl'ring, Join'ring, farming too,*
> *Almost all kinds that are to do,*
> *Blacksmithing, Tinkering, Mason work,*
> *When could I find a time to shurk?*
> *Clock work, Jenny work, keeping school*
> *Enough to puzzle any fool!*
> *An endless list of chores & notions,*
> *To keep me in perpetual motion.*

Job rotation was a smart move for many reasons. For one thing, it kept the Shakers from being bored at their work: no one ever had to do the same thing day in, day out. For another thing, it made self-sufficiency a reachable goal. When, for example, a blacksmith died or left, there were always other Brothers who knew the trade to take over right away. It gave the members the chance to learn many skills and the satisfaction of doing a number of things well; even more important, the Shaker felt that he was showing his thanks to God for

Opposite: An ingenious tin paint can saved time and tempers. Workers wiped their brushes against the inner lip to keep paint from dribbling down the outside; the brush stayed in the can during breaks because the lid fitted snugly over the handle. Best of all, Shakers painting ceilings didn't wind up with arms covered with paint: because the brush was held in the lid, drips collected in the lid instead. (Canterbury, N.H.)
Thrifty Shakers saved horsehairs to weave sieves, like the one below, for sifting paint powders.

the gift of talents by using them all. But most important of all, job rotation eliminated envy in the village. Since everyone had to share the "grievous" jobs, too, whether scouring floors for the Sisters or shoveling manure for the Brothers, no one could complain of in-equality in a society based on brotherly love.

A *Manual of Good Manners* written in 1844 stated plainly, "Always be willing to take your share of the disagreeable chores." Even the Elders and Eldresses and other leaders put their hands to work at all of the jobs in the village. Shaker visitors to Canterbury noted in 1854 that the Ministry there worked "at Tayloring." Often members who were being considered for leadership were deliberately assigned menial jobs, to see if they had enough humility to become great. According to records of all the skills possessed by the Shaker leaders, it seems that their willingness to work hard at every kind of job was one reason they were considered especially fit for leadership.

As the Shakers saw it, the members with the greatest abilities were obviously most favored by God because they weren't wasting their God-given talents. Mother Ann said, "If you improve in one talent, God will give you more." The accomplishments of Shakers like Elder Giles Avery (1815–90) of Mount Lebanon proved that he believed in "Waste not, want not" as far as skills were concerned. In his later years he tallied up his occupations—notice that his hard work contin-ued *after* he became an Elder:

> At twenty-five years of age I was appointed to the Order of Elders, as an assistant with Elder Amos Stewart. My manual employment was the repairing of buildings, digging cellars for foundations, stone masonry, sawing stone for a new dwelling, plumbing, carpentering and plastering. I had some experience at cabinet work and wagon making, and even made wooden dippers. I took an interest in orcharding; trimmed and grafted many hundreds of old apple trees; and prepared cisterns for holding liquid manure for fertilizing.

He continued,

> Evenings were passed in keeping a family diary, writing copies of anthems, hymns and songs, which originated in our Societies, amounting to some thousands. Besides writing for myself, I did

considerable copying for the singers. I also copied a book on music of about two hundred octavo pages, memorized its rules, and learned all the tunes and songs, given as examples of rules and modes.

When Elder Giles was out plowing, he didn't even waste a moment when the team was resting, but "frequently wrote a song on the plough beam."

Hervey L. Eads (1807–92) of South Union, Kentucky, was another Shaker who didn't waste his time or talent. He could make shoes, drive a team, raise seeds, make a pair of trousers, bind books, card wool, spin, whitesmith, fix teeth, print, make hats, and write for publication—all in addition to his duties as an Elder.

If we ordinary mortals can stand one more example, Elder Henry Blinn was the most active of the three. He wrote books, printed them, bound them, surveyed land, kept bees, blacksmithed, printed the Shaker newspaper, made furniture and boxes, worked as a dentist, made false teeth, kept night watch, sawed staves for pails, carved gravestones and Canterbury's holy stone, worked on the farm, carded wool, taught school, made paint and painted the Meetinghouse in 1878, braided whips—and in his spare time planted the now magnificent sugar maples in the Meetinghouse lane and the first arboretum in New Hampshire in 1886. Behind the Schoolhouse grew all the trees native to the area, so children could learn them first-hand at recess; he even had time to play marble games with the children he loved so much.

One of the nicest accomplishments of Elder Henry, though, was his sense of humor. Despite the fact that he hated dishonesty, he managed to find some wry humor when he was cheated by the porter on his trip to Kentucky in 1873. On June 17, he wrote,

> Leave Louisville at 6 o'clock A.M. having paid $3.50 for our supper, lodging & breakfast, & then paid the porter 50 cts for telling a lie. He gave us to understand that our trunk would be all right when it reached the cars, but the baggage man who took the trunk to the Depot demanded of us 25 cts more & then said the porter deceived us. The lie may have been cheap after all. We have bought printed lies & paid dearly for them, but in that case we had the paper to sell again!

Always the thrifty Shaker, Elder Henry naturally thought of recycling the paper. Indeed, the Canterbury Shakers saved all paper scraps and made their own cardboard boxes.

Elder or youth, quick or slow, everyone worked together according to, and to improve, his talents. No one was too old or too young to be of real help to the family. Children from an early age were taught simple chores: girls stitched and stirred, boys hammered and hoed. When Eldress Nancy Moore of South Union, Kentucky, visited Enfield, New Hampshire, in 1854, she approvingly wrote, "While visiting the brethren shops we saw in the Taylors room a boy of eleven years. He commenced to learn the trade at five years old has been in the shop six years and is quite expert with the needle."

The little girls' Caretaker Sister Catherine Damph of Watervliet, Ohio, noted in 1845 that eight girls from age four to twelve in one year:

    Wove 14 yds of towel loops
        ″   180 yds of Carpet bindings
    spooled 260 runs of yarn
    bordered 40 nets
    knit   10
    made   17 shifts
       ″   4 proper aprons
            7 checked aprons
           27 collar
            5 peticoats
          19 gounds
        sleaved 12
    knit   11 pair stockings
    footed 4 pair
    made 13 waistcoats
          10 pocket handkerchief
         two nightcaps
    foulded the close and ironed every week
    knit   22 pair of sail footings
    bottomed 15 chair with list and bindings

—All this besides innumerable chores, their mending, working in the kitchen, tending to their school lessons, went to school three months and a half.

Shakers practiced thrift with scrap paper by recycling it into pasteboard boxes, like the one opposite. The Gospel Monitor *taught: "Never burn up the least bit of cloth or thread that would be useful, for anything, or that would make paper." Glue-soaked layers dried to a sturdy shell on wooden forms that were sometimes plain blocks, sometimes shaped like this miniature trunk, below. One box had layers of newspapers, letters, medicine labels—even a page from an old diary. (Canterbury, N.H.)*

Even recess at school wasn't wasted when the weather was too bad for playing outside. The children put their hands to knitting or whittling, no doubt glad to have a break from arithmetic or spelling.

But no matter how versatile each member was, the Shakers never forgot that it took a community of people working together to make their way of life a success, and work together they did to make good use of their time, talent, and buildings and land. Always thrifty, Shakers didn't waste a thing—and found their saving ways a fitting method of thanking God for all his help. After all, hadn't God sent a Saviour to save them all? They saved bits of string and kernels of corn, but they knew that in the end the greatest thing that could be saved was a soul.

Elder Frederick Evans of Mount Lebanon felt that even death couldn't stop a Shaker from being of some good use. According to Elder Frederick, he could just adapt himself to a new use, and in his last act of thrift recycle all that he had left—himself. Elder Frederick always thought it would be appropriate to have "a tree planted by every grave, that thus death should lose its sting, the grave its victory over the living, and the fear of death be supplanted by a spirit of rejoicing." And besides, he felt that it was only right to return the favor of life to the earth: "Each human being, having been comforted and benefited by the scenery thus furnished while living, would add to earth's fertility and beauty by the deposit of a body for which he no longer had any use."

For over a century, one simple stone inscribed "Shakers" has marked the graves of nearly five hundred members in the Canterbury Cemetery. Believers agreed that carving and maintaining individual headstones was a waste of time. More important, they felt that one stone for all continued the communal spirit, even in rest. Because they couldn't abide waste, however, Shakers found a new use for their used headstones: turned upside down, they made dandy dripstones under the eaves of buildings to prevent mud from splashing when it rained. Visitors can still see them today. (Canterbury, N.H.)

Honesty

The late nineteenth century deserved its title, The Gilded Age. It could just as well have been tagged The Decades of Deception, considering the amount of trouble people took in order to make everything look like something else: painted "marble," stucco "gold," "flowers" made of human hair, phony mahogany graining—and last but hardly least, the bustle. When Hervey Elkins left the Shakers in Enfield, New Hampshire, he reacted with disgust to the pretentious artificiality of the outside World after a life with the simple and honest Shakers. In the cities he found

> bonnets and hats, manufactured from straw, said to have been grown in India; but which were probably made from an inferior rye straw, grown on Cape Cod; colored glass, set in gilded tinsel, sold at exorbitant prices for precious gems; paste-board hats, covered with a glossily napped cotton for the genuine beavers; galvanized watches, warranted to be pure gold, for only one hundred dollars.

In a way, the pretensions of Victorian furnishings and fashions epitomized the Victorians themselves. Nineteenth-century Americans longed for the magnificence of an ancient aristocratic past—and settled for the trappings and tinsel of grandeur. In one sense, their desire to disguise reads like discontentment with the World the way it really was: and indeed the Victorians did their best to pretend that certain facts of life simply did not exist. Women, poor creatures, weren't even allowed the possession of legs—they had "limbs" instead. On a more somber note, the artificiality of the era's fashions suggests the sweet icing of morality that often disguised a Devil's food of corruption below.

All this is not to say that our century has behaved much better, just because we prefer the fake rustic to the fake ornate. After all, it took twentieth-century technology (and taste) to transform the honest wooden ceiling beam—necessary for centuries to support the timber frame house—into plastic foam "decorator beams," hand-hewn look and all, that glue onto a ceiling perfectly capable of supporting itself. Fake brick, fake electric "candlelight," even (God forgive us) fake "old wavy glass" will reveal as much about us to the twenty-first century as Roman villas in New England and Great-Grandma's bustle tell us about the nineteenth.

On the whole, however, the twentieth century has shown a refreshing honesty in its architecture and design. We've come a long way from the turn of the century. The bad names that concrete and plastic had for years were no real fault of the materials themselves, which can be very good looking in their own way; they were the result of our own former misuse of them. Now that we realize that concrete should look and act like concrete and not imitate stone, the material takes on a new dignity. We are beginning to appreciate plastics for their own beauty, instead of forcing them to imitate wood, leather, flowers, or ivory. Artists and architects demand honesty in the relation of the design to the materials used.

Small wonder, then, that the fullest appreciation of the Shaker style of furniture and architecture has developed only in the recent past. Few Victorian visitors could appreciate the simplicity and honesty that characterized the Shaker environment. No marbling, no gilding, no graining, no *trompe l'oeuil*—nothing but honest plaster, honest wood, and honest labor.

The Shakers, unlike modern designers, were not concerned with honesty of construction from the standpoint of a stylistic creed. The honesty of their work was based on another, more permanent creed—their faith in God. The Shaker demanded honesty in the work of his heart and his soul; his demand for honesty in the work of his hands was just another expression of total spiritual honesty.

The Shakers' insistence on truthfulness as an ideal to be put into practice every day when they put their hands to work was, like most Shaker ideals, a way of life from the earliest days. The Shaker life meant sacrifice, something that other religions did not really demand. After all, becoming a Shaker meant giving up marriage and a family of one's own; it meant giving up all property to share in common with others; and it meant the discipline to sacrifice the self for the good of all. It was a faith that required its believers to give, rather than take; and members were expected to give all.

Shakers had to have a conviction of the truth of their way of life strong enough to balance the demands it made of them. Convincing newcomers in Mother Ann's time that her teachings were indeed the Truth with a capital T was the most crucial task that faced the early Believers. Mother Ann's visions and her remarkable insight into human nature convinced the superstitious, suspicious, or just plain skeptical that she had powers decidedly greater than natural and probably downright diabolical.

Besides, the early Shakers' worship must have seemed strange and frightening to onlookers: they whirled, leaped, shook, and shouted in religious agony or joy (in Harvard, they could be heard for two miles on a clear night).

Early converts like Sister Prudence Hammond needed considerable conviction to face accusations of blasphemy and witchcraft. In 1827, she stated firmly, "I found no deception or witchcraft here—nothing but the plain and honest truth ..." The conviction that Shakerism was the honest truth attracted and sustained thousands of members during the two hundred years of Shakerism in America. In spite of the gradual decline in numbers that became evident in the late nineteenth century, the members who remained never lost their faith. When a Sister was asked in 1880 whether the shrinking membership bothered her, she said "with great fervor and earnestness, that was nothing to her; she would still be a Shaker if there were only one more in the world, as the number did not alter the truth."

Convinced as they were that their way was the truth, the Shakers demanded total honesty in every part of that way: in their confession of sins; in the quality of the things that they made, used, and sold; and in their refusal to lie. Their complete devotion to honesty made the community a haven of trust. Shaker villages had no jails and no stocks. Shaker desks and boxes rarely had locks because they just weren't necessary. A section of the *Millennial Laws* entitled "Orders concerning Locks & Keys" specified that only "public stores" and "Cider if it is kept at all" were to be secured under lock and key. Locks were forbidden on possessions, and they were not to be used in the Dwellinghouse at all. The last rule in the section sums up the Shakers' attitude toward honesty best: "It is desirable to have all so trustworthy, that locks and keys will be needless."

The personal honesty of each member was a major part of Shaker spiritual instruction. *The Gospel Monitor* advised the children's Caretakers to teach them truthfulness by themselves being always truthful: "Never make promises to little children that you cannot fulfill, according to your word." Mother Ann's most devoted disciple and successor, Father James Whittaker, emphasized from the beginning the importance of being honest, saying, "Be what you seem to be, and

The hay fork, above, is a single piece of wood split and held open with curved wooden bows. Opposite: A wooden rake from Canterbury. In 1800, "Rakes were made and the stales of these were all made by hand with a plane. The bows were planed out square and then tenoned into the heads." (Canterbury, N.H.)

Instead of painting or graining, Shaker craftsmen let the honest beauty of tiger maple—and fine workmanship—shine through plain varnish. This chest was made c. 1880 at North Union, Ohio.
(Old Chatham, N.Y.)

seem to be what you really are. Don't carry two faces. You that dare use deceit, remember what I say: God will yet meet you in a strait place."

Father James's warning applied to Shaker business and craftsmanship as much as it did to Shaker souls. Elder Giles Avery of Mount Lebanon called the "dressing" of plain pine furniture "with the veneering of bay wood, mahogany or rose wood" out-and-out sinful deception, just as cheating was. Veneered Shaker pieces are almost totally unknown. To the Shaker, it was clear that honesty in the workshop was as vital as honesty in the Meetinghouse or in confession. Deception was deception, whether in veneering or in lying—and according to the *Youth's Guide* a sure way to the Devil: "Deception is the inroad of Satan, and leadeth many vices into the soul of man. Let no sin enter thy spirit upon this path."

Most Shaker furniture is unpainted, since even paint and varnish were suspect as disguises for poor workmanship. Semitransparent stains were often used, if color was used at all. An entire section of the *Millennial Laws*—"Concerning Building, Painting, Varnishing and the Manufacture of Articles for Sale, &c. &c."—was devoted to rules about paint: "Oval or nice boxes may be stained reddish or yellow, but not varnished." The floors in the Dwellinghouse, "if stained at all," were to be "of a reddish yellow, and shop floors should be of a yellowish red." Artificial wood graining was, of course, entirely discouraged. When Elder Henry Blinn of Canterbury visited the Dwellinghouse at North Union, Ohio, in 1873, he noted with disapproval the "improvements" Victorian Shakers had made there: "One part of the house has been repainted & is in striking contrast with that which is left. Some of the doors were grained, others had drab pannels & pink trimmings. Some of the wood work was marbled."

Shaker gardeners were just as careful to avoid deception in the quality or quantity of the seeds that they raised, packaged, and sold. To guarantee the quality, the Shakers of Hancock, Massachusetts, and New Lebanon and Watervliet, New York, made this agreement in 1819:

We, the undersigned, having for sometime past felt a concern, lest there should come loss upon the joint interest, and dishonor upon the gospel, by purchasing seeds of the world, and mixing them with ours for sale; and having duly considered the matter, we are confident that it is best to leave off the practice, and we do hereby covenant and agree that we will not, hereafter, put up, or sell, any seeds to the world which are not raised among believers (excepting melon seeds).

That the Shakers considered the practice of mixing seeds not only bad business but actual "dishonor upon the gospel" is good evidence how important they felt it was to practice what they preached.

To make complete honesty a real part of their way of life, the Shakers were careful to take in members who sought a better way or who needed a good home, instead of scroungers who were trying to escape the responsibilities of Worldly debts. Converts had to fairly settle all personal debts before the Shakers would accept them.

The Shakers themselves from the time of Mother Ann avoided debts to the World as they did the Devil. Certainly Mother Ann and her followers could have relied on charity to help them through the first difficult years—if they had been willing to give up their independence. They chose to work, instead: Mother Ann as a washerwoman, her disciple Father James Whittaker as a weaver, and her brother William Lee as a blacksmith.

Shakers after that chose to rely on their own efforts so completely that, according to the *Millennial Laws,* it was "contrary to order" to "borrow money among the world" or even to "go without money among the world," for fear the need to borrow might arise. It was especially important for the Trustees, who represented the Shaker community in dealings with the business world, to "avoid running into debt with the world."

This iron-bound firewood carrier made at New Lebanon, New York, is typical of Shaker honesty in design and construction. (Hancock, Mass.)

The practice of confession to the spiritual leaders (Elders for the men and Eldresses for the women) was as important for spiritual honesty as pure ingredients and honest labor were for honesty in business. Full confession was the very first step a new member took as the beginning of his Shaker life and a regular part of his life after that. The *Millennial Laws* stated: "All who ignorantly, carelessly, or willfully break the sacred orders of the gospel, are required to confess the same in the line of order. . . ." A hymn from 1833 called "The Last Woe" spelled out the dire consequences of neglecting confession:

And a woe to the liar—he is doom'd to the fire,
Until all his dark lies are confess'd—
Till he honestly tell, what a spirit from hell
Had its impious seat in his breast.

The spirit of one-for-all and all-for-one in a Shaker village made every member more aware of his duty to be honest. As a visitor observed in 1875, the Shaker village was "not a comfortable place for hypocrites or pretenders." As a sign of their general honesty, the Shakers did not have a court system in their villages, neither judge nor jury. Members who were not living up to Shaker ideals were corrected by their Elders or Eldresses, and if they persisted in their wrongs, they were welcomed to take their leave.

The Shakers had such confidence in their ability to make honesty a daily part of their lives that they did not make any kind of oath or feel it necessary to swear to something for a special occasion. According to Elder Frederick Evans, oaths were simply unnecessary because Shakers told the truth all the time: "the simple *word of a Believer* is of the same force as the *oath of a worldly, Gentile Christian,* Catholic or Protestant."

Honest in their work, in their words, in their hearts—the Shakers put their ideal into practice. George Budinger, one of the last children to grow up in the village at North Union, Ohio (near Cleveland), remembered even in his eighties the way of life he'd known as a boy: "You haven't got an organization in the world—or at least in Cleveland that I do know—that are as honest, and preach and do what they preach." The influence of his Shaker boyhood shines in his words: determined to stay strictly within the limits of truth, he amended his claim to Cleveland instead of the World!

In 1869, Shakers at Enfield, New Hampshire, were "coopering, making a substantial article of Tubs & buckets of pine timber (none of your swiveled up trash)." Smaller buckets like this were useful and beautiful, ornamented naturally with contrasting woods. (Canterbury, N.H.)

Permanence

In 1774, Mother Ann Lee and her small group of eight followers crossed the Atlantic to escape persecution in England, having suffered beatings, imprisonment, and humiliation at the hands of mobs. The insecurity of the existence they left behind was more than matched by the tossing of their ship on the stormy sea and the uncertainty of the days to come. After all, they knew no one in the colonies; they had nothing but their hands to put to work; and they had no assurance that persecution would not await them in America, too. As time proved, it did, and the years ahead were often as difficult as the years in England.

Yet their faith never wavered. The confidence Mother Ann felt in the success of her mission had a fitting symbol in her vision of two angels, calming the waves, during the worst point of the voyage. Inspired by the example of Mother Ann's steadfast faith, the determination of the early converts to build homes that would stand forever is evident in the Shaker villages that stand today. They hewed and set wood, brick, sandstone, and granite into homes and shops that defy the attempts of time, weather, or man to bring them down. The feeling of permanence—in the eternal truths of their faith and in the homes and furnishings they built and used—became a characteristic of the Shaker way of life. The buildings they made, the everyday things they used, and the faith they believed in were all designed to last. Most important, they felt that their way of life was going to last forever, and that the Shaker spirit would endure for a millennium. Even the Shaker people themselves seemed to be "built to last"; life spans of 70, 80, and 90 were so common that it seems if the Shakers couldn't quite achieve eternity on earth, they came as close as humanly possible. Eldress Dorothy Durgin (1825–98) spoke for all Shakers with her "one interest at heart" . . . for her, building a home meant "Building for Eternity."

The Shakers chose permanence as an ideal for practical and spiritual reasons. They tried to imitate the way of God by making their villages as nearly like their notion of heaven as they could. If the city of heaven were eternal, then the Shaker village as "the external body of a true Christian church" should be the nearest thing to eternal as was possible on earth. Both figuratively and literally, the Shakers were interested in sound unshakable foundations to sustain a permanent success.

Top: The permanence that Shakers sought is symbolized by steps at the Canterbury Dwellinghouse, carved from a single enormous block of granite by Brother Micajah Tucker—who worked at stonecutting into his seventies. Over a half-dozen such steps remain in the village, each as durable as the Rock of Ages. Also pictured, dry-laid granite fences like this one were solidly built of huge chunks of stone, nearly a yard across. Canterbury Shakers constructed their wooden fences, opposite, on granite bases to prevent the wood from rotting.

One part of their spiritual bedrock was the eternal nature of God Himself and of the soul in heaven. If the Word of God stood forever, then so would Shakerism. Another eternal principle, the oneness with God that each member felt, was a firm foundation for their faith. Elder Frederick Evans spoke for all members when he called revelation "from a Christ Spirit in each individual" the rock that was "the true foundation of the Shaker Church." The visionary experience of the spiritual world that Mother Ann had of angels at the helm was indeed fundamental to the Shaker faith. The inspirational dancing of Shaker worship; the messages from the spiritual world through Shaker members under inspiration as go-betweens; and the spirit drawings, inspirational hymns, and even book-length writings done while under the influence of the holy spirit all testify to the importance of revelation as a basis for their faith.

But the Shakers were a unique blend of intense spiritualism and the most down-to-earth common sense. Important as these spiritual revelations were, the real challenge of the Shaker life was to put all the ideals they held into daily practice. To provide a firm foundation for the everyday life of the Shakers, Elder Frederick added that *"Well-defined fixed principles,"* which were "perfectly understood and cordially received by all the members," were the foundation of the Shaker government. "Fixed principles" such as celibacy and shared property were basic Shaker spiritual requirements that ensured the most perfect unity with God.

Other fixed principles like charity, patience, and industry provided the basis for unity among the Shakers themselves. Elder Henry Blinn of Canterbury called for fixed principles, without which, he said, "We are left like a ship upon the ocean without a pilot or a rudder, and subject to be dashed upon the rocks." Considering the way the original Shakers made it to this side of the ocean, he chose a fitting metaphor.

The success the Shakers had in maintaining their spiritual foundations is clear from the words of a nineteenth-century visitor, who wrote that "it was their boast that they were the same in their habits and manners as they were sixty years before." It was not that the Shakers opposed progress—on the contrary, they believed wholeheartedly in it; it was just that they thought their ideals, like the perfection they sought in their manners and morals, were too permanent to need change. John Partington, one of the original group that followed Mother Ann to America, said that "God of Heaven has laid the foundation." The Shakers, after two centuries, still believe this; the Golden Rule still has meaning, after two thousand years.

The unshakability of the Believers' spiritual foundations was matched by the solidity of their actual physical foundations: the buildings themselves were built to last for centuries. A visitor to the North Family at Mount Lebanon wrote in 1880 about the "solidity and durability" of everything he saw. He concluded in admiration, "Their walls seem laid as if for all time . . ." His description could have as well suited any of the buildings in the other villages, for example, the new Dwellinghouse at Union Village, Ohio, built in 1847. This was of brick, and covered with slate, "a very durable, plain and handsome house." The villages in Maine and New Hampshire used granite dug from their lands; Western Shakers used their native sandstone.

One of the most impressive buildings must have been a mill at North Union, Ohio, described in 1852 by Elder Daniel Boler of New Lebanon:

> The mill is built adjoining a summit of solid rock, rising almost perpendicular about 40 feet. . . . Their floom [sic] or penstock is a curious piece of architecture. It is hewn out of the solid rock on 3 sides, and the front is built up with solid hewn stone, with the two ends dove tailed into the rock to prevent it from bursting out. The penstock rises perpendicular with the cliff nearly 50 feet. A thorough piece of work it is, and as durable as the rock of ages.

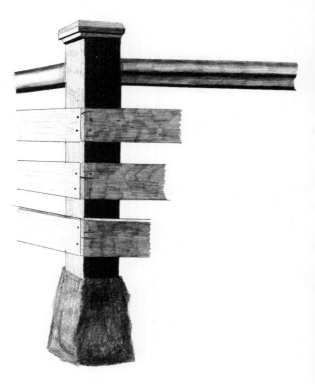

As durable as the rock of ages . . . an ideal put literally into practice.

The fact that so little remains of the nineteen Shaker villages which once stood so solidly is sadly ironic. The buildings came down not through decay, but for the most part through the decision of the Shakers themselves to take down buildings that their shrinking numbers could no longer use or maintain. Always practical, the Shakers felt that they could save on taxes with fewer buildings; they also felt that it was better to take down buildings which they couldn't keep in repair, rather than see their neat, well-built homes become shabby ghost towns. Sometimes the buildings were sold to outsiders for the bricks, wood, stone, and so forth. To make sure that the purchasers would take down the whole building instead of stripping off the valuable wood and leaving an ugly shell, the Shakers at Canterbury set time limits on the razing and required that the entire building be demolished. Often the men who bought the buildings found themselves wishing the Shakers hadn't built quite so solidly. One man found that inside what he thought was a simple clapboard structure was a solid wall of insulation brick.

The Shakers' reasons for building a home and a way of life that would last forever were not the usual ones that people have for trying to make a kind of immortality for themselves. Nothing was further from their intentions than the pride that makes a man buy the biggest marble monument he can find for his tomb. For one thing, they lived as a community and tried to devote their lives to the good of all. Anonymity was a Shaker ideal—they didn't even believe in signing their works for the praise of future ages. Instead of building monuments to their own memory on earth, they built living communities to foster lives of devotion and love to God and man, not only for themselves but for those who were to follow them. "Believers ought to be faithful with their hands, & give their hearts to God, & lay a foundation in temporal things for those who come after, or succeed us &c," wrote one member in 1837.

The graveyards at Canterbury and Sabbathday Lake today each have one simple monument labeled "Shakers" to serve as the only

The Dwellinghouse (1837) at Enfield, New Hampshire, was built to last forever. The solid granite blocks are "laid as if for all time."

stone for all the Shakers buried there. What you notice when you visit a Shaker village is the enduring nature of the buildings and shops; you may not even be aware that a cemetery exists, without the individual headstones that in most graveyards mark the only kind of permanent record most of us will ever leave.

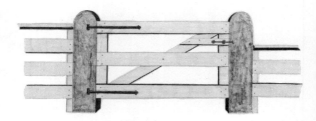

Another wooden fence at Canterbury on granite posts; note the hand-forged hardware.

Besides demanding sturdy foundations, Shakers also felt that things should be able to withstand constant use. This held true for their faith and for the things they made and used. Elder Frederick Evans said in 1859 of the Shaker way of life that "instead of attending *solely* to his *spiritual* necessities for only *one day in seven*, IT cares for and supplies all his *temporal* as well as *spiritual* wants *seven days in the week*." This meant that their faith had to be sturdy enough and practical enough to work all the time, not just for a brief hour weekly.

No wonder the Shakers made sure that all the things they made were as sturdy and practical for hard use. Since they felt that their earthly home was a visible reflection of the inner spirit, permanence in the things they saw meant that the Shaker spirit was enduring well. Virtually everything illustrated in this book is in beautiful condition today because all these things were built to last.

One of the reasons the Shakers' things lasted so well is because they took good care of them. The fact that nothing really belonged to the individual to use or abuse, but to the Family as a whole, increased the respect the members had for the things they lived with. In 1854, a visitor to Enfield, New Hampshire, described the condition of the ovens in the kitchen there, saying, "They have two soap stone ovens here which will bake bread all day if they are well heated in the morning. They have been in use 13 years, and look now like they were not more than a year old."

Another visitor in 1875 commented on the floor of the assembly hall in the Dwellinghouse at Mount Lebanon. It was so "astonishingly bright and clean" that he imagined it had been recently laid. He was amazed to learn that it had been used for twenty-nine years and had only been scrubbed twice. But, as he found out, it was "swept and polished daily; and the Brethren wear to the meetings shoes made particularly for those occasions, which are without nails or pegs in the soles, and of soft leather," so they wouldn't mark the floor. He added that they had invented many such "tricks of housekeeping."

To keep the Sisters' woven palm bonnets from crushing while on the road, Shakers at New Lebanon made a sturdy pine bonnet box—in effect, a portable section of the handy Shaker pegboard wall, packaged to go.

Another such trick, according to the *Millennial Laws,* was the way the Shakers walked on their stairs:

> When brethren and sisters go up and down stairs, they should not slip their feet on the carpet, or floor but lift them up and set them down plumb, so as not to wear out the carpets or floor unnecessarily. Also when they turn at the head or foot of the stairs, they should not turn their feet on the floor, lest they wear holes in it.

Even when tilting back in their chairs, the Shakers took pains "to prevent wear and tear of carpets and marking of floors" by adding tilting buttons or swivel feet to the hind legs. Brother G. O. Donnell of New Lebanon patented this metal device in 1852; other tilters were made of wood.

The concern for built-in permanence characterized every step of an operation, from the bottom up—sometimes literally. The Meetinghouse at Canterbury, for example, built in 1792, would make a good earthly counterpart to the biblical house built on the rock: the solid granite foundations are just as secure. The way Father Job Bishop of Canterbury described his faith could as well have described the actual Meetinghouse where he and his fellow Brothers and Sisters met every Sunday: "But the truth prevails, and the foundation of the Church remains unshaken; the revelation, on which it is built, is sure and stedfast, and never can fail."

Good foundations were only the first step, however. Inside the Canterbury Meetinghouse, the blue paint on the wooden pegboards and ceiling beams is another marvel of planned permanence. It has been repainted only twice since the Meetinghouse was built in 1792. The last coat has lasted about a century without peeling or cracking. The earlier coat from 1815 would have lasted just as well (so would the original 1792 coat which is in perfect condition upstairs), but Elder Henry Blinn and the Shakers preferred a lighter shade of blue and so repainted it in 1878. The Sabbathday Lake Meetinghouse takes the endurance prize, however. It still has the original coat of lovely dark blue paint inside on the trim since the year it was built, 1793. The Shakers felt that when they did something, it was worth doing once and for all.

The goods such as chairs that Shakers sold to the World had to show the same resistance to wear and tear. First of all, the wood was seasoned for months properly to ensure permanent soundness. Experience taught the carpenters how much wood they could remove as unnecessary weight, while retaining all the strength that was needed. The slats on the back were pegged in with wooden pegs, which couldn't rust out as nails would.

The result was a sturdy chair which looked so light and graceful that skeptical buyers often couldn't believe such slim and delicate legs could really support a large rump. The chairs were actually so strong that an *Illustrated Catalogue and Price List* prepared for the 1876 Centennial Exposition in Philadelphia, where the Shakers had an exhibit, included this guarantee: "Our largest chairs do not weigh over ten pounds, and the smallest weigh less than five pounds, and yet the largest person can feel safe in sitting down in them without fear of going through them." Time has not bowed the legs or bent the backs of these wonderful chairs; we should all stand as straight and strong when we pass the century mark.

The solid structure of Shaker-made items like these plain sturdy chairs was more important to the Shaker craftsman than useless frills which only camouflaged shoddy construction. Because they didn't rely on ornament for the appeal of their furniture, they didn't waste time on fleeting styles. Said the Shakers, "All beauty that has not a foundation in use, soon grows distasteful, and needs continual replacement with something new." The Shakers were free to develop a single simple style and then refine and perfect it infinitely. And because the things they made were not designed to suit a passing fancy, but to suit their needs forever without "continual replacement," they were also built to last forever. Brother Isaac Youngs, the clockmaker, knew that for his work as much as for his fellow man, more was necessary than just a pretty face. On the back of one of his clocks he wrote,

O where shall I my fortune find
When this shall cease to measure time?

The care that went into the things they sold was one reason the Shakers felt that patenting wasn't necessary. They reasoned that anybody with a jot of common sense would simply prefer Shaker-made items because they lasted longer. As the Shakers put it, the Worldly

Some Shaker baskets have lids permanently attached to their handles; large ones were called feather baskets, since they prevented down collected for pillows from blowing away. (Canterbury, N.H.)

copies of their work, which might have "looked like their goods before being used" but proved themselves lacking in the long run, "came to an end of their usefulness much sooner."

In spite of the satisfaction of the Shakers in their business success, their real motive was not financial profit. Instead, the Shakers told themselves to "seek the durable riches, and bid adieu to the unprofitable things of time." Having risen from poverty (but not of the spirit), they well knew how uncertain were the fortunes of this World. The true permanence they sought lay in another realm. As Brother Benjamin Youngs of Watervliet, New York, said, "The principal motive, desire, and labour, of the children of this world, is to gain a temporal interest.... But the principal motive, desire, and labour, of the people of God, is to *lay up a treasure in heaven.*"

One can't help but feel that the Shakers' love of permanence played a significant part in the remarkable longevity that distinguished Shaker communities. They valued durability more than disposability, so age took on a new dignity.

Maybe it is hard for us today in the "paper cup culture" of planned obsolescence to appreciate how different the Shakers' environment was. Everything that makes ours the era of the "youth cult" simply played no part in the Shaker world. For one thing, the Shakers' general refusal to adapt themselves periodically to new fashions resulted in a timeless quality to the village itself. No Shaker had to watch as old chairs or tables were stuck away in an attic or dumped during redecorating; the Shakers didn't redecorate. The tables and chairs were as useful when they were seventy-five as when they were new—and so were the Shakers who used them.

For another thing, celibacy meant people were not bothered that growing old would lessen their attractiveness or worth as human beings. Even if an older Sister had wanted to, she couldn't have imitated the style of the younger girls—young and old dressed alike. The generation gap was minimized, since the fixed principles of Shakerism made the social and moral standards of young and old identical. It is significant that the most respected members of the village, the spiritual leaders, were called Elder and Eldress, no matter how young they were. The greatest value in a Shaker community was associated with the wisdom that can come with age.

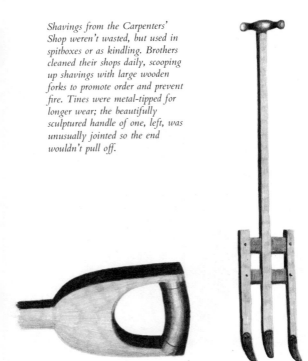

Shavings from the Carpenters' Shop weren't wasted, but used in spitboxes or as kindling. Brothers cleaned their shops daily, scooping up shavings with large wooden forks to promote order and prevent fire. Tines were metal-tipped for longer wear; the beautifully sculptured handle of one, left, was unusually jointed so the end wouldn't pull off.

Most important, the Shaker home was meant to be permanent. That meant more than granite blocks or solid beams—it meant that when a person chose the Shaker way, that home was his for life. In a way that most people today find no longer possible or desirable, the aged member remained with the Family: this was his rightful place, there was always room for him, and most of all there were always younger Brothers and Sisters to love him and make him feel needed.

Whatever the reasons, the fact is that Shakers lived long lives. Too many reached their eighties and nineties for the reasons to be mere coincidence. Accounts of spry and lively elderly fill the pages of old journals. There was Elder John Lyon of Enfield, New Hampshire, who continued to preach at seventy-four and who still had "the pith of the matter in him." Elder Frederick Evans of Mount Lebanon, at age eighty, was "still bent on reforming the world"; while brother Joseph Dyer, also of Enfield, New Hampshire, at eighty-three was content to spend his energy reforming the weeds in his watermelon patch. Elder Joseph Brackett of Sabbathday Lake at seventy-six was found plowing his garden, "which is the first ploughing done this season"; two years later, he was squiring four Sisters to the village at Alfred, Maine, a good day's journey by covered carriage—"Pretty smart business for an old man in the 78th year of his age."

One of the most remarkable was perhaps an Elder at Enfield, New Hampshire, in the middle of the nineteenth century, whom the younger Brother Hervey Elkins revered. Even though Hervey later left the Shakers, he wrote,

> Never shall I forget the neatness, the industry, and the economy of that aged father. He arose every morning, at the signal of a little alarm clock, ever kept in his room, one hour before the rest of the family. He built all the kitchen fires, and rang the large bell, the signal for general rising. He then resorted to his work-shop, a large room in a cream colored building, where he manufactured pails, and commenced his daily labor. How often have I seen him, before breakfast, his white locks floating in the breeze, drawing a light hand cart manufactured by himself, containing staves, from the machine shop, where he had previously planed and grooved them.

The long lives of members like these has always fascinated those

Love to lay a good foundation,
In the line of outward things.
    —Shaker hymn

The Meetinghouse fence at Canterbury is a good example of "outward things" literally laid on a good foundation. In the Shaker tradition, the fence stood with granite feet firmly on the ground, while the wooden pickets soared to a heavenly goal. Since the wood is supported above wet ground, it has remained rot-free and without replacement since the 1840s.

Sturdy "fingers" on heavy-duty woodenware like the canteen, top, and piggin or dry measure, bottom, were interwoven for greater durability.

who knew them. A hundred years ago, observers like Charles Nordhoff (the journalist who visited American communal societies) noted that the average life span of Shakers at that time ranged from sixty years to well into the seventies—at least a decade and more often twenty years over the national average at the time.

A particularly interesting study of Shaker longevity was done by Eldress Mary Antoinette Doolittle (1810–86) of Mount Lebanon, who herself lived to be seventy-six. In the autobiography she wrote when she was seventy, she figured that nearly seventy per cent of the Shakers who had died there during her life as a Shaker had been over seventy years of age. Out of the five hundred or so members who had passed away during that time, 123 were over seventy; 125 over eighty; and 123 over ninety. There was even one Sister, still living, who was 104 and who wanted to live at least another year so she could say she'd spent one hundred years as a Shaker—she'd been brought to the Family when she was only five years old.

The Shakers had their own ideas about why they lived longer. They took good physical care of themselves, especially as they aged. Older members ate special diets, if need be, and took exercise. Long years of sensible hours, hard work, fresh air, and abstinence from tobacco and alcohol also made their benefits known.

According to Shakers, celibacy was not only good for the soul, it was better for the body, too. They said of their spiritual kind of love that "Shaker love never grows old or cold, but is new every day." Not only was this kind of love permanent and rejuvenating spiritually—it was considered actually physically rejuvenating. In an article entitled "Celibacy: Its Relation to Longevity, and As an Essential to Divine Life," written in 1880, Elder Daniel Fraser of Mount Lebanon at age seventy-six declared, "The vital statistics of our Order show that those who from youth and upward live a virgin life average greater length of years" than ordinary people. When the Shakers looked at celibacy in this light, as a guarantee for eternal spiritual life and as a good chance for a long earthly life, it made all the more spiritual and common sense.

The Shakers knew that it was just as important for an aged Brother or Sister to keep up a healthy outlook on life as it was to maintain his healthy habits. Shakers *wanted* to live longer. They never retired at an arbitrary age, regardless of their capabilities, but worked right along with the younger members. One of countless typical members was Brother Moses Gage of Enfield, New Hampshire. An admiring younger member, Eldress Nancy Moore of South Union, Kentucky, wrote in 1854: "He was 84 years old yesterday. He is very much afflicted in his bowels, yet he is all the time engaged at some hand labor, such as braiding or other light setting work. He is a very interesting person; Is very much alive in the spirit and power of the Gospel."

Eldress Nancy was typical of Shakers in respecting older members of the village for their years of work and worship. Shaker rules for good manners advised young members to "always respect and reverence the aged" and "never laugh at them, nor mock them." Eldress Nancy, who herself reached the age of eighty-two, wrote in the same diary that a visit with the elderly Brothers at Canterbury was actually the high point of her day, instead of a tiresome duty. She said,

> The next & most interesting part of our days visit, was an interview we had with the aged brethren, the ancients of the place who lived in Mothers day. They interested us for an hour and a half telling about Mother and the first Elders. An aged brother ninety four years old who retains his intellect and is quite bright seemed pleased to converse all the time about Mother.

Even by the middle of the nineteenth century, there remained those who had seen and heard Mother Ann, on earth; no wonder the older

A section of the Canterbury Cemetery chart shows where members lie (since there are no longer individual headstones) and their ages—the average age in this section was seventy-three. The members include a remarkable group:

Dorothy Durgin, Eldress, inspired song writer, friend of Mary Baker Eddy, designer of the "Dorothy cloak";

Micajah Tucker, stonecutter, maker of Canterbury's dining chairs;

Francis Winkley, Deacon, maker of wool cards and spinning wheels;

Joanna Kaime, Ministry;

Joseph Johnson, woodworker;

Benjamin Smith, Elder, carved original tombstones, set out sugar maples;

Thomas Corbett, physician, maker of Sarsaparilla Syrup, clockmaker, designer of village fire engine;

Abraham Perkins, Elder;

Eli Kidder, cabinetmaker and tool maker;

David Parker, Trustee, first postmaster at Canterbury Shaker Village in 1848, designer of Shakers' water-powered washing machine.

The cemetery was one spot in the village where Brothers and Sisters were not separated, left and right. (Canterbury, N.H.)

325	Dorothy A. Durgin. Aug. 24, 1898. 1. Age 72 yrs.	327	Joanna J. Kaime. Dec. 31, 1898. 1. Age 71 yrs.	329	Benj. H. Smith. July 20, 1899. 1. Age 70 yrs.	333	Abraham Perkins. Aug. 12, 1900. 1. Age 93 yrs.
157	Micajah Tucker. June 27, 1848. 1. Age 84 yrs.	181	Joseph Johnson. Aug. 11, 1852. 1. Age 71 yrs.	197	Zilpha Whitcher. Nov. 8, 1856. 1. Age 82 yrs.	241	Eli Kidder. Jan. 9, 1867. 2. Age 83 yrs.
149	Francis Winkley. June 20, 1847. 1. Age 88 yrs.	182	Anna Carr. Oct. 21, 1852. 1. Age 86 yrs.	201	Betty Lougee. Feb. 24, 1857. 1. Age 77 yrs.	242	David Parker. Jan. 20, 1867. 1. Age 59 yrs.
145	Abigail Yarland. Feb. 2, 1847. 1. Age 60 yrs.	183	John Wadleigh. Oct. 23, 1852. 1. Age 75 yrs.	203	Thomas Corbett. June 13, 1857. 1. Age 76 yrs.	243	Abbie J. Trull. Feb. 9, 1867. 1. Age 25 yrs.

members, who took part in the actual founding of the faith, were treasured.

The Shaker Eldresses Anna White and Leila Taylor of Mount Lebanon, who wrote a history of the Shaker movement when they were aged seventy-three and fifty respectively, spoke for all Shakers when they said,

> Have Shakers any deadline of usefulness? Have they any room for the old folks? "There are no old folks among us; we are all young together!" was the answer given to the question, "What do you do with your old people?" It is more than a trick of speech. The absence of anxiety and foreboding has banished old age.

In living to ripe old ages, the Shakers achieved the nearest thing to permanence in life on this earth they could. But they knew in the end that everything in the material World must pass because heaven alone was the home of all that was truly everlasting. Old age didn't upset them because it did not mean decay—it meant the final ripening of the soul before the harvest. An obituary column in the Shaker newspaper was labeled simply *Harvested.*

They did not fear death, but saw it as the final chance to fulfill their ideal of permanence, as undying souls in an eternal salvation. Older Shakers did not dwell on the past. Instead, they turned their thoughts cheerfully to the future of the others in their villages. In 1904, an Eldress wrote that she often saw Brothers in their eighties planting fruit and shade trees "for the blessing of generations to come." They generously sowed what they couldn't hope to reap in this life. Quite literally, members like this took to heart the lines they had learned in their early days from the *Youth's Guide:* "If thou plant thy faith in a good soil, it will yield to thy spirit a great increase of gospel fruit in abundance; and thou shalt taste the goodness thereof in time. But the final harvest is in the world to come, after the stalk to thy spirit is decayed."

Visitors to Canterbury and Sabbathday Lake, the two remaining Shaker villages, are often amazed to discover that the Shakers today don't drive in buggies or do all their laundry by hand on Mondays. They blink at refrigerators, nudge each other when they see an electric blender in the kitchen, and positively gasp when they spot a TV antenna sticking out of the Dwellinghouse. We are so used to the image of classic Shakerism—say, 1840—when furniture was simple, all the work done by hand, and members stayed close to home, that it's easy to forget that the Shakers changed with the times along with the rest of America.

And yet nothing could be truer to the spirit of Shakerism than the outward signs of progress. The Shakers were not like the American Amish, the "plain people" who refuse to use cars, telephones, or electricity for religious reasons. The Canterbury Shakers were the first in their area of New Hampshire to have electricity, when Brother Irving Greenwood wired the village himself in 1910. They bought their first car, a Reo, two years before that, and installed battery phones four years before that, circa 1904, along with indoor toilets.

In fact, in many ways the Shakers were so far ahead of their time that it's no wonder the outside World is only now beginning to appreciate them fully. From women's liberation to recycling paper—from racial equality to population control—from the metric system to opposition to capital punishment—and even from job rotation to permanent press—the Shakers' knack for forward-looking trends seems almost uncanny.

The belief that Shakers had in progress was just as much a part of their faith as their belief in honesty or simplicity. Spiritual progress was a fundamental Shaker concept. Feeling as they did that the village they saw reflected the inner spirit, it was natural for the Shakers to welcome the outward signs of progress in their homes as a clear sign of spiritual progress within.

Mother Ann, as usual, was the first to teach about spiritual progress, characteristically using a completely down-to-earth example to make her point. When some of her followers admired an apple tree, she likened the process of ripening to the spiritual progress of the soul:

How beautiful this tree looks now! But some of the apples will soon fall off; some will hold on till they are full half grown and will then fall off; and some will get ripe. So it is with souls that set out in the way of God. Many will set out very fair and soon fall away; some will go further and then fall off; some will go still further, and then fall; and some will go through.

Progress was so important to the Shaker spirit that those who left the faith were called "backsliders," the exact opposite of those going forward.

Continual spiritual progress was important for each Brother and Sister, but it was also necessary as a way to perfection for the whole village. The Shakers saw their communities as "a system which was established by, and open to, increasing Divine revelations," and as such, progressive to the point where it would "cleanse itself from all existing errors." The goal of spiritual progress was, of course, moral perfection; it is significant that a Shaker described heaven as "the land of immeasurable progress." Since a Shaker village was meant to be a place where heavenly ideals were put into practice on earth, it's not surprising that the Shakers became known for their progressiveness.

Spiritual progress found a natural counterpart in social progressiveness. Eldress Mary Antoinette Doolittle, who wrote the study of longevity, likened social reform to the path of spiritual progress, saying, "As we feel deeply interested in all moral reformatory movements in the outside world, as underlying spiritual progress, and stepping stones thereto, we keep our eyes open to discern and read the signs of the times concerning future events."

That it is a woman quoted here is also significant. The most notable form of Shaker social progress was the notion that men and women deserved equal treatment: there were always Elders and Eldresses, Deacons and Deaconesses, and Brothers and Sisters acting as Trustees. No doubt the fact that Mother Ann was herself a woman had something to do with this forward-looking attitude. She taught her followers that God was not a male Trinity, but both Father and Mother. Man *and* woman were created in the image of God, and, as such, woman deserved equal respect.

Women in the nineteenth century who became Shaker Sisters were not meek *hausfraus,* and they certainly were not kept "barefoot and pregnant." Eldress Mary Antoinette was particularly vocal on this state of affairs. In the Shaker village, she declared,

Woman was no longer a slave in bonds, forced as it were to bear down the name of some man to posterity, and bend over the cradle and sing lullaby as her only right, and the highest aim of her existence; but she became co-worker with her brother man in every department of life. Hence they stood shoulder to shoulder, each occupying their own sphere, yet working in harmonious relations together.

Does this sound like a women's lib manifesto? Eldress Mary Antoinette said it in 1880.

What exactly was a woman's rightful place in the Shaker village? In general, it was where the Brothers weren't. Shaker women were liberated, but they still did the cooking, cleaning, sewing, and washing—not the stonecutting, farming, or carpentry. Listen to a Shaker's explanation. In 1875, a visitor asked Elder Frederick Evans (Eldress Mary Antoinette's counterpart in the Ministry at Mount Lebanon): "Suppose a woman wanted, in your family, to be a blacksmith, would you consent?" Elder Frederick replied, "No, because this would bring men and women into relations which we do not think wise." The Shakers, after all, were a celibate community and had a strong sense of order for men in their place and women in their own.

According to the *Millennial Laws,* men and women were equal in privilege and responsibility, but definitely separate: "Brethren and Sisters must not work together, except on special occasions, and then by liberty from the Elders. Brethren's and sisters' shops, should not be under one and the same roof, except those of the Ministry." A Brother was generally appointed, however, to help the Sisters with the heavy work of the laundry, dairy, or kitchens.

In the earliest years, Sisters were not allowed to go into the Brothers' shops alone without permission from the Eldress, and when they went at all, it was for work and not to "partake of melons, fruits, or nuts," or to learn songs; the same rules applied to the Brothers when they went to the Sisters' shops. So women did not do heavy farm work, make furniture, or shoe oxen. Their place in the barn was on milking stools. Milking, incidentally, was one of the few occupations that was done either by Brothers or Sisters, the men in bad weather, and the women when it was warm.

Shaker women were content to stick with traditionally feminine

Although equal to her Brothers, the Shaker Sister still did the ironing in the Family. A narrow "goose" slipped into corners; when the Sister left the room, a tin "goose pan," bottom, insulated the iron and kept it hot so she didn't waste time reheating it. (Canterbury, N.H.)

Sister Tabitha Babbitt of Harvard, Massachusetts, is credited with inventing the circular saw in 1810. (Old Chatham, N.Y.)

occupations; they worked as hard or harder than their Worldly sisters, but they worked along with their men as helping Sisters, not slaving wives. When a visitor to Union Village, Ohio, found in 1875 that some of the Sisters there "thought women might do some other things besides cooking," he also found that they were considered a little too "progressive." There was even a Sister who went so far as to say she wished the Shaker Sisters' caps would be abolished, but according to the visitor she was known as a downright "radical."

Nevertheless, Sisters did contribute several important innovations in the world of mechanical progress. One mother of invention was Sister Tabitha Babbitt of Harvard, credited with inventing the circular saw in 1810. According to the story, Sister Tabitha watched the Brothers saw one day and observed that the back-and-forth motion of their saws wasted half their effort. Returning to her own workroom, she rigged up a simple circular saw of notched tin on her spinning wheel and did her part to revolutionize industry.

Eldress Emeline Hart of Enfield, Connecticut, was another who advanced technology by thinking in circles: she invented the revolving oven at Canterbury, in 1876, a prototype of all such ovens.

For the most part, though, the Shaker Sister's equality lay in the opportunities she had for leadership in the village. From the time that Father Joseph Meacham appointed Mother Lucy Wright in 1787 to be the head of the Sisters, every position of leadership in the Shaker village was shared equally by male and female. The success of women like Eldress Dorothy Durgin of Canterbury, noted for progressive reforms within Shakerism such as bringing musical instruments into the faith; or Eldress Mary Antoinette Doolittle, who edited the Shaker newspaper from 1873 to 1875 (and "liberated" its title from *The Shaker* to *Shaker and Shakeress* in 1873), proved that the women were equal to the responsibilities. Apparently the Shaker Sisters felt that women were so capable as leaders that they thought the outside World of politics could benefit from their example: a pamphlet published around 1890 suggested "an exchange of women for men legislators" for more effective action.

Equality of the races was another important Shaker belief. Even though the pacifist Shakers didn't fight in the Civil War, they opposed slavery heartily. Elder Daniel Boler of New Lebanon joined a discussion about abolition with a Worldly slaveholder when he vis-

The famous revolving oven at Canterbury was invented in 1876 by Eldress Emeline Hart. Sisters baked sixty pies at a time on four pierced iron revolving shelves, which turned to ensure even baking. Finished pies were lifted out from the front—no burned hands, no dropped pies. Isinglass windows on each door let Sisters check without wasting heat; there was even a temperature gauge. Details, left to right: top, revolving shelves; hinge; center, isinglass window, ironwork, handle; oven with side arches.

ited his home state, Kentucky, in 1852, saying: "I had a pretty smart talk with a Kentucky slave holder, about the propriety or impropriety of holding slaves, he thot of course I was an eastern man, but I told him I was a Kentuckian by birth, and yet I could not approve of slavery."

What the Shakers preached, they put into practice. At South Union, Kentucky, slaveholders who joined the Shakers not only set their slaves free but encouraged them to join the Shakers, where they could find real brotherhood with all men. A visitor to South Union in 1875 found that for years there had been a black Family with a black Elder, "living upon the same terms as the whites," and that when that Family became too small it moved in with the white Families with no problems. For a few years after 1846, there was even a Shaker Family of black Sisters in Philadelphia, who later joined the Shakers at Watervliet, New York.

The Shakers believed in the equality of God's love for all people, and themselves loved and respected all people in order to follow God's example. Elder Richard McNemar (1770–1839) of Union Village, Ohio, wrote at the beginning of the nineteenth century,

> *Whatever your profession,*
> *Your sex or color be,*
> *Renounce your carnal pleasures,*
> *Or Christ you'll never see.*

The Shakers' deep respect for orderly life included the realization that population control was becoming increasingly necessary to maintain the dignity and even the level of tolerable existence for all life. Despite the warnings of men like Malthus, one of the commonest criticisms of the Shakers during the nineteenth century was that celibacy was unnatural and a violation of God's command to go forth and multiply. When Uncle Sam had so much undeveloped land that he offered free homesteads to settlers, this charge of not producing more helping hands to gather in the country's wealth was almost akin to un-American activity.

Shakers answered by pointing out that orphans and other homeless children found good homes in the Shaker Children's Order. Like today's zero population growth organizations, which encourage adoption instead of production, the Shakers felt that they could serve mankind—and God—better by taking care of the children already in need of loving homes instead of bringing more children into the World. One thing the Shakers didn't expect was that the whole World would convert to Shakerism and stop having children altogether; they fully recognized that their way of life was just one choice and that there would always be people who would never choose the Shaker way.

Mechanical progress was just as important to the Shakers as moral progress. In 1859, Elder Frederick Evans explained the link between

Above: The famous Shaker round barn was built by Hancock Shakers in 1826 and rebuilt after burning in 1864. In front rests a Shaker side hill plow; at left, a Brother plants corn with the Shaker corn planter (see illustration, page 36). (Hancock, Mass.)
Below: Herb presses were an important part of the Shakers' herb and medicine business. Double screw action compressed dried herbs into square blocks, a form efficiently handled, stored, and shipped. (Old Chatham, N. Y.)

new machinery and salvation: it was the power of man's mind. On the one hand, he said, man's intellect was responsible for progressive methods and machinery, "which facilitate and increase the means of physical subsistence, and greatly enhance the enjoyment of the moral faculties." On the other hand, man's intellect "prepared the soul for the opening of its spiritual capacities."

Elder Frederick's words were not just high ideals—they were put into practice in Shaker workshops. When in the early nineteenth century Brother Elisha Myrick of Harvard successfully developed an herb-pressing machine, he wrote that "every improvement relieving human toil or facilitating labor" gave man the time and opportunity for "moral, mechanical, scientific and intellectual improvement and the cultivation of the finer and higher qualities of the human mind." No wonder the Shakers put their best efforts into inventiveness, when such double-barreled encouragement aimed toward progressive ingenuity. Since an ordinary member like Brother Elisha sincerely believed that designing a better machine was not only practical and good for business but good for his spirit, too, he naturally was always thinking up new and better methods.

A member like Brother Elisha also believed sincerely that God was the source of his ability to think and create, and that he should do his best to use his creative powers in thanks for having been given them. J. M. Peebles, a friend of Elder Frederick, although not a Shaker himself, observed that as far as his friends were concerned, "Inventions

relating to industrial activities, or the spiritual exaltation of the races, have their first birth in the inner life."

It was up to the Elders and Eldresses to decide what innovations were in order in the Shaker way of life, however. According to the *Millennial Laws*, "No new fashions, in manufacture, clothing, or wares of any kind" were permitted without the consent of the Ministry. This was mainly to prevent pride in ingenuity developing into full-blown vanity. Father Joseph Meacham said to his fellow Shakers, "We have a right to improve the inventions of man, so far as is useful and necessary, but not to vain glory, or anything superfluous." In spite of their considerable contributions in technology, the Shakers never exchanged their faith in God for faith in mechanical marvels. It seems that the rest of the World did, from wonder drugs to test-tube babies to the atomic bomb. Who needs to believe in divine powers any more? Today the average Space Age American literally finds it easier to believe in the man in the moon than in God.

With all the encouragement in heaven and earth, with a good strong dose of ordinary Yankee ingenuity, the Shaker went about his daily business of constant improvement. Since he hated waste, including waste of time and motion, his biggest concern was getting rid of inefficiency. As Anna White and Leila Taylor put it, "He aims to employ his whole being and all his time in the service to which he has devoted himself, yet he sees no virtue nor economy in hard labor when a consecrated brain can work out an easier method."

Shaker architecture offers outstanding examples of efficient design, the most well known being the round barn at Hancock, Massachusetts, built in 1829, burned and rebuilt in 1865. The barn has three levels: the top, for hay; the middle, for the cattle stalls; and the bottom, for manure. Simply and efficiently, the design followed the natural course of feeding and gravity. Hay was pitched down to the cattle, and manure was shoveled through a trap door behind each stall into the manure pit below. The circle of stalls meant feeding the cows was more efficient; Brothers had merely to walk a few steps around the center to feed the ring of cattle around them. Hay wagons could drive in, around, and out the barn without turning around or backing up inside.

The large rectangular barn at Canterbury, built in 1858, was

Opposite: The 200-foot-long Canterbury barn (originally covered with 87,000 pine shingles) had ramps at the east and west ends so hay wagons could pass through and out in quick succession. This monument to Shaker progressiveness and ingenuity was tragically destroyed by fire in 1973 after 115 years of peace and prosperity. The west entrance, above, had a clever door-within-a-door. Large doors swung open for hay wagons; Brothers on foot used the regular door at the left. Hinged panels at the base were possibly raised for ventilation.

Metal pens are another invention attributed to the Shakers, although metal points were made by others as well. Shaker metal pens telescoped to fit into a pocket.

another ingenious example of progressive engineering. With a length of 200 feet and a width of 45 feet, it was called the longest barn in the state. Ramps at each end extended the total length to a whopping 240 feet. The main level of the barn was not entirely floored over; instead, a narrow "bridge" for hay wagons ran down the center. Brothers pitched hay down into storage, instead of up, saving effort by letting gravity do the work. When the barn was completely filled with the harvest, hay reached from the lower level to the ceiling high above on both sides of the ramp.

Below the hay level there were stalls for one hundred registered Guernseys. Like the Hancock barn, the Canterbury barn had trap doors behind each stall for manure, which landed in the manure pit on the bottom level. For a full house of cattle, that saved a lot of shoveling and hauling.

The barn in nearby Enfield, New Hampshire, was likewise noted for its convenience and comfort for man and beast. An admiring Brother visiting in 1869 from Kentucky wrote home that the barn had a "chimney up thro' it well secured against fire for cooking food and a room to warm in." He also noted the manure trap doors; it is easy to see why visiting back and forth among the villages was such a good way to spread progressive ideas.

The most remarkable barn, however, was the "splendid Brick Barn" at Shirley, Massachusetts. The same Brother wrote home in amazement that it had running water for the cows. He described "a trough of water supplied with a running stream, the whole length of the Barn, where the cows can drink at their leisure at all times Winter and Summer when in the Stable and it does not freeze in Winter. Another set of convenient troughs contain the food."

If running water in the barn seems like the height of cow-coddling, then the cows at North Union, Ohio, must have lived in bovine bliss—they ate hot home-cooked dinners! George Budinger, one of the last people to have lived and worked in the village (which closed in 1889), recalled in 1962 not only the cows' menu but just how dinner was served. Cooked bran and warm mash rolled into the barn on small wooden railway cars, complete with steel rail. He added, "By gosh they used to get milk there, it was surprising." Hardly—with treatment like that.

Shaker farm machinery was every bit as progressive as the barns themselves. The North Union Shakers may have gone to extra trouble to cook the cows' food, but they made up for lost time with their hay-raising tongs. Instead of pitching hay into the upstairs loft, the Brothers hitched up a horse to a set of tongs with a pulley arrangement. The horse walked, the hay went up into the loft, and Brothers forked the hay off the hook and spread it evenly into the corners.

Shakers were also quick to appreciate some of the World's more progressive inventions. According to an early issue of *The Plumber & Sanitary Engineer,* in 1880, the knowledgeable Brothers were often consulted as the neighborhood "consumer guide" because they were bound to be interested in the most efficient machinery to be had. Some of the Shakers' recommendations were no doubt for their own agricultural inventions: a revolving harrow for breaking up the soil, the design of Brother Daniel Baird of North Union, Ohio; a threshing machine designed in 1815; Charles Greaves's fertilizing machine; and the first horse-drawn mowing machine.

Brothers' and Sisters' workshops likewise exhibited progressive equipment. Shakers designed their tools and machines to take over laborious steps or to perform the specific task involved in any operation. Shaker carpenters made good use of a tongue-and-groove machine for joining boards, the invention of Brothers Henry Bennett and Amos Bishop of Mount Lebanon. Brothers in Harvard developed a machine for sizing broom-corn bristles and an improved lathe with a "screw feeder" for turning broom handles for the flat broom industry. Shaker basket weavers saved time with a machine for splint-making, the invention of Elders Daniel Boler and Daniel Crossman of New Lebanon. The North Union Brothers used water power to run a machine for making wooden tubs and pails; they also had a "self-operating" shingle saw.

For making wool carders, Brother Benjamin Bruce's invention "for cutting and bending machine card teeth and punching the leather for setting" did the trick. Shakers working in the Seed Shop had Shaker-invented machines for printing seed bags and herb packages, and for filling them with the seeds.

The Sisters' workshops were just as progressive as the Brothers'. The laundries and kitchens were models of mechanization and centralization of utilities. The laundries were particularly noted for their convenience and progressiveness. The significance of clean laundry to

Shaker Families with several hundred members produced dirty laundry by the bushel, but there was only one Monday washday per week. No wonder Sisters said that washing "was truly made worship" when Brother David Parker of Canterbury perfected a "Wash-mill" in 1858. They efficiently followed their divine command,

Come let us all in love unite,
And keep our garments clean and white.

(From an old advertisement)

IMPROVED SHAKER WASHING MACHINE, BUILT AT SHAKER VILLAGE, N. H.

PATENTED July 23 1877.

Sisters had special irons for coat sleeves. The iron side was heated on a wood stove, then inserted, wooden base down, into a sleeve. With heat from inside and another flatiron doing the job on top, Sisters did twice as good a job.

Opposite: A typical ironing room had long ironing tables and high chairs to make the job easier. A large iron stove at Hancock heated dozens of flatirons at once, so Sisters never had to wait for a hot iron. Towels dried on a wood box with its handy built-in rack; dustpan and brush hung on the side. Brothers' coathangers had a bar below for trousers.

the Shakers was great, not only for health and appearance but also as an interpretation of certain passages from the Bible. A passage from Revelations in particular was applied to Mother Ann by some of her followers: " 'And to her was granted that she should be arrayed in fine linen, clean, white,' that is, 'the righteousness of saints.' " If clean clothes were the outward sign of saintly virtue, so much more the reason for the Shakers on earth to scrub their own linens clean. As mentioned earlier, Mother Ann herself worked as a washerwoman during the first difficult years in America.

The Sisters at Sabbathday Lake, Maine, were so pleased with their efficient new laundry in 1878 that one wrote with reverence, "Labor is truly made worship." She continued on a more down-to-earth note,

> Steam does all, heats water, and boils clothes. A large copper kettle holding three barrels of water is suspended in which the water is heated for Sisters to draw into their tubs where in less than ten minutes the clothes are made to boil. They have only to turn a faucet to get hot or cold water and when done using it turn a key and the water all runs off into the drain.

Her enthusiasm was so great that it's easy to imagine her hopping out of bed on washday and running to the laundry when it was finally complete—they had yet to add a "Centrifugal Wringer" (spin dryer) and a washing machine.

The washing machine in question may well have been another noted Shaker invention, the creation of Brother David Parker of Canterbury in 1858. It used water for cleaning *and* mechanical power and was so efficient that it was welcomed not only in Shaker villages but in big city hotels. Establishments from the Parker House in Boston to the Tremont in Chicago bought them; when the Girard House in Philadelphia bought one in 1857, fourteen washerwomen left—that's how efficient the thing was. In 1876, the Canterbury Shakers exhibited the washing machine in the Philadelphia Centennial Exposition and returned with a medal for their ingenuity.

Incidentally, the near reverence that Shakers had for the power of steam shows how much they valued it as a time- and work-saver. The increase in efficiency that steam power brought about was so appreciated by Shakers as a giant step in their path to progress and perfection that this down-to-earth source of power was sometimes used as a symbol of the spiritual power of the Gospels:

> *While our steamboat, Self-denial,*
> *Rushes up against the stream,*
> *Is it not a serious trial*
> *Of the pow'r of gospel steam?*

Serious trial or not, gospel steam and ordinary steam both powered the Shakers along their way to progress.

The Canterbury Shakers were particularly progressive in their laundry in adapting sources of energy to more than one use: an "engine of sixteen horse power" in 1854 helped with the washing and with sawing the wood. Even in rainy weather the laundry was always dry by the next day for ironing. The wet clothes were hauled upstairs in a large dumbwaiter to wooden racks; steam pipes from the boiler below did double duty to dry them.

The "horse power" washing machine used at North Union, Ohio, before the turn of the century was the real thing—an actual horse operated it. According to George Budinger, it was a big wooden tub fitted with rollers that turned as a horse walked around the tub. Inside, the rollers "would smash down and squeeze the dirt out" of

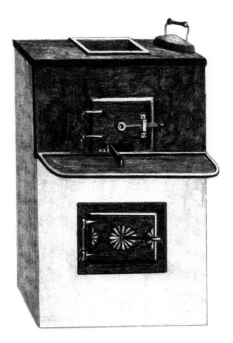

Canterbury Sisters had a "steam-iron" stove in their Sisters' Shop (1816). Flatirons heated on the sides; water for sprinkling the laundry heated in the central well. (Canterbury, N.H.)

Opposite: Canterbury Sisters cooked soup by the tubful with their enormous built-in soup kettles. The South Family at Mount Lebanon used the slicing table; the built-in blade saved time cutting hundreds of slices a day. In the back, a Sister lifts dishes from a hanging dish shelf. (Old Chatham, N.Y.)

the clothes. The only thing the Shakers had to wash separately were the men's socks, which they put into a barrel with "a stomper to stomp them up and down like a butter churn."

Ironing in a Shaker village was another marvel of progressive efficiency. At Hancock, a special stove shaped like an Apollo space capsule on stilts not only warmed the laundry where it stood; it also helped to dry the clothes and heat the irons which fitted inside. Sisters in all communities sat comfortably in high chairs to iron at the ironing tables.

As efficient as ironing was made, the ideal of course would have been to eliminate the need for it altogether. The Sabbathday Lake Shakers did just that when in the 1840s they produced what is credited with being some of the first wrinkle-resistant fabric in America. Linen was pressed between layers of chemically treated paper and heated in a screw press designed for the purpose. The fabric, which looked shiny on one side and dull on the other, also resisted moisture.

Kitchen Sisters used apple parers while other devices cored and quartered the fruit. Pea shellers and butter workers were more Shaker contributions. The Church Family at Union Village, Ohio, even had a "machine for kneeding bread which is carried by horse power, also a simple machine for washing potatoes." In 1850, the Enfield, New Hampshire, Sisters had a "new fashion churn, to churn by air."

The most remarkable inventions, however, were the ovens and ranges themselves. The main bake oven at Hancock, built in 1830, had shelf space for thirty loaf pans and seven dampers to regulate the heat. The same chimneypiece supported another oven, used exclusively for baking pies and cakes, which was round and had three shelves.

The most progressive design was the revolving oven designed and patented in 1876 by Eldress Emeline Hart of Enfield, Connecticut. Apparently Eldress Emeline got good and tired of baking only a dozen or so pies at a time for the Family. Her new oven could handle sixty pies at a time, or about seventy loaves of bread, on its four round revolving shelves.

The kitchens at villages like Canterbury and Hancock were on the basement floor of the Dwellinghouses. Heat from the ovens was kept to a minimum in the summer, and the cooking facilities were conveniently near the cool cellars where fruits, vegetables, and milk were stored. In spite of their basement location, the kitchens were anything but damp or gloomy. Here is a description of the Enfield, New Hampshire, kitchen in 1853:

> The kitchen is 40 feet in length and 24 in width. In this apartment, where so much labor is performed, the same neatness prevails as in other parts of the edifice. Carpets protect the floors, the walls are pure white and the inside of the cupboards and closets of a sky blue. Large ranges, twenty feet in length, protected by a frame of cast iron, form the laboratory of the kitchen.

In the nearby bake room, "Solid masonry as high as the room, painted a sky blue, is the only object which distinguishes this room from the others. Within these beautiful polished walls are free stone ovens, seven feet in length."

Sisters' sewing and knitting shops were just as pleasantly progressive. Enfield, New Hampshire, had a model shop. In 1850, Shakers visiting from Mount Lebanon wrote with approval, "Here the Sisters have the use of water power to help them do their work, One power Loom, a machine to twist and spool yarn, and 4 knitting machines to knit flannel drawers for sale." Four years later a Sister added, "One

Above and opposite: Details from Shaker wood-burning stoves, so efficient that most villages didn't have a single fireplace. Note the tiny draft door in the stove door. (Canterbury, N.H.)

sister attends to two machines & can knit some on her knitting needles at the same time."

Sisters like that help explain why the Shakers never considered "replacing" human beings with mechanical wonders. No matter if the knitting machine *was* "a sensible little thing . . . acting out intelligence in all its parts," it still couldn't beat a Sister who managed to keep up with her hand-knitting at the same time; and though it may have had "intelligence," it could never have a loving soul. So when Eldress Dorothy Durgin of Canterbury stated proudly in 1854 that the Wheeler and Wilson patent sewing machines in the Sisters' shop "would do the work of 12 sisters," there was no danger that the twelve women would lose their importance in the village. They could simply turn their time and talents to other good works.

One last important example of Shaker progressiveness deserves comment. Now that the energy shortage era is really upon us, we could learn a valuable lesson from the thrifty Shakers. As supplies of fossil fuels go down, prices go up—and so does the popularity of small wood-burning stoves like the ones the Shakers used.

Even though the fuel nineteenth-century Shakers used was wood (which is replaceable unlike coal, oil, and gas), the fuel-conserving Shakers didn't see any reason to squander it. They carefully saved shavings and scraps from the carpentry shops to recycle into kindling. The Shakers' famous and distinctively designed iron stove was so much more efficient than fireplaces that most Shaker villages didn't even have a single fireplace. The stove could be put in the center of the room, and heat radiated out in all directions instead of rising straight up the chimney. The stovepipe itself could act as a radiator. Double stovepipes were sometimes used to heat dwelling rooms; the stovepipe in the Schoolhouse at Canterbury in 1862 crossed the length of the room, keeping more of the students warm. Shakers were so emphatic about replacing old fireplaces with stoves that Elder Henry Blinn of Canterbury wrote in 1878 that the large fireplaces at each end of the Meetinghouse at Watervliet, Ohio, gave it "rather an old fashioned appearance."

When the Shakers did use coal, they were just as sparing in its use. The large Dwellinghouse of the Second Family at Harvard was heated throughout with only one and a half bushels of coal a day, in 1854. The heat, which was "conducted in Tin pipes from the furnace into every room & Hall in the house," could be regulated "at pleasure by means of a little cast Iron valve which could be turned either way to let the heat thro, or shut it off."

The Shakers were so concerned with saving fuel that when in 1873 Brother Hewitt Chandler of Sabbathday Lake invented a machine for making barrel staves, he designed it to burn the shavings from the stave itself to heat the stave for bending. This not only saved fuel—"nearly two cords of wood which is worth at least $3.00 per cord"—it saved his time, too. The machine chamfered, hollowed, bent, heated, and edged the staves, "leaving no hand work to be done only to pack them."

Ideas such as Brother David Parker's washing machine and Eldress Emeline Hart's revolving oven didn't benefit only Shaker villages. Hotels from Boston to Chicago bought the washing machine because of its efficiency, capacity, and durability; the oven with its revolving shelves became a standard feature of Worldly bakeries. The appeal of inventions like these was responsible for what the Shakers considered the problem of patenting. The Shakers, a truly progressive group, were reluctant to patent, believing it a form of monopoly and a selfish, un-Christian practice. Nevertheless, Brother David's washing machine was patented on January 26, 1858, and Eldress Emeline's oven on May 23, 1876. What were their feelings and why did they change?

The Shakers' original attitude toward patenting was painfully clear to Brother Elijah Brown of Canterbury, whose story was recorded by the historically minded Elder Henry Blinn there. In 1809, he invented "a mill for the grinding of bark for tanning" and went to the head Society of New Lebanon to get permission to have the machine patented. But it was "too early in the history of the Church, to enter so fully into the relations of the World, after the severe struggle of the Believers to get out, and Elijah returned without the coveted privilege." Elder Henry added that no record was made of the mill after 1809, and "it evidently became the property of all who chose to use it."

Shakers originally avoided patenting for fear that they would become too Worldly and too concerned with the financial rewards of their work. Besides, the early leaders no doubt feared that patenting might bring undue fame to the individual inventor and ruin the communal spirit.

Eventually, however, as the World and the Shakers developed mutual trust and friendship, their reasons for avoiding patenting became genuinely altruistic. God helped those who helped themselves, and so did the Shakers. If they felt they could help someone else arrive at a better way for everybody, they freely shared their inventions and ideas. Gail Borden was one inventor whom the Shakers helped to fame and fortune through their generosity. Although Borden was not a member himself, the New Lebanon Shakers let him experiment with their vacuum pan. They used it for condensing fruit juices and extracts, which evaporated at a lower temperature in a vacuum than otherwise. Gail Borden successfully condensed milk in it in 1853 and went on to found the Borden Company.

The same spirit of sharing prompted Sister Mary Whitcher of Canterbury to write in her *Shaker Housekeeper* (the first Shaker cookbook, published in 1882): "Our SHAKERS' SARSAPARILLA is not a secret or a quack remedy, nor are its ingredients withheld from those who desire to know them." However, the shrewd Shaker business head on her shoulders made her add that the Shakers' "claim to superiority" was based on the care they put into it, from gathering the ingredients in it, to curing them, to compounding them. The recipe was freely shared, but the painstaking care that went into the Shaker product could not be bought. Most people preferred to buy the Shakers' rather than make their own.

The result of the Shakers' generosity was a host of inventions attributed to but not patented by the Shakers, among them the circular saw, the flat broom, the clothespin, and a threshing machine. Unfortunately, Worldly businessmen were quick to recognize the advantages to themselves in the generosity of the Shakers. Outside businessmen could patent Shaker ideas for their own benefit, a practice that clearly violated the Shakers' intentions.

Partly from a desire to prevent this and partly from a desire to protect their own interests, the Shakers gradually began to accept the practice of patenting, though never wholeheartedly. They always tended to regard it more as a necessary evil than a source of good, and the total number of inventions they patented is small in proportion to those that were given freely. At all times, the Shakers preferred that the popularity of their goods represented the voluntary decision of consumers who chose the built-in quality of Shaker goods.

While Shakers as a rule would have liked to be completely self-sufficient, they were not opposed to taking good advantage of progressive ideas from Worldly inventors. If something was built on a sound idea and with sound construction, Shakers saw no reason why they shouldn't buy it. The Canterbury Shakers, for example, bought a "hose knitter" in 1856 in nearby Sanbornton. It was hand-powered and used for ribbed work. But, as one member added, "The feet of the hose were, as formerly, knit with the common needles." New machines were used only where they could do the work better than people, but handwork never lost its place.

This attitude helps explain some things about Shakerism in general. Brother Delmer Wilson of Sabbathday Lake, Maine, the last living Shaker Brother, made oval wooden boxes almost until his death at age eighty-eight, in 1961, that are indistinguishable in style and workmanship from ones made a century earlier. Brother Delmer took as much time to make them by hand and to make them right as his Brothers did a hundred years before him. The difference was that Brother Delmer kept to the traditional methods of craftsmen in an age when nearly everything we use is made faster and cheaper by machine.

The Shakers' refusal to compromise their standards was one of the reasons their numbers eventually began to decline. They chose to abandon various industries altogether rather than to produce quicker, cheaper, entirely machine-made items of poorer quality; as a result, they began to lose customers.

If they had chosen Worldly profit instead of perfection, perhaps Brother Delmer would not have been the last Shaker Brother. But Shakerism as it was known and respected would long since have ceased to exist. Progress, in the true Shaker sense, really had only two meanings. It meant the improvement of the community and the growth of a spirit of loving brotherhood:

> Be not anxious to go forward,
> And to leave your brother dear;
> You may happen to fall backward,
> And your brother forward stear.

Similar to the candleholder illustrated on page 47, this one was also height-adjustable.

In 1910, Canterbury Shakers had the first electricity in the area when Brother Irving Greenwood wired the village and set up a powerhouse, at right, with steam generator and wet cell batteries. At left was the garage. Canterbury's first "horseless carriage" was a 1908 Reo; later models included a Packard and a Stanley Steamer. Rather than crush their woven straw and palm headgear—or give it up—Shakers custom-ordered their cars with higher roofs. Note the pressed metal siding, another sign of the times. The tower was for fire hoses.

And progress meant coming closer and closer to achieving completely in their villages all the ideals they had chosen—honesty, purity, health, permanence, simplicity, utility—and especially brotherly love. In the words of Elder Daniel Fraser of Mount Lebanon, "The secret of all true progress: 'Thou shalt love thy neighbor as thyself.'"

Epilogue

The success of the Shakers in making their heavenly ideals a working part of their everyday life and work is evident in all things they made. Looking at Shaker chairs and barns in this light makes it seem clear that whenever they put their hands to work, they put their hearts to God, too.

Even more important, though, is something else they succeeded in making—something we can't see in a museum anywhere. More than any other ideal, they made love a part of their daily lives. They loved each other and they loved God with all their hearts; and they worked together, for each other, not against each other, without competition or pride. The proof that men and women can work together in harmony and accomplish great things at the same time is the greatest gift the Shakers can give us today. For them, at least, God's kingdom *did* come, and His will *was* done, on earth as it is in heaven.

> *And now I'll close the scrabble*
> *That has employed my pen*
> *My journal now is finished*
> *And I will say—Amen.*
>
> —*from a Shaker journal, 1846*

INTRODUCTION

page 8 "one will stand"
Valentine Rathbun: *An Account of the Matter, Form, and Manner of a New and Strange Religion* (Providence, R.I.; printed and sold by Bennett Wheeler; 1781), pp. 7–8.

10 "We aim"
Mary Antoinette Doolittle: *Autobiography of Mary Antoinette Doolittle* (Mt. Lebanon, N.Y.; 1880), p. 43.

11 "I'll work"
Harold E. Cook: *Shaker Music: A Manifestation of American Folk Culture* (Lewisburg, Pa.: Bucknell University Press; 1973. Cranbury, N.J.: Associated University Presses, Inc.; n.d.), pp. 17–18.

12 "A good many Christians"
The Shaker Manifesto, Vol. X, no. 3 (March 1880), p. 71.

14 "five hundred spectators"
"Sabbathday Lake Church Record and Journal 1874" (manuscript), p. 131. The Shaker Museum, Sabbathday Lake, Maine.

22 "I fear you will"
Mary Julia Neal, ed.: *The Journal of Eldress Nancy* (Nashville, Tenn.: The Parthenon Press; 1963), p. 16.

"this was a little too"
Elder Henry C. Blinn: "A Historical Record of the Society of Believers in Canterbury, N.H., East Canterbury, 1892" (manuscript), pp. 189 ff. Shaker Village, Inc., Canterbury, N.H.

23 "There is a great many"
Isaac N. Youngs: *Tour through the States of Ohio and Kentucky, by Rufus Bishop and Isaac N. Youngs, In the summer of 1834*" (manuscript). Western Reserve Historical Society, Cleveland, Ohio.

24 "William Shaw left"
Thomas Damon: "Journal, Enfield, Conn., 1834–45" (manuscript). The Henry Francis du Pont Winterthur Museum, Andrews Collection.

29 "We used to have"
Charles Nordhoff: *The Communistic Societies of the United States from Personal Observations.* (New York: Harper & Brothers, Publishers; 1875. Dover Publications, Inc.; 1966), p. 161.

30 "Really it seems"
Elder Henry C. Blinn: "A Journey to Kentucky in the Year 1873," *The Shaker Quarterly,* Vol. IV, no. 2 (Summer 1966), p. 64.

32 "Those who're faithful"
Giles B. Avery: "Daily Journal: A Journal of Times, Rhymes, Work & Weather, Very much mixed up together, Feb. 1836 to Jan. 1838" (manuscript). Western Reserve Historical Society.

TIME

34 "O let each one"
Edward Deming Andrews and Faith Andrews: *Shaker Furniture: The Craftsmanship of an American Communal Sect* (New York: Dover Publications, Inc.; 1950), p. 112.

No matter what size his head, a Brother's hat fit—it was made "to order" on his own hat form, like Benjamin Gates's. (Old Chatham, N.Y.)

34 "Now's the time"
Edward Deming Andrews: *The Gift to Be Simple: Songs, Dances and Rituals of the American Shakers* (New York: J. J. Augustin; 1940. Dover Publications, Inc.; 1963), p. 18.

35 "I sleep seven hours"
Richard McNemar: *A Selection of Hymns and Poems; For the Use of Believers* (Watervliet, Ohio; 1833), p. 39.

"O swiftly see!"
Andrews and Andrews: *Shaker Furniture*, p. 112.

"Even the farmers"
"Hand Cards," *The Shaker Manifesto*, Vol. XX, no. 8 (August 1890), p. 170.

36 "A few crooked, headless pins"
Elder Henry C. Blinn: "A Historical Record of the Society of Believers in Canterbury, N.H., East Canterbury, 1892" (manuscript), p. 138. Shaker Village, Inc., Canterbury, N.H.

"attempted to cross the Bark Mill pond"
Blinn, ibid., p. 206.

"My whole stay"
Edward Deming Andrews: *The People Called Shakers* (New York: Dover Publications, Inc.; 1953, 1963), p. 71.

37 "Whether you pass"
A. B. Harris: "Among the Shakers," *The Granite Monthly*, Vol. I, no. 1 (April 1877), pp. 21–2.

"Even in what is seen"
William Hepwroth Dixon: *New America* (Philadelphia: third edition; 1869), pp. 304–5.

38 "Elder William Dumont"
"Gleanings from Sabbathday Lake Church Journals, 1872–84," *The Shaker Quarterly*, Vol. VI, no. 4 (Winter 1966), p. 130.

"Slug:"
Charles Nordhoff: *The Communistic Societies of the United States*, p. 216.

"he would never allow"
Eldress Nancy E. Moore: "Journal of a Trip to Various Societies Sept. 1854–Oct. 1854" (manuscript), pp. 19–20. Western Reserve Historical Society.

40 "I must . . . consider"
Elizabeth Lovegrove: "Journal, New Lebanon, N.Y., 1837–41," (manuscript). The Henry Francis du Pont Winterthur Museum, Andrews Collection.

"August 1836"
Andrews and Andrews: *Shaker Furniture*, p. 40.

"October 1816."
Isaac N. Youngs: "Clock maker's journal with remarks and observations, experiments, beginning in 1815. New Lebanon, 1815–35" (manuscript). Western Reserve Historical Society.

41 "to banish from the mind"
Blinn: "Historical Record," p. 8.

43 "When at work"
Blinn, ibid., p. 108.

43 "Elder Otis Sawyer"
"Gleanings from Sabbathday Lake Church Journals, 1872–84," *The Shaker Quarterly*, Vol. VI, no. 3 (Fall 1966), p. 104.

44 "an impromptu thought"
Blinn: "Historical Record," p. 53.

"When he conceits"
Nordhoff: *Communistic Societies*, p. 218.

"YOUNG brethren"
Andrews and Andrews: *Shaker Furniture*, p. 93.

ORDER

49 "Every great man"
Alonzo Hollister: Notes from an addition to Isaac N. Youngs's "Clock maker's journal" (manuscript), p. 23. Western Reserve Historical Society.

50 "Where they both stand"
Seth Youngs Wells, comp.: *Testimonies of the Life, Character, Revelations and Doctrines of Mother Ann Lee* (Albany, N.Y.: Weed–Parsons Printing Co., Printers; second edition; 1888), p. 21.

"To accomplish this purpose"
Some Lines in Verse about Shakers (New York: William Taylor & Co.; 1846), p. 35.

51 "How could these"
Eldress Aurelia G. Mace: *The Aletheia: Spirit of Truth* (Farmington, Me.: Press of the Knowlton & McLeary Co.; second edition; 1907), p. 75.

"The great Architect"
Richard W. Pelham: *A Shaker's Answer to the Oft-Repeated Question, "What Would Become of the World If All Should Become Shakers?"* (Boston, Press of Rand, Avery, & Co.; 1874).

"All the members"
Edward Deming Andrews: *The People Called Shakers*, p. 59.

54 "They are our every day companions;"
Hervey Elkins: *Fifteen Years in the Senior Order of Shakers: A Narration of Facts Concerning That Particular People* (Hanover, N.H.: Dartmouth Press; 1853), p. 126.

"evidently called"
Testimonies Concerning the Character and Ministry of Mother Ann Lee and the First Witnesses of the Gospel of Christ's Second Appearing (Albany, N.Y.: Printed by Packard & van Benthuysen; 1827), p. 172.

"for the time,"
Giles B. Avery: *Sketches of Shakers and Shakerism* (Albany: Weed–Parsons Printing Co.; 1884) p. 9.

56 "If sacred places"
Giles B. Avery: "Sacred Places, Sacred Seasons," *The Shaker Manifesto*, Vol. IX, no. 4 (April 1879), p. 74.

57 "spoke appropriately"
Daniel Boler: "A Journal or Memorandum of a Journey throughout the Western

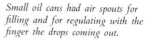

Small oil cans had air spouts for filling and for regulating with the finger the drops coming out.

Societies of Believers, New Lebanon, 1852" (manuscript). Western Reserve Historical Society.

57 "It can not be denied"
B. J. Lossing: "The Shakers," *Harper's New Monthly Magazine*, Vol. XV (1857), p. 169.

"Feb. 5, 1856"
Brother Daniel Miller: "A Church Journal, Union Village, Ohio, 1856–65 (manuscript), p. 4. Western Reserve Historical Society.

"All around the walls"
Eldress Nancy E. Moore: "Journal of a Trip to Various Societies Sept. 1854–Oct. 1854" (manuscript), p. 28. Western Reserve Historical Society.

58 "All things must"
Mary Antoinette Doolittle: *Autobiography of Mary Antoinette Doolittle*, p. 35.

59 "every stick of wood"
Elder Henry C. Blinn: "A Journey to Kentucky in the Year 1873," *The Shaker Quarterly*, Vol. VI, no. 3 (Fall 1966), p. 95.

"Good Berries,"
"A Short Sketch of Our Journey to the East, Hancock, 1850" (manuscript), p. 12. The Henry Francis du Pont Winterthur Museum, Andrews Collection.

60 "villages as neat"
James Fenimore Cooper: *Notions of the Americans, Picked Up by a Travelling Bachelor* (Philadelphia; 1828), Vol. XI, p. 248.

"There was a neatness"
Blinn: "Journey to Kentucky," *The Shaker Quarterly*, Vol. VI, no. 4 (Winter 1966), p. 135.

"on the 4th of July 1846"
Elder Henry C. Blinn: "A Historical Record of the Society of Believers in Canterbury, N.H., East Canterbury, 1892" (manuscript), p. 82. Shaker Village, Inc., Canterbury, N.H.

61 "All work done,"
Andrews: *People Called Shakers*, p. 60.

"We ought to get on"
Charles Nordhoff: *The Communistic Societies of the United States*, p. 162.

"Such a dwelling,"
Elkins: *Fifteen Years*, p. 52.

62 "Pass the dairy house,"
"Items of a Journey to Harvard, Shirley, and Lynn; New Lebanon, N.Y., 1846" (manuscript). Western Reserve Historical Society.

"The first thing"
Richard McNemar: *The Kentucky Revival* (New York: reprinted by Edward O. Jenkins; 1846), p. 119.

SPACE

63 "The low, dark . . . structures"
Hervey Elkins: *Fifteen Years in the Senior Order of Shakers*, p. 52.

66 "Green painted bed steads,"
Edward Deming Andrews and Faith Andrews: *Shaker Furniture*, p. 54.

67 "plain chairs, bottomed"
Elkins: *Fifteen Years*, pp. 25–6.

"A bed stands"
William Hepworth Dixon: *New America* (Philadelphia; third edition; 1869), pp. 308–9.

69 "In the large family diningroom,"
Charles Edson Robinson: *The Shakers and Their Homes* (East Canterbury, N.H.; 1893), p. 110.

72 "In every room"
Robinson, ibid., p. 110.

"800 drawers"
Eldress Nancy E. Moore: "Journal of a Trip to Various Societies Sept. 1854–Oct. 1854" (manuscript), p. 49. Western Reserve Historical Society.

74 "The buildings are large"
John Humphrey Noyes: *History of American Socialisms* (Philadelphia: J. B. Lippincott & Co.; 1870. New York: Dover Publications, Inc.; 1966), p. 606.

"Their buildings were made"
David R. Lamson: *Two Years' Experience among the Shakers* (West Boylston, Mass.: published by the author; 1848), p. 17.

"The interior of the edifice"
Elkins: *Fifteen Years*, p. 36.

75 "to preserve the carpets"
"Carpets," *Shaker and Shakeress*, Vol. III, no. 6 (June 1873), p. 44.

"Good and evil"
Eldress Aurelia G. Mace: *The Aletheia: Spirit of Truth*, p. 140.

"A robe that is spotless,"
From a spirit drawing: *From Father Joseph, to Eliza-Ann Taylor*. Western Reserve Historical Society.

76 "perfectly smooth,"
Peculiarities of the Shakers . . . By a visitor (New York; 1832).

"It is fifty-eight by forty feet,"
Elkins: *Fifteen Years*, p. 40.

"Sab. 11 June"
Elizabeth Lovegrove: "Journal, New Lebanon, N.Y., 1837–41" (manuscript), p. 13. The Henry Francis du Pont Winterthur Museum, Andrews Collection.

"10 lbs. White Lead,"
Andrews and Andrews: *Shaker Furniture*, p. 118.

SIMPLICITY

77 "dignified without being proud,"
Eldress Nancy E. Moore: "Journal of a Trip to Various Societies Sept. 1854–Oct. 1854" (manuscript), pp. 16–17. Western Reserve Historical Society.

Shaker tools were simple but pleasing: note the chalk line, carved as finely as any chair finial, below; and the graceful handle on the iron drill, opposite. (Canterbury, N.H.)

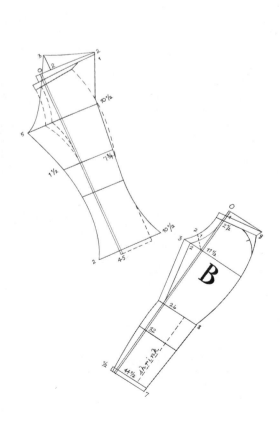

77 "... the design was based upon"
George Heard Hamilton: *Nineteenth and Twentieth-Century Art* (New York: Harry N. Abrams, Inc.; 1970), pp. 339–40.

80 "We all ought to be simple,"
David R. Lamson: *Two Years' Experience among the Shakers*, p. 83.

"The deliberate simplicity"
B. B. Dunlavy: "South Union, Ky., June 9, 1869, Visit of Pleasant Hill Ministry to Mt. Lebanon and Other Eastern Societies" (manuscript), pp. 23–4.

81 "I love to feel simple,"
Charles Nordhoff: *The Communistic Societies of the United States*, p. 231.

"I will be simple"
Nordhoff, ibid., p. 223.

"use no compliments,"
Valentine Rathbun: *An Account of the Matter, Form, and Manner of a New and Strange Religion*, p. 4.

"Simplicity scorneth pride,"
The Youth's Guide in Zion, and Holy Mother's Promises (Printed at Canterbury, N.H.; 1842), p. 16.

82 "Rye Indian bread,"
Moore: "Journal of a Trip," pp. 27–8.

"What a dish is Lobster!"
"Items of a Journey to Harvard, Shirley, and Lynn; New Lebanon, N.Y., 1846" (manuscript), p. 75. Western Reserve Historical Society.

"O dear!"
Elder Henry C. Blinn: "A Journey to Kentucky in the year 1873," *The Shaker Quarterly*, Vol. VI, no. 2 (Summer 1966), p. 56.

"Never put on silver spoons"
Seth Youngs Wells, comp.: *Testimonies of the Life, Character, Revelations and Doctrines of Mother Ann Lee*, pp. 267–8.

"You may let the moles"
Wells, ibid., Chapter XXX.

83 "very deep, or long waisted"
Lamson: *Two Years' Experience*, p. 60.

"Certainly ... if I understand"
Moore: "Journal of a Trip," pp. 18–19.

"The sisters are required"
Lamson: *Two Years' Experience*, p. 39.

84 "A woman whom fashion"
"The Bird Craze," *Mount Lebanon Cedar Boughs: Original Poems by The North Family of Shakers* (Buffalo: The Peter Paul Book Company; 1895), p. 63.

"employed for several days"
Edward Deming Andrews and Faith Andrews: *Shaker Furniture*, p. 19.

85 "No image or portrait"
Hervey Elkins: *Fifteen Years in the Senior Order of Shakers*, p. 26.

86 "Our Zion home"
"Home," *Mount Lebanon Cedar Boughs*, p. 49.

PERFECTION

88 "a perfect pattern"
Testimonies Concerning the Character and Ministry of Mother Ann Lee . . ., pp. 29, 94, 115, 163.

"so conscientious"
Josephine E. Wilson: "A Farewell to Elder Benjamin H. Smith," *The Shaker Manifesto*, Vol. XXIX, no. 9 (September 1899), p. 134.

89 "like that of the brethren"
David R. Lamson: *Two Years' Experience among the Shakers*, p. 55.

"right over this"
David Sellin: "Shaker Inspirational Drawings," *Philadelphia Museum Bulletin*, Vol. LVII, no. 273 (Spring 1962), pp. 95–6.

"Each of these communities"
Edward Deming Andrews and Faith Andrews: *Shaker Furniture*, p. 56.

90 "the waves of the Ocean,"
Eldress Nancy E. Moore: "Journal of a Trip to Various Societies Sept. 1854–Oct. 1854" (manuscript), pp. 92, 94. Western Reserve Historical Society.

"the Shakers believe"
John Humphrey Noyes: *History of American Socialisms*, p. 602.

91 "the women all had on"
"Letter from Pittsfield, Mass., Oct. 23, 1845" (manuscript). Pocumtuck Valley Memorial Libraries, Deerfield, Mass.

"contrary to order"
William J. Haskett: *Shakerism Unmasked, or the History of the Shakers* (Pittsfield, Mass.: published by the author; 1828), p. 173.

"all exactly twenty feet square,"
Hervey Elkins: *Fifteen Years in the Senior Order of Shakers*, p. 40.

"The Ministry here"
Moore: "Journal of a Trip," p. 42.

92 "keeping the top, middle, and bottom"
Anna White and Leila S. Taylor: *Shakerism: Its Meaning and Message* (Columbus, Ohio; 1904. New York: AMS Press, Inc.; 1971), p. 310.

93 "Anything may,"
Calvin Green and Seth Y. Wells: *A Summary View of the Millennial Church, or United Society of Believers (Commonly Called Shakers)* (Albany, N.Y.: Packard & van Benthuysen; 1823), p. 320.

94 "a chart"
"Gleanings from Sabbathday Lake Church Journals, 1872–84," *The Shaker Quarterly*, Vol. VI, no. 4 (Winter 1966), p. 126.

"Your proportions"
Caroline B. Piercy: *The Shaker Cook Book: Not by Bread Alone* (New York: Crown Publishers Inc.; 1953), p. 59.

"Precept on precept"
Edward Deming Andrews: *The Gift to Be Simple*, p. 126.

Handwrought iron tailor's shears, above, were as simple as the clothes Shakers cut with them. Tailors based their patterns on right angles, straight lines, and precise measurements. This sketch for a trouser pattern, opposite, comes from a New Lebanon notebook, c. 1850.

*Brushes like this one were designed
for cleaning dustpans.*

95 "all walks"
"Gleanings," *The Shaker Quarterly,* p. 131.

"A Man can Show"
"Family Record, Hancock, 1829–77" (manuscript). The Henry Francis du Pont
Winterthur Museum, Andrews Collection.

96 "March 12, 1852"
"Arms family letter, from Sacket's Harbor, N.Y., March 12, 1852" (manuscript).
Pocumtuck Valley Memorial Libraries, Deerfield, Mass.

"They kneel"
Sister Marcia Bullard: "Shaker Housekeeping," *Good Housekeeping* (July 1906).

"The hair shall not"
Lamson: *Two Years' Experience,* p. 38.

97 "nearly as smoothe"
Elder Henry C. Blinn: "A Historical Record of the Society of Believers in
Canterbury, N.H.; East Canterbury, 1892" (manuscript), p. 132. Shaker Village,
Inc., Canterbury, N.H.

"I can yet remember"
Freegift Wells: "Ministry Journal including Trips to Pleasant Hill & South
Union, Ky., and North Union, Watervliet & Whitewater, Ohio, 1836–7"
(manuscript), p. 64. Western Reserve Historical Society.

98 "One, two, three steps,"
Andrews: *Gift to Be Simple,* p. 103.

"more than a score"
Elkins: *Fifteen Years,* p. 42.

"graves are laid out"
"Journal of a Trip to Harvard and Lynn, Mass.; Alfred and New Gloucester,
Maine; and Enfield and Canterbury, N.H." (manuscript; Enfield, Conn.,
1850–99). The Henry Francis du Pont Winterthur Museum, Andrews
Collection.

UTILITY

99 "These people"
David R. Lamson: *Two Years' Experience among the Shakers,* p. 17.

100 "An arbitrary inhibition"
Hervey Elkins: *Fifteen Years in the Senior Order of Shakers,* p. 29.

"Beauty rests"
Edward Deming Andrews and Faith Andrews: *Shaker Furniture,* p. 21.

"if they were to build"
Charles Nordhoff: *The Communistic Societies of the United States,* pp. 164–5.

101 ". . . Hannah Bronson"
Elder Henry C. Blinn: "A Historical Record of the Society of Believers in
Canterbury, N.H., 1892" (manuscript). Shaker Village, Inc., Canterbury, N.H.

104 "it will avail nothing"
Peculiarities of the Shakers . . . By a visitor, p. 44.

105 "In years past,"
Andrews and Andrews: *Shaker Furniture*, p. 19.

"The rose bushes were"
Sister Marcia Bullard: "Shaker Housekeeping," *Good Housekeeping* (July 1906),
p. 37.

106 "whatever of truth"
Catharine Allen: *Biographical Sketch of Daniel Fraser of the Shaker Community of
Mt. Lebanon, N.Y.* (Albany, N.Y.: Weed, Parsons & Company, Printers; 1890),
p. 10.

"We have given you"
Testimonies Concerning the Character and Ministry of Mother Ann Lee . . . , p. 45.

CLEANLINESS

107 "She had at one time"
Anna White and Leila Taylor: *Shakerism: Its Meaning and Message*, p. 365.

108 "Sweep sweep"
Edward Deming Andrews: *The Gift to Be Simple*, p. 58.

"I have come,"
Andrews, ibid., p. 60.

"Bow down low"
Andrews, ibid., p. 125.

"They are remarkably neat"
William J. Haskett: *Shakerism Unmasked*, p. 221.

110 "The brothers must clean"
John Humphrey Noyes: *History of American Socialisms*, p. 610.

112 "of course with piles of dust"
Charles Nordhoff: *The Communistic Societies of the United States*, p. 165.

113 "if there is"
Nordhoff, ibid., pp. 136–7.

114 "In each village"
William Dean Howells: "A Shaker Village," *The Atlantic Monthly*, Vol.
XXXVII, no. 219 (June 1876), p. 709.

HEALTH

115 "A pearly brow"
"Health," *Mount Lebanon Cedar Boughs*, p. 30.

"an offense"
Charles Nordhoff: *The Communistic Societies of the United States*, p. 133.

116 "His faithfulness"
Elder Henry C. Blinn: "A Historical Record of the Society of Believers in
Canterbury, N.H.; East Canterbury, 1892" (manuscript), pp. 269–70. Shaker
Village, Inc., Canterbury, N.H.

"I need not"
William J. Haskett: *Shakerism Unmasked*, p. 299.

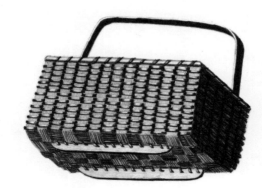

*Special kindling baskets had cloth linings to
keep chips and dirt in the basket; wooden
runners strapped underneath let air circulate
to keep the kindling dry.*

Sisters used sturdy wooden patterns, sized "large" to "small," for making their bonnets—cool straw for summer, warm quilted covering for winter.

117 "the subject of"
B. B. Dunlavy: "South Union, Ky., June 9, 1869, Visit of Pleasant Hill Ministry to Mt. Lebanon and Other Eastern Societies" (manuscript), p. 60. Western Reserve Historical Society.

"the sash"
Nordhoff: *Communistic Societies*, p. 152.

"The latter is"
Charles F. Wingate: "Shaker Sanitation," *The Plumber & Sanitary Engineer*, Vol. III, no. 20 (September 1880), p. 397.

119 "On Tuesday,"
Nordhoff: *Communistic Societies*, p. 167.

"There has been"
Philemon Stewart: "A Confidential Journal Kept in the Elders' Lot, New Lebanon, 1st order, 1842" (manuscript), pp. 4–5. Western Reserve Historical Society.

120 "*green tea*"
Brother Daniel Miller: "A Church Journal commencing Jan. 1st 1856 & ending Apr. 30 1865, Union Village, 1891" (manuscript), p. 1.

"Elder Joseph Brackett"
"Sabbathday Lake Church Record and Journal 1873" (manuscript), p. 95. The Shaker Museum, Sabbathday Lake, Maine.

"Men of sound reason"
Nordhoff: *Communistic Societies*, p. 219.

121 "relieved some"
Elizabeth Lovegrove: "Journal, New Lebanon, N.Y., 1837–41" (manuscript), p. 3. The Henry Francis du Pont Winterthur Museum, Andrews Collection.

122 "It seemed to uninstructed minds"
"Steam and Waterworks—What They Cost," *Mount Lebanon Cedar Boughs*, pp. 226 ff.

123 "What is cleansing"
Elder Henry C. Blinn: *The Life and Experience of Mother Ann Lee* (Canterbury, N.H.: published by the Shakers; n.d.), p. 17.

124 "As water washes"
Peculiarities of the Shakers . . . By a visitor, pp. 86–7.

"said there was"
Eldress Nancy E. Moore: "Journal of a Trip to Various Societies Sept. 1854–Oct. 1854" (manuscript), p. 4. Western Reserve Historical Society.

"Come, Come,"
Edward Deming Andrews: *The Gift to Be Simple*, p. 78.

125 "About 5 o'clock"
Moore: "Journal of a Trip," p. 24.

126 "This Cistern"
Freegift Wells: "Ministry Journal including Trips to Pleasant Hill & South Union, Ky., and North Union, Watervliet & Whitewater, Ohio, 1836-7" (manuscript), p. 12. Western Reserve Historical Society.

126 "force pump"
Daniel Boler: "A Journal or Memorandum of a Journey throughout the Western Societies of Believers, New Lebanon, 1852" (manuscript). Western Reserve Historical Society.

"Water is conducted"
Dunlavy: "Visit of Pleasant Hill Ministry," p. 18.

127 "rainwater drained off"
George Engle Budinger: "Recollections of North Union Shaker Colony" (typescript of taped interview by Frank Myers and Harrison Collister; 1962), p. 18.

128 "commenced to live"
"Sabbathday Lake Church Record and Journal," p. 84.

129 "And considering a gluttonous appetite"
Testimonies Concerning the Character and Ministry of Mother Ann Lee . . . , p. 140.

"The glutton's a seat"
Nordhoff: *Communistic Societies*, p. 220.

130 "but very little use"
Testimonies, p. 29.

"To thirty gallons"
"A Book of Remedies for the Different Ailments" (manuscript). Western Reserve Historical Society.

"Inebriation,"
Nordhoff: *Communistic Societies*, p. 215.

131 "Diet drink"
"Recipe book, Hancock, Mass. 1828–46" (manuscript). Western Reserve Historical Society.

132 "an extensive establishment"
Dunlavy: "Visit of Pleasant Hill Ministry," p. 26.

133 "The Infirmary"
Dunlavy, ibid., p. 16.

"witnessed a surgical operation"
Boler: "Journal."

134 "it was generally"
Boler, ibid.

"a splendid Rocking Chair"
Moore: "Journal of a Trip," pp. 28–9.

"A little cold"
Nordhoff: *Communistic Societies*, p. 216.

136 "Look at yourselves;"
Testimonies, p. 62.

"Shall the humpback,"
"Physical Resurrection," *Mount Lebanon Cedar Boughs*, p. 160.

"Health,"
"Health," ibid., p. 30.

Patterns for woodwork were usually made of tin; they lasted well and maintained a perfectly true edge. "Finger" joints on oval wooden boxes were drawn with a tin pattern like this.

THRIFT

137 "observe good economy;"
Seth Youngs Wells, comp.: *Testimonies of the Life, Character, Revelations and Doctrines of Mother Ann Lee,* p. 263.

138 "only stewards"
Anna White and Leila S. Taylor: *Shakerism: Its Meaning and Message,* pp. 150-1.

140 "When he was quite aged"
Elder Henry C. Blinn: "A Historical Record of the Society of Believers in Canterbury, N.H.; East Canterbury, 1892" (manuscript), p. 265. Shaker Village, Inc., Canterbury, N.H.

141 "With satisfaction"
Elizabeth Lovegrove: "Journal, New Lebanon, N.Y., 1837–41" (manuscript). The Henry Francis du Pont Winterthur Museum, Andrews Collection.

"would show respect"
Clara Endicott Sears, comp.: *Gleanings from Old Shaker Journals* (Cambridge, Mass.: The Riverside Press, Houghton Mifflin Company; 1916), p. 101.

"the small beginnings"
Elder Henry C. Blinn: *Gentle Manners, a Guide to Good Morals* (East Canterbury, N.H.; 1899), p. 20.

142 "remember this thing"
Sears: *Gleanings,* p. 104.

"it was thought best"
Edward Deming Andrews and Faith Andrews: *Shaker Furniture,* p. 41.

143 "at the underpining"
Lovegrove: "Journal."

"two old Barns"
"Sabbathday Lake Church Record and Journal, 1873" (manuscript), p. 70. The Shaker Museum, Sabbathday Lake, Maine.

144 "scalloping crumbs"
Caroline B. Piercy: *The Shaker Cook Book,* p. 50.

"You New-England people"
Testimonies Concerning the Character and Ministry of Mother Ann Lee . . . , p. 21.

146 "Three of these"
Freegift Wells: "Ministry Journal including Trips to Pleasant Hill & South Union, Ky., and North Union, Watervliet & Whitewater, Ohio, 1836-7" (manuscript), p. 96. Western Reserve Historical Society.

"Elder Cephas took time"
Elder Henry C. Blinn: "A Journey to Kentucky in the Year 1873," *The Shaker Quarterly,* Vol. VI, no. 3 (Fall 1966), p. 101.

147 "There is a small stream"
"Journal of a Trip to Canterbury, 1847" (manuscript).

"No where do"
Hervey Elkins: *Fifteen Years in the Senior Order of Shakers* (Hanover, N.H.: Dartmouth Press; 1853), p. 129.

"Went to a Cave"
William Deming: "Travel to the State of Ohio, 1810" (manuscript), p. 14. The Henry Francis du Pont Winterthur Museum, Andrews Collection.

148 "Jan. 31"
Andrews and Andrews: *Shaker Furniture*, p. 38.

"I've always found"
Isaac N. Youngs: "Clock maker's journal with remarks and observations,
experiments, beginning in 1815. New Lebanon, 1815–35" (manuscript). Western
Reserve Historical Society.

149 "At twenty-five years"
Autobiography by Elder Giles B. Avery, of Mount Lebanon, N.Y. (East Canterbury,
N.H.; 1891), pp. 5–6.

150 "Leave Louisville"
Blinn: "Journey to Kentucky," *Shaker Quarterly*, p. 93.

151 "While visiting"
Eldress Nancy E. Moore: "Journal of a Trip to Various Societies Sept. 1854–Oct.
1854" (manuscript), pp. 72–3.

"Wove 14 yds"
"A Journal containing an account of the Hand Labor Performed by the Sisters,
1845, Watervliet" (manuscript). Western Reserve Historical Society.

152 "a tree planted"
White and Taylor: *Shakerism*, p. 335.

HONESTY

153 "bonnets and hats,"
Hervey Elkins: *Fifteen Years in the Senior Order of Shakers*, pp. 134–5.

155 "I found no deception"
Testimonies Concerning the Character and Ministry of Mother Ann Lee . . . , p. 51.

"with great fervor"
"Among the Shakers," *The Shaker Manifesto*, Vol. X, no. 3 (March 1880), p. 56.

"Be what you seem"
Elder Frederick W. Evans: *Shakers Compendium* (New York: Lenox Hill
Publishing and Distributing Co.; 1972. Burt Franklin; 1859), p. 170.

156 "One part"
Elder Henry C. Blinn: "A Journey to Kentucky in the Year 1873," *The Shaker
Quarterly*, Vol. VI, no. 4 (Winter 1966), p. 141.

"We, the undersigned,"
"An Ancient Witness," *The Shaker Manifesto*, Vol. XI, no. 2 (February 1881),
p. 45.

158 "And a woe"
Charles Nordhoff: *The Communistic Societies of the United States*, p. 224.

"the simple *word*"
Elder Frederick W. Evans: *Autobiography of a Shaker, and Revelation of the
Apocalypse* (Mt. Lebanon, N.Y.; 1869), p. 99.

"You haven't got"
George Engle Budinger: "Recollections of North Union Shaker Colony," p. 23.

*Two sculptured wood forms: above, a scoop
from Hancock carved from a single chunk of
maple; opposite, a butcher block from Pleasant
Hill, Kentucky (at Old Chatham, N.Y.),
made of a slice of sycamore nearly a yard
across.*

Shaker mops had looped ends—no cut ends to fray, and a longer-lasting mop.

PERMANENCE

160 "from a Christ Spirit"
Elder Frederick W. Evans: *Autobiography of a Shaker, and Revelation of the Apocalypse*, p. 39.

"*Well-defined fixed principles*"
Elder Frederick W. Evans: *Shakers Compendium*, p. 53.

"we are left"
Elder Henry C. Blinn: *Gentle Manners, a Guide to Good Morals* (East Canterbury, N.H.; 1899), p. 14.

"it was their boast"
John Humphrey Noyes: *History of American Socialisms*, p. 602.

161 "solidity and durability"
Charles F. Wingate: "Shaker Sanitation," *The Plumber & Sanitary Engineer*, Vol. III, no. 20 (September 1880), p. 397.

"The mill is built"
Daniel Boler: "A Journal or Memorandum of a Journey throughout the Western Societies of Believers, New Lebanon, 1852" (manuscript), p. 16. Western Reserve Historical Society.

162 "Believers ought"
Freegift Wells: "Ministry Journal including Trips to Pleasant Hill & South Union, Ky., and North Union, Watervliet & Whitewater, Ohio, 1836–7" (manuscript), p. 71. Western Reserve Historical Society.

163 "instead of attending"
Evans: *Compendium*, pp. 24–5.

"They have two"
Eldress Nancy E. Moore: "Journal of a Trip to Various Societies Sept. 1854–Oct. 1854" (manuscript), pp. 60–1. Western Reserve Historical Society.

"astonishingly bright"
Charles Nordhoff: *The Communistic Societies of the United States*, p. 168.

164 "But the truth"
Testimonies Concerning the Character and Ministry of Mother Ann Lee. . ., p. 167.

166 "The principal motive,"
Thomas Brown: *An Account of the People Called Shakers* (New York: Parker and Bliss; 1812. AMS Press Reprint, 1972), p. 23.

167 "which is the first ploughing"
"Gleanings from Sabbathday Lake Church Journals, 1872–84," *The Shaker Quarterly*, Vol. VI, no. 3 (Fall 1966), p. 111.

"Never shall I forget"
Hervey Elkins: *Fifteen Years in the Senior Order of Shakers*, p. 50.

168 "A particularly interesting study"
Mary Antoinette Doolittle: *Autobiography of Mary Antoinette Doolittle*.

"The vital statistics"
Daniel Fraser: "Celibacy: Its Relation to Longevity, and As an Essential to Divine Life," *The Shaker Manifesto*, Vol. X, no. 3 (March 1880), p. 62.

169 "He was 84"
Moore: "Journal of a Trip," p. 73.

169 "The next & most"
Moore, ibid., p. 30.

170 "Have Shakers any deadline"
Anna White and Leila S. Taylor: *Shakerism: Its Meaning and Message,* p. 383.

"for the blessing"
White and Taylor, ibid., p. 306.

PROGRESS

171 "How beautiful"
Clara Endicott Sears, comp.: *Gleanings from Old Shaker Journals,* p. 30.

172 "a system"
Catharine Allen: *Biographical Sketch of Daniel Fraser of the Shaker Community of Mt. Lebanon, Columbia County, N.Y.* (Albany, N.Y.: Weed, Parsons & Company, Printers; 1890), p. 9.

"As we feel"
Mary Antoinette Doolittle: *Autobiography of Mary Antoinette Doolittle,* p. 44.

173 "Woman was no longer"
Doolittle, ibid., p. 36.

"Suppose a woman"
Charles Nordhoff: *The Communistic Societies of the United States,* p. 166.

174 "thought women"
Nordhoff, ibid., pp. 203–4.

176 "I had a pretty smart talk"
Daniel Boler: "A Journal or Memorandum of a Journey throughout the Western Societies of Believers, New Lebanon, 1852" (manuscript). Western Reserve Historical Society.

"Whatever your profession,"
Edward Deming Andrews: *The Gift to Be Simple,* p. 48.

178 "which facilitate"
Elder Frederick W. Evans: *Shakers Compendium,* p. 13.

"every improvement"
Edward Deming Andrews: *The People Called Shakers,* p. 114.

"Inventions"
Elder Frederick W. Evans: *Autobiography of a Shaker, and Revelation of the Apocalypse,* p. 159.

179 "We have a right"
Andrews: *People Called Shakers,* p. 115.

"The aims"
Anna White and Leila S. Taylor: *Shakerism: Its Meaning and Message,* p. 310.

180 "splendid Brick Barn"
B. B. Dunlavy: "South Union, Ky., June 9, 1869, Visit of Pleasant Hill Ministry to Mt. Lebanon and Other Eastern Societies" (manuscript), p. 53. Western Reserve Historical Society.

"By gosh they"
George Engle Budinger: *Recollections of North Union Shaker Colony,* p. 5.

Shakers made sturdy wooden berry boxes for their home-grown berries: the boxes stacked neatly and had airholes to let the berries dry.

182 " 'And to her' "
Evans: *Autobiography,* p. 131.

"Steam does all,"
"Gleanings from Sabbathday Lake Church Journals, 1872–84," *The Shaker Quarterly,* Vol. VI, no 4 (Winter 1966), p. 129.

183 "While our steamboat,"
Nordhoff: *Communistic Societies,* p. 225.

"a big wooden tub"
Budinger: "Recollections," p. 9.

184 "machine for kneeding"
Boler: "Journal."

"new fashion churn,"
"A Journal of the Ministry's Eastern Visit, June 1850, New Lebanon" (manuscript). Western Reserve Historical Society.

185 "The kitchen"
Hervey Elkins: *Fifteen Years in the Senior Order of Shakers,* pp. 39–40.

"Here the Sisters"
"A Journal of the Ministry's Eastern Visit."

"One sister attends"
Eldress Nancy Moore: "Journal of a Trip to Various Societies Sept. 1854–Oct. 1854" (manuscript), p. 64. Western Reserve Historical Society.

186 "a sensible little thing"
"Journal of a Trip to Harvard and Lynn, Mass.; Alfred and New Gloucester, Maine; and Enfield and Canterbury, N.H." (manuscript). The Henry Francis du Pont Winterthur Museum, Andrews Collection.

"rather an old fashioned appearance"
Elder Henry C. Blinn: "A Journey to Kentucky in the Year 1873," *The Shaker Quarterly,* Vol. VI, no. 4 (Winter 1966), p. 137.

"conducted in"
Moore: "Journal of a Trip," pp. 7–8.

187 "nearly two cords"
"Gleanings," *The Shaker Quarterly,* Vol. VI, no. 3 (Fall 1966), p. 107.

"a mill"
Elder Henry C. Blinn: "A Historical Record of the Society of Believers in Canterbury, N.H., East Canterbury, 1892" (manuscript), p. 129. Shaker Village, Inc., Canterbury, N.H.

188 "Our SHAKERS' SARSAPARILLA"
Mary Whitcher's Shaker Housekeeper (Hastings-on-Hudson, N.Y.: Morgan & Morgan, Inc.; 1882. Reprinted by Hancock Shaker Village, Hancock, Mass.; 1972).

189 "hose knitter"
Blinn: "Historical Record," p. 114.

"Be not anxious"
Andrews: *People Called Shakers,* p. 151.

190 "The secret"
Allen: *Daniel Fraser,* p. 25.

Andrews, Edward Deming: *The Community Industries of the Shakers.* Albany: The University of the State of New York; 1933.

————: *The Gift to Be Simple: Songs, Dances and Rituals of the American Shakers.* New York: J. J. Augustin; 1940. Dover Publications, Inc.; 1967.

————: *The People Called Shakers.* New York: Dover Publications, Inc.; 1953, 1963.

Andrews, Edward Deming, and Faith Andrews: *Religion in Wood: A Book of Shaker Furniture.* Bloomington: Indiana University Press; 1966.

————: *Shaker Furniture: The Craftsmanship of an American Communal Sect.* New York: Dover Publications, Inc.; 1950.

————: *Visions of the Heavenly Sphere: A Study in Shaker Religious Art.* Charlottesville: The University Press of Virginia, published for The Henry Francis du Pont Winterthur Museum; 1969.

Andrews, Faith: *Work and Worship: The Economic Order of the Shakers.* Greenwich, Conn.: New York Graphic Society; 1974.

Avery, Elder Giles B.: *Autobiography by Elder Giles B. Avery, of Mount Lebanon, N.Y.* East Canterbury, N.H.; 1891.

————: *Sketches of Shakers and Shakerism.* Albany, N.Y.: Weed-Parsons Printing Co., Printers; 1884.

Blinn, Elder Henry C.: *Gentle Manners: A Guide to Good Morals.* East Canterbury, N.H.; 1899.

————: *The Life and Experience of Mother Ann Lee.* Canterbury, N.H.: Published by the Shakers; n.d.

Brown, Thomas: *An Account of the People Called Shakers.* New York: Parker and Bliss; 1812. New York: AMS Press Reprint; 1972.

Budinger, George Engle: "Recollections of North Union Shaker Colony." Typescript of taped interview by Frank Myers and Harrison Collister; 1962.

Clark, Thomas D.: *Pleasant Hill in the Civil War.* Kentucky: Pleasant Hill Press; 1972.

Cook, Harold E.: *Shaker Music: A Manifestation of American Folk Culture.* Lewisburg, Pa.: Bucknell University Press; 1973. Cranbury, N.J.: Associated University Presses, Inc.; n.d.

Desroche, Henri: *The American Shakers from Neo-Christianity to Presocialism.* Translated from the French and edited by John K. Savacool. Amherst: University of Massachusetts Press; 1971.

Doolittle, Eldress Mary Antoinette: *Autobiography of Mary Antoinette Doolittle.* Mt. Lebanon, N.Y.; 1880.

Dunlavy, John. *The Nature and True Church of Christ Proved by Plain Evidences.* New York: Printed by George W. Wood; 1847.

Eads, Elder H. L.: "Shaker Theology." *The Shaker Manifesto* (1879).

Elam, Sister Aida, and Sister Miriam Wall: *History of the Shakers; Education and Recreation.* Canterbury, N.H.: Canterbury Shakers; 1961.

Elkins, Hervey: *Fifteen Years in the Senior Order of Shakers: A Narration of Facts Concerning That Particular People.* Hanover, N.H.: Dartmouth Press; 1853.

Evans, Elder Frederick W.: *Autobiography of a Shaker, and Revelation of the Apocalypse.* Mt. Lebanon, N.Y.; 1869.

————: *Shakers Compendium.* New York: Burt Franklin; 1859. Lenox Hill Publishing & Distributing Co.; 1972.

Frost, Sister Marguerite: *The Shaker Story.* Canterbury, N.H.: Canterbury Shakers.

The Gardener's Manual. New Lebanon, N.Y.: The United Society; 1843. Reprinted from the library at Hancock Shaker Village, Hancock, Mass., by Morgan & Morgan, Inc., Hastings-on-Hudson, N.Y.; 1972.

Gibbs, James W., and Robert W. Meader: *Shaker Clock Makers.* Columbia, Pa.: The National Association of Watch and Clock Collectors, Inc.

The Gospel Monitor: A Little Book of Mother Ann's Word to Those Who Are Placed as Instructors & Care-takers of Children. Printed at Canterbury, N.H.; 1843.

Green, Calvin, and Seth Y. Wells: *A Summary View of the Millennial Church, or United Society of Believers (Commonly Called Shakers).* Albany, N.Y.: Packard & van Benthuysen; 1823.

Haskett, William J.: *Shakerism Unmasked, or the History of the Shakers.* Pittsfield, Mass.: Published by the author; 1828.

Johnson, Theodore E., and John McKee: *Hands to Work and Hearts to God: The Shaker Tradition in Maine.* Bowdoin College Museum of Art; 1969.

A Juvenile Monitor: Containing Instructions for Youth and Children. Printed at New Lebanon; 1823.

Klamkin, Marian: *Hands to Work: Shaker Folk Art and Industries.* New York: Dodd, Mead & Company; 1972.

Lamson, David R.: *Two Years' Experience among the Shakers.* West Boylston, Mass.: Published by the author; 1848. New York: AMS Press Reprint; 1971.

Lassiter, William Lawrence: *Shaker Architecture.* New York: Bonanza Books; 1966.

Lindsay, Sister Bertha, and Sister Lillian Phelps: *Industries and Inventions of the Shakers; Shaker Music: A Brief History.* Canterbury, N.H.: Canterbury Shakers; 1961.

Lossing, B. J. "The Shakers." *Harper's New Monthly Magazine,* Vol. XV (1857), pp. 164–77.

Mace, Eldress Aurelia G.: *The Aletheia: Spirit of Truth.* 2nd edn. Farmington, Me.: Press of the Knowlton & McLeary Co.; 1907.

McNemar, Richard: *The Kentucky Revival.* New York; 1846. Reprinted by Edward O. Jenkins.

Mary Whitcher's Shaker House-Keeper. 1882. Reprinted from the library at Hancock Shaker Village, Hancock, Mass., by Morgan & Morgan, Inc., Hastings-on-Hudson, N.Y.; 1972.

Meader, Robert F. W.: *Illustrated Guide to Shaker Furniture.* New York: Dover Publications, Inc.; 1972.

Melcher, Marguerite Fellows: *The Shaker Adventure.* Cleveland: Press of Case Western Reserve University; 1968.

Miller, Amy Bess, and Persis Fuller: *The Best of Shaker Cooking.* New York: Macmillan Publishing Co., Inc.; 1970.

Mount Lebanon Cedar Boughs: Original Poems by The North Family of Shakers. Buffalo: The Peter Paul Book Company; 1895.

Neal, Julia: *By Their Fruits: The Story of Shakerism in South Union, Kentucky.* Chapel Hill: University of North Carolina Press; 1947.

———, ed.: *The Journal of Eldress Nancy.* Nashville, Tenn.: The Parthenon Press; 1963.

Nordhoff, Charles: *The Communistic Societies of the United States from Personal Observations.* New York: Harper & Brothers, Publishers; 1875. Dover Publications, Inc.; 1966.

Noyes, John Humphrey: *History of American Socialisms.* Philadelphia: J. B. Lippincott & Co.; 1870. New York: Dover Publications, Inc.; 1966.

Patterson, Daniel W.: *Nine Shaker Spirituals.* Old Chatham, N.Y.: The Shaker Museum Foundation, Inc.; 1964.

Pearson, Elmer R., Julia Neal, and Walter Muir Whitehill: *The Shaker Image.* Boston: New York Graphic Society in collaboration with Shaker Community, Inc., Hancock, Mass.; 1974.

Peculiarities of the Shakers described in a series of letters from Lebanon Springs . . . By a visitor. New York; 1832.

Beautiful proportions in a simple lap desk (c. 1850) meant that "beautification" with ornamentation was unnecessary. The slanted top was for writing; the small drawer held pen and ink. (Old Chatham, N.Y.)

Pelham, Elder Richard W.: *A Shaker's Answer to the Oft-Repeated Question, "What Would Become of the World If All Should Become Shakers?"* Boston: Press of Rand, Avery, & Co.; 1874.

Phillips, Hazel Spencer: *Richard the Shaker.* Lebanon, Ohio; 1972.

Piercy, Caroline B.: *The Shaker Cook Book: Not by Bread Alone.* New York: Crown Publishers Inc.; 1953.

————: *The Valley of God's Pleasure: A Saga of the North Union Shaker Community.* New York: Stratford House; 1951.

Poppeliers, John, ed.: *Shaker Built: A Catalog of Shaker Architectural Records from the Historic American Buildings Survey.* Washington, D.C.: Historic American Buildings Survey; 1974.

Rathbun, Valentine: *An Account of the Matter, Form, and Manner of a New and Strange Religion.* Providence, R.I.: Printed and sold by Bennett Wheeler; 1781.

Richmond, Colin Becket: *From Their Hearts and Hands: A Treasury of Shaker Poetry.* Privately published; 1974.

Robinson, Charles Edson: *The Shakers and Their Homes.* East Canterbury, N.H.; 1893.

The Round Stone Barn: A Short History. Hancock, Mass.: Shaker Community, Inc.; 1968.

Sears, Clara Endicott, comp.: *Gleanings from Old Shaker Journals.* Cambridge, Mass.: The Riverside Press, Houghton Mifflin Company; 1916.

Shaker Hymnal. East Canterbury, N.H.: The Canterbury Shakers; 1908. Reprinted in 1961 by Shaker Savings Association.

Shea, John G.: *The American Shakers and Their Furniture.* New York: Van Nostrand Reinhold Company; 1971.

Sommer, Margaret Frisbee: *The Shaker Garden Seed Industry.* Old Chatham, N.Y.: The Shaker Museum Foundation, Inc.; 1972.

Testimonies Concerning the Character and Ministry of Mother Ann Lee and the First Witnesses of the Gospel of Christ's Second Appearing. Albany, N.Y.: Printed by Packard & van Benthuysen; 1827.

Testimony of Christ's Second Appearing, Exemplified by the Principles and Practice of the True Church of Christ. 4th edn. Albany, N.Y.: Published by the United Society, called Shakers; 1856.

Thomas, Samuel W., and James C. Thomas: *The Simple Spirit: A Pictorial Study of the Shaker Community at Pleasant Hill, Kentucky.* Pleasant Hill Press; 1973.

Wells, Seth Y., comp.: *Testimonies of the Life, Character, Revelations and Doctrines of Mother Ann Lee.* 2nd edn. Albany, N.Y.: Weed-Parsons Printing Co., Printers; 1888.

White, Eldress Anna, and Eldress Leila S. Taylor: *Shakerism: Its Meaning and Message.* Columbus, Ohio; 1904. New York: AMS Press Reprint; 1971.

Wiggin, Kate Douglas: *Susanna and Sue.* Cambridge, Mass.: The Riverside Press, Houghton Mifflin Company; 1909.

Williams, John S.: *Consecrated Ingenuity: The Shakers and Their Inventions.* Old Chatham, N.Y.: The Shaker Museum Foundation; 1957.

————: *The Shaker Religious Concept Together with the Covenant, Hancock, Mass., 1830.* Old Chatham, N.Y.: The Shaker Museum Foundation; 1959.

Wingate, Charles F.: "Shaker Sanitation." *The Plumber & Sanitary Engineer,* Vol. III, no. 20 (September 1880), p. 397.

The Youth's Guide in Zion, and Holy Mother's Promises. Printed at Canterbury, N.H.; 1842. Mother's Work Series No. 1; copyright © 1963 by the United Society.

A pod auger, for reaming out bung holes in barrels, had a curved metal blade and utilitarian but shapely wooden handle. (Canterbury, N.H.)

PERIODICALS

The Shaker (monthly newspaper of the Shakers under that title 1871–72; later known as *Shaker and Shakeress, The Shaker Manifesto,* and *The Manifesto*), published by Shakers, Shaker Village, N.H., through December 1899.

The Shaker Quarterly, published quarterly by The Shaker Museum, Sabbathday Lake, Maine.

The World of Shaker, published quarterly by the Guild of Shaker Crafts, Inc., Spring Lake, Michigan.

Shaker boys learning in the Carpenter's Shop made precise rulers with an iron stamp gauged to an inch and marked with equal divisions. Then they stamped in numbers, blackened the markings, and varnished the whole as their first work in perfect cabinetry.

Shaker-made spools—more thread than wood—saved time because they didn't need rewinding as often as ordinary spools. Winding two different colors on the double spool made finding another spool unnecessary when changing colors. (Canterbury, N.H.)

Angled (rather than straight) clothing brushes were easier to use on the back and shoulders, as Shakers practiced literally what they sang:

Now we will be united and brush off pride and stiff,
Come brush, yea brush and brush again till limber as a withe.

Stonecutters like Brother Micajah Tucker carved granite rain drains to place under the eaves of buildings.

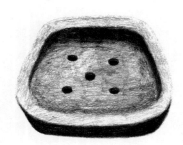

The securely fastened head on a Shaker hammer couldn't fly off the handle (notice the metal shanks bolted to the sides), so neither could the Brother using it!

Harry Houdini

A Magical Life

HOUDINI'S DEATH DEFYING MYSTE
ESCAPE FROM A GALVANIZED IRON CAN FILLED WITH
AND SECURED BY MASSIVE LOCKS.

MEANS A
DEATH

Elizabeth MacLeod